Dream's End

Dream's End

*Two Iowa Brothers
in the Civil War*

ORR KELLY

and

MARY DAVIES
KELLY

KODANSHA
INTERNATIONAL
New York • Tokyo • London

Kodansha America, Inc.
114 Fifth Avenue, New York, New York 10011, U.S.A.

Kodansha International Ltd.
17-14 Otowa 1-chome, Bunkyo-ku, Tokyo 112-8652, Japan

Published in 1998 by Kodansha America, Inc.
Maps on pages xxi, 156, 165, 169, 198, and 217 drawn by Thomas M. Palance

Library of Congress Cataloging-in-Publication Data

Kelly, Orr.
Dream's end : two Iowa brothers in the Civil War / Orr Kelly and Mary Davies
Kelly.
p. cm.
Includes bibliographical references and index.
ISBN 1–56836–226–9
1. Brayman, Andrew Jackson, 1845–1864. 2. Brayman, Barney, 1847–1871. 3.
United States. Army. Iowa Infantry Regiment, 36th (1862–1865) 4. United
States. Army. Iowa Cavalry Regiment, 8th (1861–1865) 5. Iowa—History—
Civil War, 1861–1865—Regimental histories. 7. Soldiers—Iowa—Biography.
I. Kelly, Mary Davies. II. Title.
E507.5 36th.K45   1998
973.7'477—dc21   98–15419

Book design by Tina Thompson

Manufactured in the United States of America

98 99 00 01 02   QFF   10 9 8 7 6 5 4 3 2 1

PAGE II: *Andrew, left, and Barney Brayman.* (Authors' collection.)

To our children, Charles and Barbara.

May they live in peace.

CONTENTS

LIST OF MAPS

MAPS BY THOMAS M. PALANCE

CAST OF CHARACTERS

Avera, William Franklin: young Confederate soldier at
Marks' Mills

Baker, N. B.: Iowa state adjutant general

Banks, Maj. Gen. Nathaniel P.: Union leader of disastrous
Red River expedition

Barner, Lt. Col. Horatio G.: officer in Eighth Iowa Volunteer
Cavalry

Brayman, Andrew Jackson: soldier in the 36th Iowa Volunteer
Infantry

Brayman, Flora Arabella or "Belle": younger sister of Andrew
and Barney

Brayman, Edward Barney: trooper in Eighth Iowa Cavalry

Brayman, Lewis: father of Andrew and Barney

Brayman, Mary Genette Gore: mother of Andrew and Barney

Brayman, Victoria Icebenda or "Tory": older sister of Andrew
and Barney

Brownlow, Col. James P.: survivor of Battle of Newnan

Butler, Maj. Gen. Benjamin: Union commander of the
Department of the Gulf in New Orleans

Cabell, Brig. Gen. William L.: Confederate commander at
Marks' Mills

Casey, Samuel: former member of Congress and prominent
cotton speculator

Chidester, Col. John T.: stagecoach operator and owner of
home in Camden

Cleburne, Maj. Gen. Patrick: Irish-born Confederate commander

Crawford, Col. Samuel J.: Union commander of the Second Kansas Colored Infantry

Crawford, Col. William A.: Confederate commander of Arkansas troops at Poison Springs

Croxton, Col. John T.: officer of the Fourth Kentucky Mounted Infantry; Union brigade commander during McCook raid south of Atlanta

Davidson, Brig. Gen. John W.: Union commander in advance on Little Rock

Davis, Jefferson: Confederate president

Dockery, Brig. Gen. Thomas P.: Confederate commander at Marks' Mills

Dodd, David: 17-year-old hanged as confederate spy in Little Rock

Dorr, Col. Joseph B.: commander of Eighth Iowa Cavalry

Douglas, Stephen: Democratic presidential candidate

Drake, Lt. Col. Francis Marion: deputy commander of 36th Iowa Volunteer Infantry; in charge at Marks' Mills

Fagan, Brig. Gen. James: Confederate commander at Marks' Mills

Forrest, Brig. Gen. Nathan Bedford: Confederate cavalry commander

Frémont, Maj. Gen. John C.: Union general

Garrard, Brig. Gen. Kenner: Union commander in Stoneman-McCook raid south of Atlanta

Gedney, Capt. Joseph B.: officer of Company I, 36th Iowa Volunteer Infantry; Andrew Brayman's company commander

Goodenough, Gilbert Clark: husband of Victoria Brayman

Grant, Brig. Gen. Ulysses S.: Union commander

Halleck, Maj. Gen. H. W.: Union commander

Hamilton, Maj. A. H.: acting commander of 36th Iowa Volunteer Infantry at Marks' Mills

Hammond, Alexander: Union surgeon general

Hare, M. H.: chaplain of 36th Iowa Volunteer Infantry

Hawthorn, Brig. Gen. Alexander T.: Confederate officer and lawyer; laid out defenses of Camden

Henry, Capt. C. A.: quartermaster during Steele's march to Camden

Holmes, Lt. Gen. Theophilus H.: Confederate commander in the attack on Helena

Hood, Lt. Gen. John Bell: Confederate general defending Atlanta

Johnston, Gen. Albert Sidney: Confederate general killed at Shiloh

Johnston, Lt. Gen. Joseph E.: Confederate general opposing Sherman in the advance on Atlanta

Jones, Dr. Joseph: Confederate surgeon who visited Andersonville

Kirkwood, Samuel J.: Iowa governor

Kittredge, Col. Charles A.: commander of 36th Iowa Volunteer Infantry

LaGrange, Col. Oscar H.: Union commander of First Wisconsin Cavalry; captured in battle north of Dalton

Lee, Gen. Robert E.: Confederate commander

Longstreet, Lt. Gen. James: Confederate commander

Marmaduke, Brig. Gen. John S.: Confederate general in Arkansas

Maxey, Brig. Gen. Samuel B.: Confederate commander of Texans and Indians at Poison Springs

McCauley, Maj. Mark: commander of Union cavalry at Marks' Mills

McClernand, Maj. Gen. John A.: Union general; rival of Grant

McCook, Brig. Gen. Edward Moody: leader of Union cavalry in sweep south of Atlanta; defeated at Newnan

McLean, Col. William E.: commander of 43rd Indiana Volunteer Infantry

Meigs, Montgomery C.: Union quartermaster general

Morgan, Brig. Gen. John Hunt: Confederate cavalry commander

Norris, Maj. Wesley W.: Union infantry commander at Marks' Mills

Pearson, Lt. Benjamin F.: officer in 36th Iowa Volunteer Infantry; diarist

Peetz, Lt. Charles: commander of Second Missouri Light Artillery at Marks' Mills

Pemberton, Lt. Gen. John C.: Confederate commander defeated at Vicksburg

Polk, Lt. Gen. Leonidas: Confederate general and Episcopal bishop

Porter, Adm. David Dixon: commander of the Union fleet on the Mississippi

Prentiss, Maj. Gen. Benjamin: Union commander at Helena

Price, Brig. Gen. Sterling: Confederate cavalry commander in Arkansas

Rice, Brig. Gen. Samuel A.: Union brigade commander under Steele

Roddey, Brig. Gen. Philip D.: Confederate commander at Newnan

Root, Maj. Richard: officer in Eighth Iowa Cavalry

Rosecrans, Maj. Gen. William S.: Union commander of the Department of the Cumberland; defeated at Chickamauga

Ross, Brig. Gen. L. S.: commander of Confederate cavalry that captured members of Eighth Iowa Cavalry at Newnan

Salomon, Brig. Gen. Frederick: Prussian-born Union commander of the division in which Andrew Brayman served

Scott, Maj. Gen. Winfield: veteran U.S. Army general; author of manual on tactics

Shelby, Brig. Gen. Joseph: commander of Confederate Iron Brigade; victor at Marks' Mills

Sherman, Maj. Gen. William Tecumseh: Union commander in Georgia campaign

Shoup, Brig. Gen. Francis A.: chief of staff of the Confederate army in Atlanta; diarist

Smith, Lt. Gen. Edmund Kirby, known as Kirby Smith: commander of the Confederacy's Trans-Mississippi Department

Smith, Brig. Gen. A. J.: commander of Union infantry in the Red River expedition

Stanton, Edwin M.: Union secretary of war

Steele, Brig. Gen. Frederick: Union commander in ill-fated expedition to Camden

Stinson, Mrs. Virginia: officers of both armies stayed at her home in Camden, Arkansas

Stone, W. M.: governor of Iowa succeeding Samuel Kirkwood

Stoneman, Maj. Gen. George: Union commander in raid south of Atlanta

Taylor, Maj. Gen. Richard: Confederate commander opposing Red River expedition

Thayer, Brig. Gen. John M.: judge in trial of David Dodd; later Union commander under Steele in march to Camden

Thomas, Maj. Gen. George H.: Union commander in Atlanta campaign, known as the "Rock of Chickamauga"

Varner, Capt. Martin: commander of Company A, 36th Iowa Volunteer Infantry; in charge on march from Helena

Walden, Capt. M. M.: commander of Company H, Eighth Iowa Cavalry; Barney Brayman's company commander

Wheeler, Maj. Gen. Joseph: Confederate cavalry commander opposing Sherman on march through Georgia; victor at Battle of Newnan

Winder, John Henry: in charge of the Confederate prisoner-of-war system

Wirz, Capt. Heinrich Hartmann or "Henry": Confederate officer in charge of interior of prison camp at Andersonville

Wittenmyer, Annie Turner: Keokuk widow who organized care for wounded and sick Union soldiers

PROLOGUE

This is a true story.

Andrew Jackson Brayman and Edward Barney Brayman, the brothers of Orr Kelly's grandmother, died young, leaving behind no letters, no diaries, nothing but the bare skeletons of their military careers outlined in the records of their service in the Civil War. It would have been tempting to resort to fiction to tell the story of them and their Iowa farm family, relying on the vast written record of the war.

We have not done that. Instead, we have pursued the ghosts of Andrew, and Barney, as Edward was known, through the records of the units in which they served, the after-action reports and memoirs of their officers, and the diaries, letters, and newspaper accounts of men who served in the same units as they did.

It was Mary Kelly, during her research as a genealogist, who first came across Andrew and Barney and kept digging for more information about them. The more she learned, the more she insisted: "There's a story here."

Gradually we came to know the two boys. By sheer luck we stumbled across pictures of both of them, so we know what they looked like. We even found a lock of Andrew's sandy-colored hair enclosed in the frame with one picture. We learned where they served, what hospitals Andrew recuperated in, where they fought, where one of them died, and where the other was captured. We visited the site of the infamous prison at Andersonville, where Barney was incarcerated, and sensed what it must have been like to be a prisoner there in the summer of 1864.

Our search was made more difficult by the circumstances of the two boys' service. Andrew fought in Arkansas, far from the center of attention of most Civil War historians, in a campaign that rates a footnote at most in histories of the war. Unlike the sites of the great battles of the war, with their statuary, their cemeteries, their dioramas and visitor centers, the crossroads where Andrew died contain only a small marker, a single picnic table, and a trash barrel.

Barney's activities were no easier to trace. He served in the cavalry, and while many maps show the exact position of infantry regiments in major battles, the cavalry was always off on a raid or protecting the flanks of the army or scouting out enemy positions. Finding just where Barney's cavalry company was and what it was doing posed a constant challenge.

Through all this investigation, the two boys always remained elusive to us, sometimes emerging tantalizingly from the mists, at other times mere shadows fading in and out as we sought them through the fog of time.

We ended our search with a feeling of affection for these two boys and of admiration for the bravery and fortitude of the common soldiers on both sides as they endured the long marches, hunger, heat and cold, the disease, and the bloody fighting of the long war.

Our feeling toward many of their leaders was often quite the opposite: anger rather than admiration. Would Andrew have survived the war, we wondered, if Abraham Lincoln had not, in the process of playing political games with the cotton speculators, sent an incompetent political general off on a wild-goose chase up Louisiana's Red River? Would Barney have avoided imprisonment in Andersonville, we wondered, if General William T. Sherman had thought through the consequences of sending a cavalry raid south of Atlanta or if the incompetent General George Stoneman had not disobeyed orders?

We concluded that, as so often happens in war, the men who fought were more to be admired than their leaders.

In our search, we found helpful encouragement wherever we turned. We are particularly indebted to the following:

Dr. Gregory J. W. Urwin, professor of history at the University of Central Arkansas in Conway, shared with us his own writings on the Civil War in Arkansas, especially his dramatic account of the massacre at Poison Springs, and guided us to a number of other valuable sources. Just as we were preparing to leave his office, he mentioned that he had several pictures of men who had served in Arkansas, all but one of them officers. The one enlisted man turned out to be Andrew Brayman, in his military uniform.

This led us to Roger Davis of Keokuk, Iowa, who had provided Dr.

Urwin with the picture. We contacted Davis and learned he had picked it up at a yard sale. And as it turned out, he had also found a picture of Andrew's brother, Barney. He supplied us with copies of both pictures.

In the course of our research, we spent a week at the State Historical Society of Iowa Library/Archives in Des Moines. There, Ellen Sulser, one of the archivists, proved most helpful not only in supplying materials we asked for but in suggesting others we should look at. At one point she showed up with a cart brimming with the wartime correspondence of the state's adjutant general, containing the original letters and telegrams between him and officers of the regiments in which Andrew and Barney served.

Officials at the state archives in both Nashville, Tennessee, and Little Rock, Arkansas, were also helpful in providing us with materials about the war in their states.

In Arkansas a focus of our research was the Battle of Marks' Mills, in which Andrew was killed. One of the most useful and pleasant afternoons we spent was at the rural home, a few miles from the battlefield, of Anita Knowles, whose ancestors had lived in the area since before the war. Mrs. Knowles was eighty-two years old at the time of our visit. As a schoolgirl in the 1930s, she wrote a research paper recounting interviews with residents of the area who were alive at the time of the war. Her recollections of what they told her, plus the stories passed down to her by her parents and grandparents, provided an invaluable glimpse of what life was like in rural Arkansas when the war suddenly found its way there.

In Camden we met with Townsend Mosely, who has walked the entire route of General Frederick Steele's ill-fated expedition to Camden and back, using his metal detector to find the route the soldiers followed and the fields where they fought. He was especially helpful in describing for us what he had learned about the battles of Elkins' Ferry, Poison Springs, and Marks' Mills.

We also drew on the knowledge of several persons who have studied and, in several cases, reenacted the Civil War battles in Arkansas: James Boney of New Edinburg; Jim Hearnsberger of Thornton; Mark Meyers, superintendent of the Moro Bay and Eldorado state parks; Mr. and Mrs. Edgar A. Colvin of Pine Bluff, who have erected a number of markers in the area where the Marks family mills stood.

John Teeter, who manages a museum of local history in Prescott, Arkansas, near the site of the Battle of Prairie de Ann, described that battle for us and helped orient us to visit the battlefield, which is unmarked.

In Little Rock, Mark Christ of the Department of Arkansas Heritage provided us with an article he had written on the Civil War in Arkansas and guided us to several other sources of information. We also met with James L. Northum, a staff forester with the Arkansas Forestry Commission, who described for us how the countryside would have looked to the Union soldiers on their march south from Little Rock in March and April 1864.

In Georgia one of our most rewarding mornings was spent with Kevin McAuliff, a preservation planner in Dalton for the State Regional Development Center. With him we drove and walked over the Rocky Ridge battlefield area where the Union and Confederate forces first met at the beginning of Sherman's march to Atlanta and beyond.

We also visited the Atlanta History Center, the battlefields in the area of Kennesaw Mountain, and the local historical societies and libraries in Newnan, the city near which Barney Brayman was captured, and in Helena, where the 36th Iowa Infantry was stationed.

Much of our basic research was done at the Library of Congress and the National Archives in Washington, as well as at the Fort Ward Museum in Alexandria, Virginia, and the National Library of Medicine in Bethesda, Maryland.

We are particularly indebted to Greg Urwin for reading the manuscript of *Dream's End* and helping to protect us from the errors of carelessness or ignorance that tend to creep into any attempt to cover such a broad sweep of history.

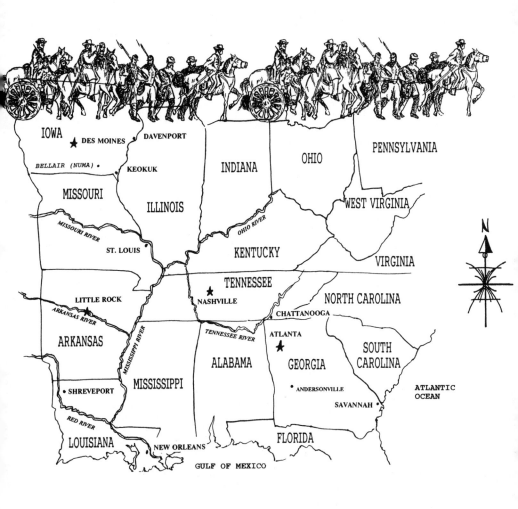

IOWA
DES MOINES
DAVENPORT
BELLAIR (NUMA)
KEOKUK
MISSOURI
ILLINOIS
INDIANA
OHIO
PENNSYLVANIA
WEST VIRGINIA
MISSOURI RIVER
OHIO RIVER
ST. LOUIS
KENTUCKY
VIRGINIA
TENNESSEE
LITTLE ROCK
NASHVILLE
NORTH CAROLINA
ARKANSAS RIVER
CHATTANOOGA
TENNESSEE RIVER
ATLANTA
ARKANSAS
MISSISSIPPI RIVER
ALABAMA
GEORGIA
SOUTH CAROLINA
SHREVEPORT
MISSISSIPPI
ANDERSONVILLE
ATLANTIC OCEAN
SAVANNAH
RED RIVER
LOUISIANA
NEW ORLEANS
FLORIDA
GULF OF MEXICO

N

Dream's End

Sudrake   C W Wittrick   A J Hamilton

Part One

The War Comes to Iowa

PAGE XXIV: *Officers of the 36th Iowa Volunteer Infantry. Seated at center are Lt. Col. Francis Marion Drake, the deputy regimental commander, and to his left Col. Charles W. Kittredge, the regimental commander.* (State Historical Society of Iowa Library/Archives, Des Moines.)

Chapter One

A Call to Arms

As Mary Brayman looked around the supper table one warm evening in the summer of 1862, her feelings of pride and pleasure in her family were tempered by a nagging sense of foreboding. It was the second year of the great conflict between the North and the South, and the winds of war were blowing uncomfortably close to their home in the tiny farming community of Bellair, Iowa.

Mary didn't worry about her eldest daughter, Tory—Victoria Icebenda—who was happily married to Gilbert Clark Goodenough. He was a graduate of her own alma mater, the Belleville Academy in upstate New York, and a promising schoolmaster.

She didn't worry, either, about little Belle—Arabella—who, at five years old, was the delight of the family.

But sometimes as she glanced at her husband, Lewis, then 55 and in poor health, and at her two sons, a painful sense of apprehension swelled up like a wave and almost seemed to overwhelm her.

The two boys were too young to join the army and thankfully would be spared service if the war ended soon. Andy was 17 and his brother, Edward Barney—known as Barney—was only 15. But the boys could talk of little but the war. Many of their slightly older friends had already signed up in response to President Lincoln's call, on July 2, for 300,000 three-year volunteers.

Their home in the village of Bellair (now known as Numa), situated on the edge of the prairie in Appanoose County, Iowa, only a few miles from the Missouri border, was not as remote as it seemed. The weekly Centerville *Chieftain*, published in the county seat a dozen miles to the north, provided a steady flow of information from the battlefronts and from the state and national capitals in Des Moines and Washington. Boys who had enlisted in the early days of the war came home or wrote letters with their eyewitness accounts of the war.

In the early months of the conflict, there was a good deal of optimism that the war would be a short one. Almost everyone assumed it would be only a matter of weeks, or at most months, before the Southern states were brought back into line. Even after the devastating Union defeat at the Battle of Bull Run, back east in Virginia in July 1861, the Ottumwa (Iowa) *Weekly Courier* offered this encouraging view:

"It is not at all likely that the volunteers will be needed longer than the first of next May, which is the time General [Winfield] Scott has set for the rebellion to be put down. The regulars will be able to finish up what remains of the mutiny after the volunteers have swept through the rebel country."

But by the summer of 1862, much of the news was not good. Even the newspaper stories of Northern victories came bordered with accounts of appalling casualties.

In February a combined force of infantry, under Brig. Gen. Ulysses S. Grant, and river gunboats took Fort Henry on the Tennessee River near the Tennessee-Kentucky border, then followed up with the capture of Fort Donelson on the Cumberland River ten miles to the east, with the surrender of 15,000 Confederate soldiers. The victory at Fort Donelson brought the first favorable attention to Grant from a Northern public eager for a winner, as well as promotion to the rank of major general of volunteers. When the Confederate commander asked for terms of surrender, Grant replied: "No terms except an unconditional and immediate surrender can be accepted. I propose to move immediately upon your works." In the press he was instantly hailed as "Unconditional Surrender Grant."

The capture of the two forts was a severe blow to the Confederacy, beginning the process of opening up the great network of internal waterways, especially the mighty Mississippi, to the movement of Northern boats and troops.

But the good news of the Confederate surrender at Donelson was followed quickly by reports of the terrible casualties taken by the Union forces: 500 killed, 2,104 wounded, and 224 missing. The four Iowa regiments involved in the battle suffered 40 killed—33 of them in a single regiment, the Second Iowa Infantry. As a sign of mourning, Iowa newspaper editors "turned the rules" on their front pages: The strips of lead that separate the columns normally make fine lines, but the editors turned them upside down, making a series of broad black lines that gave a funereal tone to the page.

Before going to the front, the Second Iowa had been detailed as guards at a prison, a converted college. When some of the college's possessions were found to be missing, the regiment was blamed. When it left for the battlefront, it was forced to march with its flags furled and without band music as a symbol of its disgrace.

At Donelson the regiment, seeking to restore its image, charged through a barricade of fallen trees, broke into the fort, and raised its flag, torn by 16 bullet holes, over the stronghold. When news of the battle reached Des Moines, the governor and the adjutant general went to the scene with a team of doctors to care for the wounded. They returned to hang the flag of the Second Iowa in a position of honor in the state house of representatives.

A month later three Iowa regiments and two light artillery batteries were involved in a major battle at Pea Ridge, just south of the Missouri border in the northwestern corner of Arkansas. That victory was especially welcome to the residents of Appanoose and other counties on the southern tier of Iowa. It meant that the threat of attack from Southern forces in Missouri that might bring the war to their own homes had been removed.

But again the casualties among the Iowa regiments were appallingly high. Iowa accounted for a third of the 1,384 Union casualties with 64 dead, 362 wounded, and 17 missing.

Less than a month later, Iowa troops bore yet another heavy burden of dead, wounded, and captured when 40,000 Confederate soldiers under General Albert Sidney Johnston caught Grant's army asleep near Pittsburg Landing in southern Tennessee in a battle whose name still has an ominous ring—Shiloh.

Grant had with him at Shiloh 11 Iowa regiments—a quarter of his entire force. Five of the Iowa regiments, joined by two from Illinois, fought all day along a sunken road that came to be known as the "Hornets Nest," holding off the Confederate assault long enough for Grant to throw reinforcements into the battle and drive the Rebels back.

The euphoria brought by news of the narrowly won Union victory at Shiloh was quickly followed by horror at the scale of the casualties. Lincoln was justifiably appalled. Grant, a hero because of his victories at Forts Henry and Donelson, was the victor at Shiloh, but he was also responsible for what was almost a disastrous defeat and for the enor-

Battle of Pittsburg Landing (Shiloh). (Authors' collection.)

mous casualties. Grant, who spent too much time drinking and too little time studying tactics, had failed to order his troops to dig trenches
and set up defensive barriers. Thus, when the Confederate soldiers
suddenly materialized out of the morning mists, the Union troops were
nearly as defenseless as sheep and were slaughtered almost as easily.

A third of the 7,000 Iowans involved in the battle became casualties: 235 killed, 999 wounded, and 1,147 missing or captured. Of the
wounded, 116 died within a short time after the battle.

It was this terribly costly "victory," coupled with other bloody battles and setbacks in the Eastern Theater, that led to Lincoln's call for
300,000 volunteers in July. And it was this call for volunteers that sent
teams of civilian recruiters out in wagons from Centerville to bring in
the manpower for what would become the 36th Iowa Volunteer
Infantry.

They came in a train of horse-drawn wagons, sometimes even
bringing along a brass band, to Bellair, Cincinnati, and the other little
towns of Appanoose County. Music from the band would draw a
crowd. Then the "war speeches" began, urging young men in the audi-
ence to heed the call to the colors. Sometimes there was a celebrity of
sorts to attract attention.

On August 11, little more than a month after Lincoln's call for volunteers, Andrew Jackson Brayman, his blue eyes shining with patriotic fervor beneath an unruly shock of auburn hair, stepped forward and enlisted as a private in Company I of the 36th Iowa Volunteer Infantry. Company I was one of four 100-man companies drawn from rural Appanoose County. The 36th was one of 23 regiments that Iowa sent off to war in 1862.

Mary Brayman had taken some comfort from the knowledge that Andy was too young to volunteer. He was. But the day after his enlistment, his father signed a paper giving his permission for his son to enlist. Although he was only two months beyond his seventeenth birthday, the document listed the new private's age as 18.

For Lewis Brayman, there was not only a father's worry at seeing his son go off to war, perhaps to suffer death or a crippling wound. The enlistment of his strapping young son was also a severe economic loss. To the Brayman family, as to agrarian families throughout history, a son was an important part of the family's wealth. Andrew and his younger brother, Barney, also embodied the family's hopes for the future. They were the ones who would continue to cultivate the family's 328 acres and eventually pass on the family name to their own children.

How much did a son amount to in cold economic terms? To a Northern farm family, a son was certainly at least as valuable as a slave was to a Southern planter. In 1860 in Arkansas the purchase of a good field hand cost about $1,500—enough money to buy a farm with a house, barn, and cattle. Ironically, the farmers of the North sent their wealth—their sons—off to war while the Southerners also sent their sons but refused—for a variety of reasons—especially the fear of armed black men—to commit a significant part of their wealth to the war, not arming their slaves until the very end of the conflict.

The few days after his enlistment were a flurry of activity for Andrew and the other young men who formed Company I—the Bellair Company. One of their first and most important tasks was to elect their officers. By acclamation, they chose as their captain Joseph B. Gedney, a prosperous 36-year-old local farmer with 155 acres of land who was the father of six children. George R. Hutson, 34, was chosen as first lieutenant and Walter S. Johnson, 27, as second lieutenant. Gedney was older than most of the men he was chosen to lead, although many of the new soldiers were married and had children, unlike the predominantly young, unmarried volunteers of 1861. Gedney seemed a born leader. But neither he nor the other two officers had any military experience.

Wearing their own clothes and carrying their own weapons, the men of Company I drilled up and down the crossroads at the center of Bellair.

On August 16, a Saturday, they formed a parade of wagons and joined the three other Appanoose County companies in Centerville. As the boys from Bellair came into the square around the courthouse, the other companies lined up and saluted them. Word quickly spread through the ranks: They would leave on August 19, only three days away, to report to Camp Lincoln in Keokuk, at the southeastern corner of Iowa, for basic training.

The troops from Bellair returned home to pack the few belongings they would take with them to camp. On the nineteenth they returned to Centerville. Family members and local residents formed a cheering crowd to see them off. But then new orders came over the telegraph: They were to remain in Centerville and drill there until the call to report to active duty came.

Disappointed, the Bellair boys drifted back home again. Although their departure for military service was delayed, the additional time at home gave them a chance to help finish the year's harvest—in itself an important contribution to the war effort.

Then word came down from Centerville of a grand rally to be held on September 2. A team was sent out to bring in a fifer and drummer to provide music for the gathering, and 150 leaflets were printed.

On the morning of September 2, the Bellair Company again took the now-familiar ride to Centerville to join the other companies north of town to drill in their formations.

While they drilled, residents of the town were busy preparing a lavish meal. The food was served in relays. First the soldiers ate, then the women, and finally the men. After the dinner two local men—including M. H. Hare, who would serve as the regimental chaplain—gave patriotic speeches. Then the troops formed up and marched back into town.

When the rally was over, the boys from Bellair went home once again.

A week later the Bellair boys were called to rendezvous in Centerville and prepare, at last, to leave for camp. For two days they bivouacked near Centerville, and then on September 11 the orders to report to camp arrived. Early the next morning they climbed into wagons for the ride to the nearest railway at Ottumwa, some 40 miles northeast.

That night the troops camped on the riverbank opposite Ottumwa. The next morning they forded the river and sat down to eat a breakfast prepared for them the day before by the women of Centerville. Then they climbed into the railroad cars for the 90-mile trip east to Burlington and then south to Keokuk.

For many of the boys, it was their first ride on a railroad train—the first of many new sights and sounds and experiences that would quickly transform these simple farm boys into worldly veterans, old beyond their years.

Chapter Two

The Dream Is Born

When Lewis Brayman was born in the rocky hills of Windham County, Vermont, on April 16, 1807, the great forces that were to shape his life and those of his sons had already been set into motion. And if one man can be singled out as setting them in motion and giving them voice, it is Thomas Jefferson, author of the Declaration of Independence and third president of the new nation.

First came the philosophy. In June 1781 Jefferson injured his wrist and was unable to ride out over the 5,500-acre estate surrounding his mountaintop home in Monticello, Virginia. Instead, he stayed home and answered a series of questions about Virginia that had been posed to him by a French diplomat—a document later published as *Notes on Virginia*. It was a detailed account of the people, geography, crops, and geology of Virginia. But it also contained a brief description of Jefferson's ideal for the future of the United States—a future in which the nation would be peopled by free, independent yeoman farmers rather than city dwellers and factory workers. This is what he wrote:

> Those who labor in the earth are the chosen people of God, if ever He had a chosen people, whose breasts He has made his peculiar deposit for substantial and genuine virtue. It is the focus in which he keeps alive that sacred fire, which otherwise might escape from the face of the earth. Corrup-

tion of morals in the mass of cultivators is a phenomenon of which no age nor nation has furnished an example.

It is the mark set on those who, not looking up to heaven, to their own soil and industry, as does the husbandsman, for their subsistence, depend for it on casualties and caprice of customers. Dependence begets subservience and venality, suffocates the germ of virtue, and prepares fit tools for the designs of ambition. This, the natural progress and consequence of the arts, has sometimes perhaps been retarded by accidental circumstances; but, generally speaking, the proportion which the aggregate of the other classes of citizens bears in any state to that of its husbandmen, is the proportion of its unsound to its healthy parts, and is a good enough barometer whereby to measure its degree of corruption.

While we have land to labor then, let us never wish to see our citizens occupied at a workbench, or twirling a distaff. Carpenters, masons, smiths, are wanting in husbandry; but, for the general operations of manufacture, let our workshops remain in Europe. It is better to carry provisions and materials to workmen there, than bring them [the workmen] to the provisions and materials, and with them their manners and principles. The loss by the transportation of commodities across the Atlantic will be made up in happiness and permanence of government. The mobs of great cities add just so much to the support of pure government, as sores do to the strength of the human body. It is the manners and spirit of a people which preserve a republic in vigor. A degeneracy in these is a canker which soon eats to the heart of its laws and constitution.

For Jefferson, it is obvious, this was more a philosophical ideal than a guide to everyday life—at least his own life. By 1796 he had set up a manufacturing plant on his own estate and was turning out 1,000 pounds of nails each month. Later, at the time of the War of 1812, he manufactured cloth, and his writings reflected a growing respect for those engaged in commerce. "Experience has taught me," he wrote, "that manufactures are now as necessary to our independence as to our comfort."

Despite Jefferson's own change of view, millions of Americans saw themselves mirrored in his earlier words. They were strong, independent, and self-reliant. They worked the land with their hands and were proud of their hard labor. With Jefferson, they opposed taxes and a strong central government. With Jefferson, they believed in the rights of the states. The echoes of Jefferson's idealism can be heard clearly even today in much of the American nation's political rhetoric.

Perhaps Jefferson's political philosophy would have had no practical effect if the population of the growing nation had been confined to the original colonial territory and the cities of the Atlantic seaboard. But an action taken by Jefferson in 1803 made it possible for Americans not only to dream the Jeffersonian ideal but to hope to achieve it in their own lives. By his action he made available what then seemed an unlimited "land to labor."

In 1803, in an action of such questionable constitutionality that it would quickly have gotten a twentieth-century president impeached, Jefferson arranged with France for the purchase, for 60 million francs or 12 million dollars, of a vast, unsurveyed, and ill-defined expanse of land extending west from the Mississippi River to the Rockies. It included all or parts of today's states of Montana, North and South Dakota, Minnesota, Iowa, Wyoming, Nebraska, Colorado, Kansas, Missouri, Oklahoma, Arkansas, and Louisiana. Neither Jefferson nor anyone else knew exactly what the nation had bought with the Louisiana Purchase. What was clear was that the nation now had, for all practical purposes, an unlimited frontier to provide room for a vast westward movement.

Although Americans were to be divided at midcentury in a bitter war, the Jeffersonian ideal appealed strongly to rural families both north and south. The families of Scotch-Irish ancestry who were moving westward across the South were much the same as those of English ancestry who were moving westward across the North. They saluted the same flag, sang the same songs, worshiped the same God—although in different churches—and nourished the same dreams of freedom and independence sketched for them by Jefferson. Until 1860 the majority of these Americans lived on and cultivated the land, just as Jefferson had wished.

Lewis Brayman and Mary Gore were both part of the westward movement. In the mid-1830s, when he was in his late twenties, Lewis moved from Vermont to Ohio to farm.

Mary Genette Gore was born June 18, 1814, near Belleville, in the far north of New York State, near the eastern shore of Lake Ontario, the daughter of Samuel and Rebecca Barney Gore. Her father had died at age 40 when Mary was little more than a year old, and she was reared by her mother, an accomplished milliner. Upstate New York had a tradition of small-college higher education for men and women, and Mary received a good education at the Belleville Academy. She was thus able to pass on to her children a love of books and learning in an age when many farm boys were thought to need little formal education and most girls could learn all the domestic skills they needed to know at home from their mothers.

Adopting the pattern followed by many families, Mary's twin brothers, Hart and Clark Gore, moved from New York to Ohio in the 1830s, cleared land for a farm, and set up a sawmill. Once they were settled, Mary and her mother moved west to join them.

Lewis and Mary were married in Franklin Mills, Ohio, on March 19, 1837. Their first daughter, Victoria Icebenda Brayman—her unusual middle name came from Lewis's sister—was born in Ravenna, Ohio, on March 13, 1840. Their second child, Andrew Jackson Brayman, was born in Rootstown, Ohio, on June 8, 1845, and their third, Edward Barney Brayman, was born in Newbury, Ohio, on January 8, 1847. Their second son's middle name was his maternal grandmother's maiden name. He was known throughout his life as Barney.

In 1856 the economy was robust, and thousands of restless residents of Ohio were able to sell their farms at a profit and migrate farther west. The Brayman family joined the migration, taking the railroad west to the Mississippi. At Burlington, Iowa, Lewis and Mary—who was six months pregnant with their fourth child—piled all their belongings into two wagons. Then, with Tory, Andrew, and Barney perched atop the load, they set out on the 100-mile trek to south-central Iowa.

They were not alone. Long columns of wagons filled the trails across the prairie. The growth of the state's population was explosive: from 192,000 in 1850 to 675,000 in 1860. Growth continued even during the turmoil of the Civil War, expanding the population to 1,194,000 by 1870.

Today, Iowa seems firmly rooted in the Midwest—in fact, at the center of the nation. But in 1856 it was considered to lie far to the west, literally on the frontier.

Although the area between the Missouri and Mississippi rivers that became the state of Iowa had been included in the Louisiana Purchase, the land continued to be occupied primarily by several Indian tribes for three decades, until the Black Hawk War of 1832. The door was then opened partially to white settlers, but even after the white men's victory in that war, large portions of the area remained off-limits to whites. Gradually more and more of the state was opened to settlement in treaties with the tribes.

Iowa became a U.S. territory in 1838, with its capital in Iowa City. It was granted statehood in 1846 as a free state, balancing the admission of Florida as a slave state. Iowa's capital was moved to Des Moines in 1857.

Although Iowa was still very much a frontier state when they arrived, the route the Brayman family followed had already been well worn. In 1832 an army cavalry troop known as dragoons had cut across the southeastern corner of Iowa on the way to Missouri, establishing what came to be called the Dragoon Trail. They are believed to have been the first white men to visit the area that became the Braymans' new home in Appanoose County—which was named for a chief of the Sac tribe.

Another trail in the same area was known as the Bee Trace because it was used by pioneers who gathered honey from a series of trees harboring bees.

These earlier designations gave way to another name after a large migration of Mormon families passed through the area in 1839 and 1840, fleeing from persecution in Ohio and then from their headquarters at Nauvoo, Illinois. After 1840 the wagon road network was known as the Mormon Trail.

In 1856, trundling over these routes already heavy with history, the Brayman family made their way to the tiny new settlement of Bellair, in Appanoose County, only a few miles north of the Missouri border. The town had been laid out with 20 lots in 1854, and a general store was opened there the following year. But it had neither telegraph nor railroad links to the outside world, and it was not until 1859 that a post office was opened in Bellair. With the proceeds of the sale of his Ohio farm, Lewis was able to buy 40 acres of farmland for $700 and, a few months later, to purchase another 211½ acres for $1,400.

To a family arriving in the fall of 1856, southern Iowa must have seemed like the promised land. The county is laced with small streams in the watershed separating the Missouri and Mississippi rivers. Streams flowing into the Fox River deliver their water to the Mississippi. Those flowing into the broad Chariton River contribute to the flow of the Missouri. The rivers and streams broke the land into picturesque, heavily forested, shallow valleys, interspersed with open prairies. Lewis and his farmer friends sifted the rich soil through their fingers and pronounced it the most fertile they had ever seen. In the wooded valleys, long used as hunting grounds by the Sac and Fox tribes, game was plentiful.

Enjoying the warm sun of the late summer and the crisp days of early autumn, the new settlers had no hint of what lay in store for them.

On the first of December 1856, an arctic air mass swept down over what is now the Midwest, heralding the fiercest winter since white men first settled in the area. None of the settlers had ever experienced the full fury of a prairie storm, and even the Indians said they had never encountered such bad weather. Heavy snow was accompanied by howling winds and temperatures that hovered at or below zero.

The new settlers in Appanoose County were relatively fortunate: The distances between the sheltering groves of trees along the streambeds were short. But farther north those trying to travel from one point to another had to cover 25 or 30 miles across the open prairie from one settlement, in a sheltering grove of trees, to the next. Many of the new settlers lost their lives while the storm raged.

After three days the storm let up. But the bad weather continued for months, with more snow, wind, and bitter temperatures. Spring came a month later than usual, frost was recorded in June, and the first strawberries didn't appear until the first day of summer.

In the midst of this bitter winter—and three days before their first Christmas in their new home—Mary Brayman gave birth to the family's fourth child. Flora Arabella Brayman was born on December 22, 1856. In rural Iowa in the 1850s, many children died in infancy or in their early years. But the Brayman family was fortunate. The new baby, her mother and father, sister and brothers all lived through that dreadful winter.

As the winter's snows finally melted, Lewis set to work with a wooden plow to open the fertile land for his first crops, probably oats, Indian corn, and wheat, the three major crops produced by the pioneers. The future looked as bright as the broad prairie skies. But just over the horizon were dark clouds of another kind.

In the summer of 1857, the nation was struck by an economic storm that today's Americans, with their multitude of safety nets, can scarely imagine. The storm began in August with the collapse of the

Ohio Life and Trust Company, a life insurance and financial-agency firm. Wall Street panicked. Banks closed or refused payments. Gold, silver, and the notes issued by stable banks in Massachusetts, New York, and Ohio disappeared. All that was left in circulation were various forms of scrip and IOUs of dubious value. Notes issued by banks in one state could not be redeemed at banks in another state.

Land values plummeted. When tax sales were held in 1858, the fortunate few with cash were able to buy previously valuable property at only a few cents on the dollar.

Appanoose County farmers, who had had a good harvest, found themselves with barns full of oats, corn, and wheat but no one with money to buy their crops. The only way to get goods or services was to trade—so many bushels of corn for an ax or a bolt of cloth, for example. The entire state and much of the nation was reduced to a barter economy.

If the state legislature had not intervened with a law extending the time allowed to redeem lands seized for taxes, three-fourths of the land in Iowa would have changed hands.

The havoc caused by the depression continued for four years. Things had only begun to return to something close to normal when the war came in 1861—and the war would cause far more disruption than the freaks of nature and the economy that preceded it. Borne along in this great tide of war, Andrew Brayman and his colleagues in Company I of the 36th Iowa Volunteer Infantry began their military careers at Camp Lincoln in Keokuk.

Chapter Three

You're in
the Army Now

On the afternoon of September 13, when the train from Ottumwa pulled into the Keokuk station on the bank of the Mississippi, Andy and the other farm boys from southern Iowa leaned out the windows, drinking in the sight of the biggest river they had ever seen, and of the steamers tied up along the levee or moving majestically up and down its waters.

Through the windows on the other side of the train, they were surprised to see two companies of infantry drawn up in ranks as a welcoming committee.

The welcome they received was a far cry from the decidedly unfriendly greeting that had been accorded some of the first troops to arrive in Keokuk a year before. Keokuk, situated in the extreme southeastern corner of Iowa, just north of the Missouri border, was notorious as a hotbed of antiwar sentiment. In fact, one of the motives for setting up Union training camps at Keokuk was to protect the area from guerrilla forces across the border in Missouri—forces that might otherwise have received a friendly welcome from local Southern sympathizers.

When one of the early Union regiments, arriving by boat in the summer of 1861, had debarked and lined up on the levee, the soldiers were startled when passengers on passing steamboats hooted and jeered at them. As they marched up the street to the tune of a band playing "The Girl I Left Behind Me," citizens of Keokuk were at the windows and on the roofs of buildings shouting derisively.

The hostility was returned a short time later when one of the sol-diers was drugged in a bar: Members of his company descended on the bar the next day and trashed it.

Tensions between soldiers and some Keokuk citizens continued throughout the war. At one point soldiers returning from the front seized the type and press of the Keokuk *Constitution-Democrat* and threw them into the Mississippi. Governor Samuel J. Kirkwood wor-ried constantly about the safety of Keokuk and other communities in the southern tier of Iowa counties and encouraged the organization of Home Guard companies to preserve order.

In the years just before the war, much money had been spent to make Keokuk into the greatest city on the Mississippi. Located at the point where the Des Moines River enters the Mississippi, its prospects as a trading center had seemed bright. But the arrival of the railroads had cut sharply into river trade. Although Keokuk did gain railroad service, the major east-west line passed to the north through Burling-ton, providing a more direct link between the growing cities of Illinois and Iowa. In effect, at the time war broke out, Keokuk was in decline. If the locomotive had not killed the town, it had hurt it severely.

By the time the 36th Infantry regiment arrived, however, many cit-izens of Keokuk realized that business stimulated by the four bustling army camps on a plateau above the town had saved the city, at least for a while, from a more severe decline.

Hence the welcoming committee that greeted Andrew and the other boys on their arrival in Keokuk. When they alighted from the cars, they lined up in a rough approximation of a military formation and marched off, trying to keep in step. But they were not a very imposing sight. They carried no weapons, and they were still dressed in the civilian clothes they had worn when leaving home.

Their new home was Camp Lincoln. Although it had been estab-lished only a month before, two other regiments had already passed through the camp and, after the briefest of training, were headed south toward the battle zone. Most of the boys were assigned to drafty, hastily built barracks, much like the distinctive two-story buildings that sprang up at camps across the country during World War II. The overflow were assigned to tents.

At Camp Lincoln the new soldiers of the 36th Iowa met the two men who were to lead the regiment through the next three years. Unlike the company officers, who were elected by the men them-

Col. Charles W. Kittredge, commander of the 36th Iowa Volunteer Infantry.
(State Historical Society of Iowa Library/Archives, Des Moines.)

selves, the regimental officers were picked by Governor Kirkwood. He made his choice based at least as much on political considerations as on the officer's military ability. The appointment of regimental officers was an important source of political patronage for Kirkwood and the other Northern governors. Even after regiments were sworn into federal service, they retained strong ties to the statehouse in Des Moines, and issued a steady stream of reports to the state adjutant general.

The men of the 36th were therefore fortunate that, in addition to their political qualifications, their colonel and his second-in-command both had had at least some limited military experience.

Appointed colonel of the new regiment was Charles A. Kittredge, 36, a resident of Ottumwa, the largest city in south-central Iowa. The year before, Kittredge had enlisted for three years as a captain of Company F of the seventh regiment of Iowa volunteers. He received his commission on July 24, 1861, and less than four months later was severely wounded in a minor battle at Belmont, Missouri.

The enemy bullet tore into his right groin. If the bullet had struck a bone, it would have shattered and he would almost certainly have died. But he was fortunate: The bullet passed through his body intact. The next few days were nonetheless a harrowing ordeal for him. The wounded captain was left untended on the field of battle until his Confederate captors took him to their base at Columbus, Kentucky. Even there, he remained without medical treatment for six days. Finally, he was turned over to the Union forces and hospitalized at Cairo, Illinois.

Kittredge tried to return to duty, but his wound was so severe that he finally gave up and resigned his commission on June 9, 1862.

Two months later, Kittredge apparently felt well enough to seek appointment as colonel of the new 36th Iowa. But Governor Kirkwood, or some of his aides, harbored doubts. On August 30 N. B. Baker, the state adjutant general, sent a frantic wire from Davenport to the postmaster at Ottumwa: "Stop & return to me here a large envelope & enclosure directed to Charles W. Kittredge, Ottumwa, Iowa, mailed here twentyeighth (28") or twentyninth (29")." On September 10 Baker wired the governor: "We were unable to stop Kittridge [sic] Commission for thirtysixth (36) Regiment. He now nominates a Quarter Master. What shall I do."

By that time, Kittredge had his commission in hand and was preparing to join his new regiment at Camp Lincoln. On September 5, apparently unaware of the effort to snatch back his commission, he wrote a brief, curious note to the governor: "I have decided to accept the commission you have tendered to me and if hereafter you have to blush for the appointment I assure you as a gentleman and a soldier it shall not be for the particular reason we discussed when I saw you recently at Des Moines."

Kittredge did not spell out the "particular reason" he had in mind. But perhaps we can assume, based on troubles he had later in his military career, that he had succumbed to what came to be known as "the old soldier's disease"—the tendency of soldiers to ease the pain of their wounds with opium or, in Kittredge's case, alcohol.

As second in command of Andrew's regiment, Kirkwood appointed Francis Marion Drake as a lieutenant colonel. Although he was only 28 years old, Drake had already had more adventures than most men encounter in a lifetime.

When he was only 18, he had organized a supply train of six six-ox wagons and, with 16 men and a boy, set out across the plains for California. As Drake later told the story, shortly after they had crossed the

Lt. Col. Francis Marion Drake, deputy commander of the 36th Iowa Volunteer Infantry. (Library of Congress, Washington, D.C.)

Missouri River at what is now the border between Iowa and Nebraska, they were attacked by 300 Pawnee warriors and faced an almost certain massacre. But Drake managed to kill the Indian chief with a shot from his musket, and the demoralized war party withdrew.

Two years later Drake set out again for California, this time driving a herd of 100 milk cows—97 of which survived the trip. When he attempted to return home, his ship ran aground on the California coast with a loss of 800 lives. Drake swung down a hawser and found a small boat with which he made three trips ashore, rescuing several passengers. He finally made his way to San Francisco and boarded another ship, which arrived safely on the East Coast despite a fire at sea.

In the spring of 1861, Drake helped organize an independent regiment in which he served as captain and major and was involved in two battles with Rebel forces in Missouri.

Even at his young age, Drake was given to what the soldiers called "corporosity," but they took his portly build as a sign of good health.

During the three years of the 36th Iowa's service, Kittredge was often absent, filling brigade or division positions or, at least on one important occasion, sick. The result was that Drake was often the senior commander in the regiment.

In the euphoria of the August days in which they enlisted, Andrew and his friends could hardly have imagined the indignities and hardships that lay ahead of them.

Four days after their arrival at Camp Lincoln, the boys of Company I were ordered to line up in one of the drafty barracks, strip naked, and submit themselves to a probing examination by what the army called "surgeons," although they were not surgeons in the modern sense and many of them barely qualified as physicians. A few of the recruits were rejected, but most of them were pronounced fit for duty.

Several days later Captain Gedney lined up Company I and read them the Articles of War, a barely comprehensible jumble of rules and regulations. But from then on, if any of the new soldiers got in trouble, the army could insist that they had been warned.

The busy days that followed were filled with almost endless drilling on the Camp Lincoln parade ground, even when rain had turned the grounds into a sea of mud. Reveille sounded at 4 A.M., breakfast call at 5 A.M., drill at 9 o'clock, dinner call at noon, drill call again at 2 P.M., dress parade at 5 o'clock, supper at 5:30, tattoo at 8, and taps at 9 P.M.

As yet the new soldiers had no weapons and were restricted to practicing close-order drill rather than marksmanship. This would seem to be a poor preparation for combat, but the drills, in which ever-larger groups of soldiers learned to march shoulder to shoulder, to change direction while keeping their formation intact, and, most important, to follow orders quickly and without question, were in fact a useful preparation for the type of warfare in which they would be engaged.

Basic battlefield tactics were spelled out in *Infantry-Tactics*, written by Maj. Gen. Winfield Scott, who was recognized as the greatest American military leader of the first half of the nineteenth century. Shortly before the war a new book of tactics was adopted, providing for more rapid and fluid troop movements. But these tactics were still very similar to Scott's. They called for massed formations of highly disciplined troops to march relentlessly on the enemy and overcome him with musket fire from a short range, then make a bayonet attack.

As the troops of the 36th Iowa maneuvered across the parade ground above Keokuk, they learned to march only 13 inches apart, close enough to maintain elbow-to-elbow touch during an advance.

As Scott wrote, if the men "do not strictly observe the touch of elbows, it would be impossible for an individual to judge whether he marches abreast with his neighbour, or not, and whether there be not an interval between them."

Scott also feared that the attacking formation would disintegrate if the men moved too fast. He therefore advised advancing on the foe with a steady, deliberate 28-inch step at a rate of 90 steps a minute, sometimes speeded up to a "quick time" rate of 110 steps a minute. But except in the final moments of a charge, he ruled out double quick time, or the run.

The assumption on which Scott's tactics were based was that a formation could approach close to the foe before it came within range of enemy smoothbore muskets. This assumption had been borne out in a number of battles in the war with Mexico in 1848, a war in which the generals who were to lead troops on both sides during the Civil War served as junior officers. But, by the time of the Civil War, these tactics failed to take into account the fact that many troops on both sides were now armed with rifles, which, with their greater range and accuracy, could decimate an advancing formation well before it got within bayonet range. The advance in weapons technology was startling: While the smoothbore musket had a killing range of 100 yards, the rifled musket was accurate and deadly at 300 to 400 yards and could kill a man at more than half a mile.

Scott's tactics, by failing to take into account this dramatic change, were to cost thousands of lives during the conflict and may even have been responsible for the South's loss of the war.

By September 28, the 36th Iowa was sufficiently well trained that it put on its first dress parade, and Colonel Kittredge pronounced it "well done." "Dress parade" was of course a misnomer, since the new soldiers had yet to be issued uniforms. They were still wearing their civilian clothes, which were rapidly becoming threadbare from the stress of constant drilling.

In their spare time the young soldiers wandered the streets of Keokuk wide-eyed. It was still a small town, but it was bigger and more bustling than anything they had ever seen.

In the towns and villages from which they had come, moreover, black people were a rarity. But Keokuk had become a refuge for hundreds of former slaves—"contraband," as they were known—who wandered the streets seeking work and the protection of white sponsors who would shield them from those trying to return them to their former owners across the line in Missouri. But the soldiers also heard the tales of former slaves who had made their way from as far away as South Carolina.

The streets of Keokuk also, of course, offered all the temptations to which armies are always subjected: liquor, gambling, and loose women. The regimental chaplains, who served to remind the troops of what their mothers would warn them against if they were there, seemed to focus their attention on gambling and swearing although one regiment—the 24th Iowa—was known as the temperance regiment. Less heed seemed to be paid to the temptations of drinking and prostitution, although the spread of venereal disease later became a major concern of army authorities.

One company in particular attracted attention by its volunteer effort to combat the evils of profanity. The members agreed that anyone heard swearing would read aloud a chapter from the Bible. At almost any hour of the day, those passing the company barracks heard the sound of a repentant sinner reading his assigned chapter.

On October 4, nearly two months after most of the men had enlisted and a full three weeks since they had arrived in camp, the troops of the 36th Iowa were finally lined up and mustered into Federal service by Lt. Charles J. Ball of the regular army. The delay in putting them formally on active duty was to become an issue in the summer of 1865 when, with the war over, the veterans were eager to go home but the army insisted they had not served their full three years.

Although it was late summer and still quite warm when the 36th Iowa arrived at Camp Lincoln, by early October the first icy winds of winter were sweeping down from Canada. Despite the cold, it was not until October 9 that each man was issued a single blanket. Kittredge sent a message to the state's adjutant general complaining of the poor quality of the blankets.

He was not the only one complaining. Throughout the army the shortage of blankets was severe. In a frantic effort to provide protection for the troops in the approaching winter, orders were placed as far away as Canada and even England. The more unscrupulous mill owners took the money and produced blankets of what was known in the trade as "shoddy"—material that had been spun into yarn and woven into cloth and then ground up, respun, and rewoven.

Andrew Brayman in uniform. (Roger Davis, Keokuk, Iowa.)

One journalist of the time described shoddy as "a villainous compound, the refuse stuff and sweepings of the shop, pounded, rolled,
glued, and smoothed to the external form and gloss of cloth, but no
more like the genuine article than the shadow is to the substance."

The day before the issue of blankets, the men each received a pair
of shoes, or bootees, as they were known. These ankle-high shoes were
made in a uniform shape so that the same shoe could be worn on either
the right or the left foot.

It was not until October 26, nearly a month and a half after they
had arrived in camp, that the men received additional parts of their
uniforms. Under army regulations, they were supposed to be issued two
caps, one hat, one overcoat, two dress coats, three pairs of trousers,
three flannel shirts, three pairs of flannel drawers, four pairs of stock-
ings, four pairs of bootees, and one blanket.

But on October 27 Kittredge reported to the adjutant general that
his men had received only one dress coat, one pair of pantaloons, one
undershirt, one pair of socks, and one cap. They still were in need of
overcoats, blouses, drawers, and hats.

They did, finally, on October 30, receive rifles and could begin to look and feel like soldiers. Most of the recruits were already familiar with firearms. In many families it was the practice, as a kind of coming-of-age rite, for a boy to be measured for his own custom-made rifle. At $14 it was a sizable investment but also a necessary one for families that depended on game for a good part of their diet. It usually did not take long for a boy to become so skilled with his new rifle that he could "bark" a squirrel—hit the bark so close to a squirrel that it would kill the animal without piercing its fur.

To these boys, who had grown up on or close to the frontier, it was obvious that the weapons provided to them by the army were, for the most part, junk. Kittredge, somewhat more charitably, told the adjutant general, "The guns are many of them defective."

When war broke out, the U.S. Army had in its arsenals half a million old-fashioned smoothbore muskets and about 90,000 weapons with rifled barrels. The changeover to the more accurate rifle, with its longer range, had begun in 1855, while Jefferson Davis, who became president of the Confederacy, was the U.S. secretary of war. At the outbreak of fighting, some of the machinery for manufacturing rifles and some 119,000 muskets and rifles fell into Confederate hands. This left both sides scrambling to provide weapons for their rapidly growing armies.

Ships were soon arriving from Europe at both northern and southern ports carrying weapons originally intended for British, Austrian, French, and Belgian soldiers.

Both the Union and the Confederacy rapidly expanded their arms industries, taking advantage of recent developments in the industrial revolution that permitted mass production of weapons with fully interchangeable parts. By 1863, the U.S. armory at Springfield, Massachusetts, was turning out 600 high-quality rifle muskets a day. The South, with a much smaller industrial base, was never able to produce enough weapons for all its soldiers and had to rely on imports, plus the weapons the troops scavenged from battlefields after their early victories over the Union forces.

In 1862 the North was still issuing imported weapons. What the Iowans received was the eight-pound, Austrian-made Lorenz rifle, firing a .54-caliber bullet and technically known as a rifle musket. Caliber is a measure of the diameter of the bullet or rifle barrel. The bullet for the Lorenz rifle was thus about half an inch in diameter. The rifle came with a long, pointed, angular bayonet that could be attached to the muzzle. Thousands of these rifles were imported and used by both North and South during the war.

In the few weeks they remained in camp after receiving their weapons, the soldiers were taught rudiments of the manual of arms, a series of precise movements in which a soldier bit open a paper cartridge, poured some powder down the barrel, dropped in a bullet, and tamped them both down with a rammer. Then he placed a percussion cap at the other end of the barrel, where it would be struck and ignited by the hammer when he pulled the trigger. In combat three buckshot were often rammed down on top of the bullet. Loading the musket was a cumbersome process whose mastery required a good deal of practice. But the soldiers got good at it: A trained man could get off three shots a minute.

The shortage of supplies in the early days of the war was understandable. An army that at the outset had numbered only 16,000 officers and men—many of them in frontier posts—was expanding by the tens of thousands. The Union quartermaster general, after a few weeks of preparing the army for war, resigned his commission and took a leading role as a Confederate general. He was succeeded by Montgomery C. Meigs, an engineer corps captain who had designed and built the aqueduct that supplied the District of Columbia with water and who supervised the construction of the dome of the U.S. Capitol.

Meigs quickly organized a highly efficient supply force. But graft, bribery, and corruption were a constant problem. At Meigs's urging, the secretary of war ordered the doors to the War Department in Washington to be closed at 3 P.M. each day so his men could get at least some work done without being pestered by the contractors, lobbyists, and speculators who had descended on Washington like a swarm of locusts, seeking to profit from the war effort.

By the spring of 1862, Meigs had made great headway in equipping the rapidly expanding army. But then in July, Lincoln made his call for 300,000 more three-year volunteers and, shortly after that, for another 300,000 militia. As the recruits streamed into training camps, supply shortages were inevitable.

By late October, the men of the 36th Iowa were suffering intensely from the cold. On October 27, in fact, it was so cold that the scheduled drill was canceled. Each barracks was furnished with only a single stove, hardly enough to provide warmth for 80 or 90 men. But the worst part of the day was mealtime. The troops were fed outdoors at "cooking sheds," where their fingers became so cold they could hardly get the food to their mouths.

The cold undoubtedly aggravated what was already becoming an overwhelming problem for the regiment—sickness. In a message on October 24, Kittredge wrote: "I doubt not that our sick list is much increased from exposure to the cold. We have lost four men since we have been in quarters who died of disease. The number of sick reported today is 99."

All 961 members of the regiment had come from small towns and isolated farms. Many of them had never traveled more than a few miles from home. Most of them had never been exposed to, or had the opportunity to build up an immunity to, infectious disease. In Keokuk they were as defenseless against disease as the Native Americans had been when the early explorers imported European diseases.

On October 27, the same day Kittredge reported the partial issue of clothing, he also reported 106 men sick. He was soon reporting more deaths from disease as both measles and smallpox swept through the regiment. Deaths in infancy and early childhood were painfully common in Iowa's frontier communities. But it was a shock to the soldiers and their families to see boys who had left home a few weeks before in the bloom of youthful health simply waste away and die.

Keokuk, in addition to serving as a training base, was also rapidly becoming a major hospital center. Andrew and the other members of the regiment who managed to remain healthy were appalled and frightened to see their friends cut down by disease and to see sick and wounded men, in pitiful condition, carried ashore from steamers arriving from battlefields to the south. One soldier wrote home that the sight of so many sick and disabled soldiers made his heart ache.

On November 24, after little more than two months of training, Andy's Company I and five other companies of the 36th Iowa formed up in ranks and marched down to the riverbank to begin their journey south toward combat. On the following day two of the remaining four companies boarded another packet, and the final two were assigned to two barges towed by the ship.

A number of those who were sick were brought along with the regiment as it headed south. On November 21, a few days before the 36th Iowa departed, Kittredge had reported that, of 953 officers and men, 310 were sick, 17 had died, one had deserted, and one had been discharged since October 4. The regiment had, before it exchanged a single shot with the enemy, lost at least 25 percent of its effective strength. Had such a loss been suffered in battle, it would have been considered disastrous.

Disembarking at St. Louis, the soldiers marched through the city to

Benton Barracks. After their makeshift camp at Keokuk, Benton Barracks seemed to have every convenience, much to their delight. The barracks were roomy and well ventilated, with coal stoves for heat. The kitchens were fitted out with new stoves and comfortable tables and benches. Near each kitchen was a water hydrant with fresh water from a nearby reservoir.

The troops credited Maj. Gen. John C. Frémont for the quality of their new accommodations, although he was no longer in charge of the Western Department. In the early days of the war, Frémont, a politically well-connected general, had spent lavishly—an estimated $12 million—to construct posts such as Benton Barracks, build elaborate fortifications, and purchase supplies for the troops. With a war on, he was in a hurry to get the job done and had had little regard for such technicalities as army regulations. As a result of his haste, the supply system he created was chaotic.

When Maj. Gen. H. W. Halleck took over from Frémont, he was appalled. "The most astonishing orders and contracts for supplies of all kinds have been made and large amounts purport to have been received but there is nothing to show that they have ever been properly issued, and they cannot now be found," he reported.

If the troops, snug in their accommodations at Benton Barracks, had known the full story, they would have realized that Frémont was also at least partially responsible for the Union Army's long delay in providing them with uniforms and even with blankets. Frémont himself escaped prosecution, but his quartermaster, Maj. Justus McKistry, was arrested, tried by court-martial, convicted of favoritism and corruption, and dismissed from the service.

The men were surprised to find that a sizable commercial area had been set up inside the military reservation, offering a great variety of foodstuffs for sale to the troops to supplement their plain army diet. Many of the merchants were recently discharged servicemen. But their prices were high for a soldier making $13 a month: Irish potatoes, $1.05 a bushel; sweet potatoes, $1; chickens, $3; butter, 23 to 27 cents a pound; and eggs, 23 cents a dozen.

The soldiers' stay in the relative comfort of Benton Barracks was brief. On December 19 the 36th Iowa marched down to the levee and embarked for the South. After barely three months of training—much of it without weapons—the army considered the regiment ready to be thrown into battle.

The area south of St. Louis into which they were sailing was in tur-

moil. On December 11 Confederate Brig. Gen. Nathan Bedford Forrest, one of the most skilled and feared Southern cavalry commanders,
had launched an assault on Grant's communications lines in Tennessee. On December 21 Rebel Brig. Gen. John Hunt Morgan began
his own cavalry raids on Federal supply lines in central Tennessee. The
Rebels seemed to be able to strike almost any place at any time. At
Columbus, Kentucky, the 36th Iowa stopped briefly to reinforce the
Federal garrison there in preparation for an enemy attack. To the disappointment of the new soldiers, however, the Rebels withdrew without attacking, and they were denied their baptism of fire.

Although the soldiers could not see the big picture, they were bit
players in a great gathering of forces whose goal was to open up the
entire Mississippi River to Federal boat traffic and thus split the Confederacy in two. The target of this gathering of forces was the Rebel
strongpoint at Vicksburg, Mississippi, whose guns were currently preventing the passage of Union boats.

Chapter Four

Down the Big River

To General Grant, the Rebel fortress at Vicksburg was like a barbed thorn stuck deep in his flesh. No matter how hard he worked at pulling it out, Vicksburg remained steadfast, a threat both to the Union cause and to Grant's own military career.

Vicksburg, which was then little more than a village, lies on the western edge of the state of Mississippi, on the eastern side of the river roughly halfway between New Orleans and Memphis, both of which were in Union hands. The river approaches Vicksburg from the northwest. At a point almost due west of the town, it swings sharply to the east and runs directly toward the high bluffs on which Vicksburg sits. It then curves away to the southwest.

The cliffs that dominate the riverscape at Vicksburg are nearly 300 feet high. They continue off to the northeast where they are known as Haines's Bluff and the Chickasaw Bluffs. As Union officers stood helplessly by on the western side across from Vicksburg, the Rebel guns dominated the river's big curve and effectively blocked all traffic on the Mississippi at that point. Even Union ironclads risked damage, and if other, more vulnerable ships tried to slip past the town, they were in danger of destruction.

Grant began his efforts to take Vicksburg in the fall of 1862, feeling himself under severe pressure to give the people of the North and, particularly, Abraham Lincoln, a victory. In September the North had won a victory of sorts in the Battle of Antietam at Sharpsburg, Maryland. But it was a painfully costly victory—the bloodiest single day's battle ever fought on the North American continent. And Gen. Robert E. Lee had been allowed to slip across the Potomac with his battered army and prepare for another offensive into the North.

To add to Grant's worries, an antisecession Democratic politician named John A. McClernand had organized a body of troops in his home state of Illinois and was heading south with the intention of taking over the war from Grant and winning lasting glory for himself. Although McClernand was technically under Grant's command, he had secret orders from Lincoln that encouraged him to feel that insubordination would not be punished and that he was free to run his own little war.

It was not the first time McClernand had given Grant problems. In the attack on Fort Donelson the previous February, McClernand had charged some Confederate artillery batteries—in violation of orders from Grant—and had been thrown back with heavy losses.

Grant also had to contend with swarms of cotton speculators and other civilians who followed closely behind the army, and sometimes even got out in front of it, in their effort to obtain cotton, which was in desperately short supply in the cotton mills of New England. Fortunes could be, and were, made overnight from cotton lying ready for the picking in Southern fields. As we shall see, cotton speculators were at least partly responsible for an ill-advised military operation the following year that would have a devastating impact on the lives of many Iowa soldiers, especially the men of the 36th Iowa Volunteer Infantry.

Grant became so angered by the speculators that he injudiciously issued an order barring Jews—or "Israelites," as he called them—from the rail lines running into the area where his army was operating. Grant, for some reason, thought of the cotton speculators as Jews even though they were not all, or even mostly, Jewish. On instructions from Washington, the order was quickly withdrawn.

The Department of the Tennessee, which Grant commanded, was also confronted by another human tide: former slaves fleeing northward by the thousands. Their numbers grew rapidly after the Emancipation Proclamation, freeing all slaves in areas in rebellion against the Union, was issued on January 1, 1863. Grant's response was to gather them into "contraband" camps, guarded by soldiers who were instructed to protect them from their former owners and to keep them in the camps. They were put to work picking cotton at a wage of a few cents a day. They were "free," but for many of them life in a Union camp must have seemed little better than life on a Southern plantation. As soon as it was picked, of course, the cotton was eagerly bought up by the speculators.

When he could spare time to think about military matters, Grant —sometimes stimulated by suggestions from Lincoln himself—toyed with, or put into effect, at least six attempts to extract the Vicksburg thorn. One of these attempts was to bring the 36th Iowa into combat for the first time.

Grant's first plan was a good one, although not without serious risks. He would head south down the center of Mississippi. Meanwhile, Grant's friend and confidant, Brig. Gen. William Tecumseh Sherman, would work his way up the Yazoo River, to where it entered the Mississippi 12 miles above Vicksburg, and assault the Confederate positions on Chickasaw and Haines's Bluffs. Grant would arrive as Sherman captured the bluffs, flanking the enemy position. Together they would sweep into Vicksburg from the east and north, silencing the enemy guns.

With an army of 30,000 men in a fleet of gunboats and transports, Sherman moved up the Yazoo. The crews literally had to cut their way through the trees and undergrowth hanging over the banks as they crept through an old river channel known as the Chickasaw Bayou. When they came within view of the bluffs, Sherman was dismayed at the strength of the enemy positions. True, the enemy force numbered about 15,000—only half the size of his own army. But from their carefully placed artillery and sniper positions, the Rebels could not only fire down on his men but also catch them in deadly cross fires.

Sherman spread his forces out so it would appear that he intended to make a frontal assault all along the bluffs, but his plan was to hit hard at just two points. He called Brig. Gen. G. W. Morgan aside and pointed out the position he was to hit.

"General, in ten minutes after you give the signal, I'll be on those hills," Morgan assured him.

On the morning of December 29, Sherman's forces were all in position, and he gave the order to attack.

Things went wrong from the beginning. One general got lost and didn't attack his position. Morgan, despite his promise, did not personally lead his men, and their attack failed. At one point, as the Union assault faltered, men of the Sixth Missouri dug little caves in the face of the cliff with their fingers and huddled there as Confederate riflemen leaned out over the parapet, held their rifles vertically, and fired straight down.

Throughout the battle Sherman listened anxiously for the sounds of Grant's guns approaching from the north. Grant, however, had been out of telegraphic communication since he left Memphis. He had no way to let Sherman know that he had gotten only as far south as Oxford, a good 170 miles from Vicksburg, and had turned back after Confederate raiders had destroyed his supply base at Holly Springs and torn up the railroad tracks that he relied on to keep his forces supplied.

Sherman prepared another assault for the following day, with Brig. Gen. Frederick Steele's forces prepared to make a dash for the bluffs at daylight. But morale on the Union side had begun to collapse. From their position on Chickasaw Bayou, Sherman's troops could hear the whistles as trains arrived in Vicksburg carrying Confederate reinforcements, and they could even see battalions of Rebel soldiers marching toward Haines's Bluff. Sherman had to place armed guards on the ships gathered in the bayou below the bluffs to keep the skippers from turning and heading back downstream.

Perhaps fortunately, a dense fog engulfed the area on the morning of December 30. Sherman gave up and pulled his force back away from the bluffs. He put his losses at 175 men killed, 930 wounded, and 743 captured.

While the battle at Vicksburg was coming to its foggy end, the 36th Iowa was marching to the levee at Memphis, where it had stopped briefly on the way down from St. Louis. There it boarded three packets—the *Anglo Saxon, Ida May*, and *Lebanon*—and headed downriver toward Helena, Arkansas. On the afternoon of December 31, it tied up at Helena and remained aboard the boats overnight. Looking out over the levee, the soldiers were not impressed by Helena. It appeared to be a small village of wood-frame houses, a low, muddy place with numerous ponds of green-looking water.

Margaret E. Breckinridge arrived in Helena a short time after the Iowans as a nurse on a riverboat. The Helena she described was certainly not the garden spot of Arkansas.

> You never saw so wretched a place as Helena; low damp,
> and enveloped in a continual fog, the rain poured down the
> whole time we were there, and the camps stretching for

miles up and down the river looked like the constant and abiding dwelling-place of fever and ague, and it is without doubt a most sickly post, and why it is held still though known and proved to be a most unhealthy place, nobody seems able or willing to tell. The mud is enough to frighten anybody who does not wear cavalry boots, and the soldiers, who with all their hardships and privations have a joke for everything, tell grave stories of mules and wagons being lost forever in the streets of Helena, two pointed ears being the self-erected monuments to tell where each mule is buried.

Miss Breckinridge was deeply moved by the condition of the former slaves—the "contrabands"—who had settled at one end of town. "Such wretched, uncared for, sad-looking creatures I never saw." Smallpox, she reported, was "making terrible havoc among them."

"The soldiers," she added, "seem to have a latent notion that the contrabands were in the beginning the cause of the war, and feel a little spiteful toward them accordingly, forgetting that they, poor souls, are innocent."

When the 36th Iowa arrived, ten or twelve infantry and cavalry regiments were already camped in and around Helena, so the newcomers did not have much choice of a campsite. They were marched to an expanse of bottomland lying between the levee and the river. It was about a quarter of a mile wide and was dotted with many ponds of standing water, some of them covered with green scum.

The next day and on into the night, their tent city was hammered by heavy rains and high winds. The tents kept out the rain, but the wind was so heavy that the men spent the night worried that their tent pegs would pull out.

The depressing sight of Helena and their new home was softened by the first word they had heard as they debarked on New Year's morning: "Vicksburg is ours!"

Over the next ten days, conflicting reports filtered in from the battlefront. But the news became steadily worse. All lingering hope that the battle had been a victory was resolved on Saturday, January 10, when the *City of Memphis* steamed up the river and tied up on the levee at Helena, carrying 750 wounded and sick soldiers from Vicksburg.

Members of the 36th Iowa were appalled, especially since two of the badly hit regiments were also from Iowa. Many of the men who were crowded aboard the ship, they were told, had lain for ten days since the battle with little or no medical attention. It was obvious that a great many of them would soon die.

The very next day, the 36th Iowa received orders to prepare to depart. They were not told where they were headed or when, but that did not stop the rumor mill: Word quickly spread through the camp that they would soon go downriver toward Vicksburg. But days passed with no orders to begin the move. Actually, Sherman, encamped near Vicksburg, had sent word: "For God's sake send no more troops here. I can find no place to land them on account of the high water. Waters still rising."

Despite the dampness and the cold—and an unusual six-inch snow on January 15—the regiment was fairly comfortable. After 12 days in the miasmic bottomland where they had first been ordered to set up their tents, they moved to higher ground, where another regiment had just vacated a cluster of little wooden huts. But the sickness that had plagued the regiment since the early days in Keokuk seemed only to flourish the more in Helena. Every morning, 20 or 25 men reported sick.

Andrew had begun feeling ill in early December, while the regiment was still at Benton Barracks, and was admitted to the regimental hospital on December 8 and again on December 16. He was well enough to make the trip to Helena, departing on December 19, but on January 5 he was again admitted to the hospital, suffering from diarrhea. On January 25 he was so sick that the regimental surgeon sent him upriver to St. Louis, where he was admitted to the army hospital at Jefferson Barracks.

For months, Andrew languished in hospitals at St. Louis and Keokuk before finally regaining enough strength to rejoin his regiment.

The regiment remained at Helena for a month after Andrew's departure, alternating guard duty with drill. Rumors that the soldiers would soon become part of a renewed effort to take Vicksburg continued to circulate.

Helena itself was giving every indication of being a war zone. Every day and long into the night, the area reverberated with sounds of an army on the move: the footsteps of marching men, the clop-clop-clop of horses and mules, the rattling of wagons, the shouts of teamsters, the music of bugles, fifes, and drums, and the whistles of the steamers.

At 11 o'clock on the evening of January 6, drummers beat the long roll, and parts of two infantry regiments and several cavalry regiments were alerted to meet a possible attack. But the next morning dawned clear and very cold, with thick ice on the ponds and no sign of the anticipated attack.

At the end of January, the most exciting news in months flashed through the camp: Union cavalry had raided a wedding party in the small town of Lagrange, 15 miles west of Helena. The troopers had swooped down on the festive gathering and captured five Rebel soldiers in Union uniforms. One man ran; as he tried to escape he was shot, and he died within a few minutes.

The routine of camp life was punctuated by Sunday religious services in which regimental chaplains and lay preachers together fought an often uphill battle against what they saw as the work of the devil. At one meeting a large gathering of troops listened to an impassioned speech by Brig. Gen. Clinton B. Fiske, who scathingly criticized officers who gave a bad example to their men by swearing. Such religious or moral lectures by high-ranking officers were not unusual. In fact, one important Confederate general was also an Episcopal bishop. Fiske, who later founded a college for African-Americans that bears his name, was an especially outspoken moral as well as military leader.

The camp routine was finally broken on February 7, when 400 men were sent downriver and ordered to cut the levees on the eastern, or Mississippi, side of the river a short distance below Helena. This move was in preparation for a major new effort to get at Vicksburg and silence those troublesome guns. It was an effort so unusual and difficult, however, that even the most imaginative rumormongers had not included it in their diet of speculation.

The plan was this: With the levees open, the farmland lying to the east of the river would flood, permitting riverboats to make their way from the Mississippi into Moon Lake and then through an old river channel known as the Yazoo Pass to the Coldwater River, which flows southward, roughly parallel to the Mississippi. It flows into the Tallahatchie River, which then joins the Yalobusha River to form the Yazoo River. By this backwater route, it was hoped, an army could be slipped in behind the Vicksburg defenses.

This was not the only plan under way. At the urging of Lincoln, Grant had men at work trying to cut a canal from one section of the Mississippi to another, below Vicksburg. Supposedly this canal would permit ships to bypass the Rebel guns. Another plan called for creating a 200-mile detour, through a series of lakes, bayous, and canals, so boats could get around Vicksburg and reenter the big river 100 miles south of the town. The canal-building plans never came to much. Despite the difficulties involved, the Yazoo Pass Expedition, of all the proposals for approaching Vicksburg from the north, seemed to offer the most hope.

On February 24 the 36th Iowa embarked on the expedition in two small steamers—the *Mariner* and the *Levina Logan*—and anchored that night in Moon Lake. As it set out, the regiment numbered only 600 enlisted men and 30 officers. It had lost a third of its strength to illness, even though not a shot had yet been exchanged with the enemy.

Looking across the lake the next morning, the soldiers counted 20 other steamers waiting their turn to work their way through the narrow, twisting Yazoo Pass toward the broader Coldwater River. Soldiers of the 36th entered the pass the next day and hacked their way through the brush, trees, and vines that hung down over the water. Men were stationed on each deck with long poles to push tree branches aside and prevent them from damaging the boat. At several points, where tree stumps blocked the way, hundreds of soldiers spread out in the mud, took their places on long ropes, and pulled the stumps out in a kind of one-sided tug-of-war.

For hours and then days, the soldiers simply sat and waited for the boats up ahead to move forward. The area they were passing through seemed deserted. But when they noticed that men in other boats were eating beef and pork, they found two cows and killed and butchered them. Finally, on March 5, they emerged into the Coldwater. They found it broad, muddy, and no colder than the water they had been moving through. From that point they were able to travel more rapidly southward.

In all this time the enemy had fired not a single shot. The soldiers were beginning to think they could go wherever they wanted to in Mississippi unmolested.

But as they moved down the Coldwater River, they realized that someone knew they were coming. On March 9 they saw cotton burning at as many as 20 places along the way. On some plantations the cotton had been moved outside to be burned, but at others the buildings were burning as well. The only white people seen along the way were women and children. The men were either all gone off to war or in hiding.

On the following day two local men stepped out of the woods and fired at the troopships, wounding two men. They were the first members of the regiment to be injured by the enemy. As they neared the confluence of the Tallahatchie and Yalobusha Rivers, they found the water filled with thousands of bales of burning cotton, presumably thrown into the river to impede their progress.

At noon on March 11 the boats carrying the regiment tied up at a large beautiful plantation. About two miles farther downstream, at the point where the Tallahatchie and Yalobusha Rivers combine to form the Yazoo River, stood Fort Pemberton, where Confederate forces blocked their passage. The men debarked, formed up in line of battle, and hurried the two miles to the fort, where two other regiments were already skirmishing with the enemy. As they fought, artillery shells whistled over their heads, aimed at boats in the river. One ball struck the gunboat *Chillicothe*, killing four men and wounding ten more. After a desultory, inconclusive engagement of about two hours, the men were ordered back to their boats, talking excitedly among themselves about their first exposure to enemy fire in a real battle.

The next day the Iowans were pulled back to guard a road along the Tallahatchie, about a mile above its junction with the Yalobusha. Although they were within cannon shot of the fort, the men felt themselves almost out of danger. Bored, they amused themselves by fashioning fans from palm leaves and by swinging on the grapevines that hung down from the large trees bordering the road.

Over the next few days, there were sporadic exchanges of fire, but little damage was done on either side. Senior officers debated whether to attack Fort Pemberton, but no one told the troops what was going on. On March 20, the decision to avoid a battle as too risky having been taken, the two boats carrying the 36th were ordered back up the river. A wave of disappointment swept through the regiment: The men were confident they could have taken the fort easily if the generals had only had the courage to order an attack.

The following day they met reinforcements coming downriver, so they turned around and headed back to where they had spent the previous days, near a mound that had presumably been constructed by prehistoric occupants of the area. The mound—called Shell Mound because of a nearby ridge of clamshells—stood about 40 feet high and about 150 feet across at the bottom. It appeared to be perfectly round, with a path winding its way around to the top, which was flat and about 35 feet across. Spring had just come in these southern latitudes, and the mound was dotted by peach, pear, and plum trees in full bloom. It was a surprising sight to the Iowa farm boys. Where they lived, winter had not yet lost its grip.

Despite its beauty, Shell Mound was to leave a melancholy memory in the minds of the soldiers of the 36th Iowa. They left three of their members behind, buried next to a rosebush on the slope of the mound. H. N. Swallow of Company F was buried first. Then John Myers of Company G died of typhoid fever and was buried next to him. The most disturbing death of all came a few nights later. John E. Walker of Company G ate supper as usual and then went to bed in a tent with his brother-in-law. They talked quietly as a storm raged outside. Suddenly Walker made a strange sound. By the time his tentmate got a candle lit, he was dead of some unknown illness. He was buried next to the other two soldiers on the side of the mound.

In all, ten men of the regiment died of illness on the expedition, and many became so ill that they were unfit for service for months.

The expedition was finally abandoned on April 4; no serious effort had been made to attack the fort and open the way to Vicksburg. The 36th arrived back in Helena on April 8, having accomplished nothing.

Grant now turned all his attention to a plan that had been in his mind at least since early February. In fact, most if not all of the other efforts—the canal-building, even the Yazoo Pass Expedition—may have been ordered more to keep the army busy than because of any realistic hope that they would be successful. That may explain why Fort Pemberton was not attacked, even though deserters said it probably could have been captured with relative ease.

Grant's plan was to move his army south past Vicksburg on the Louisiana side of the Mississippi, partly on the roads as soon as they dried out and partly on boats on the bayous. Then a flotilla of gunboats and transports would make a nighttime run down the Mississippi past the Vicksburg guns; the hope was that enough of them would get through to transport the army across the river below Vicksburg. Grant would then be in position to approach Vicksburg from the rear and either capture the post or force its surrender.

Sherman argued that Grant would be better off going back to his original plan of approaching from the north, down the middle of the state of Mississippi. But Grant was afraid of the political consequences of moving his army, which was then spread out for 60 miles on the western side of the river, back north: It would appear to be a retreat. The Northern press and politicians were already buzzing angrily about the delay in taking Vicksburg, and Lincoln was under growing pressure to fire him. Grant decided he could not afford to back up one step. Instead, he would put his plan into effect.

In late March, Sherman tried making one more amphibious assault to get in behind the Vicksburg defenses. It failed, as he knew it would; its purpose was merely to make the Vicksburg defenders believe the next assault would come from the north. As Sherman pulled back, Grant set his army in motion to the south, heading toward a settlement known as Hard Times, Louisiana, on the western side of the Mississippi, across from the Confederate forts at Grand Gulf, 40 miles south of Vicksburg.

Everything then depended on Adm. David Dixon Porter, who was in command of the brown-water navy that operated on the inland sea—the great network of rivers in the drainage basin of the Mississippi. On the night of April 17, Porter sent his fleet into the Vicksburg gauntlet. The gunboats went down the center of the river, trading shells with the guns on the cliffs above. Meanwhile the transports ran as close to the west bank of the river as they could, protected by barges lashed to their sides and filled with coal, bags of grain, and bales of cotton.

The gunboats escaped serious damage, but the transports were badly battered. Some of them were sunk and others were set afire. But on the seventeenth and subsequent nights, the daring crews brought through enough boats to provide Grant's army with the transportation it needed to cross the river.

The Union soldiers quickly defeated the Confederate defenses at the crossing point. Then Grant made a daring decision: He ordered his army to march northward, without any supply line to the rear. The men were issued three days' rations. When that was gone, they and their animals would have to live entirely off the land.

Grant's forces then marched to a point between two Rebel armies headquartered at Vicksburg and Jackson, Mississippi. It was a dangerous, perhaps even foolhardy move. If the two enemy forces coordinated their attack, they could smash Grant's army. But Grant moved fast. He sent part of his men to drive the enemy from Jackson. Then he swung toward Vicksburg, pushing the Rebel forces back within their defenses.

Grant's daring maneuver was a splendid success. His army marched

200 miles in 19 days, defeating the enemy in five separate engage-ments. It has been called the most brilliant campaign ever fought on American soil.

Lt. Gen. John C. Pemberton, the Confederate commander at Vicksburg, had made a grievous mistake. Instead of abandoning Vicks-burg, he kept his forces within the city's defenses, permitting his men to be surrounded. All Grant had to do was wait, and he would capture not only the city but a 30,000-man enemy army.

But Grant, perhaps responding to political pressure, got impatient. On May 19 he ordered an assault on the Vicksburg defenses. A few of the Union soldiers got to the top of the parapet, but they were then thrown back with severe casualties. After meeting with his generals on May 20, Grant ordered another attempt for May 22. Again, the attackers were repelled with severe casualties. Although the reason may have seemed obvious to the soldiers, the generals had not yet learned that an attempt to take a heavily fortified position manned by soldiers with rifles was almost certain to end in bloody defeat.

As Sherman contemplated the carnage of the day's assault, Grant, who had left his horse back out of sight, approached on foot. While the two men talked, a messenger brought a penciled note from McClernand claiming that he had captured an enemy parapet and proclaiming that the Union flag waved over Vicksburg. He demanded a renewed assault by the other forces.

"I don't believe a word of it," Grant muttered. But Sherman reminded him that an official communication such as this couldn't be ignored. As Grant left to check the situation, he told Sherman that, if he hadn't received new orders by 3 o'clock, he should send his men in a new attack.

When no word came, Sherman again attacked, and his troops, as he knew they would, suffered another bloody repulse.

It was later learned that McClernand's report was a lie. He was relieved of his command.

After their repeated assaults had failed, the Union forces settled down for a siege, which lasted until the Rebel forces finally surren-dered on July 4. As the Confederate soldiers marched out of their fortress and laid down their arms, the Union troops stood quietly and respectfully. Then the men of the two sides embraced and celebrated together. One side had lost and one had won. But they both felt pride at having taken part in an historic event.

Siege of Vicksburg. (Authors' collection.)

While Grant was making his daring move on Vicksburg, the men of the 36th Iowa remained in their camp at Helena, disappointed to be left out of the action. But Helena soon became a center of action itself. Increasingly, Union cavalry patrols ran into small Rebel units that were feeling their way toward Helena.

On May 10 the sound of distant cannon fire was heard and the drummers beat the long roll, calling out every man able to bear arms. Scouts from the Fifth Kansas Cavalry reported contact with the forces of Confederate Brig. Gen. John S. Marmaduke about ten miles from the city, but the enemy forces came no closer.

Of more immediate concern to the commanders at Helena was the increasing guerrilla activity along the river, as passing ships took fire from sharpshooters hidden in the woods. On May 24 a Marine brigade stationed in Helena sailed north to the town of Austin, Mississippi, where it had been fired upon the previous evening.

The Marines swept through the little town, killing a number of men believed to be guerrillas in a brief but intense battle in which four of the Marines were killed and a dozen wounded. Then they set fire to the town. When they left, only the chimneys still stood above the ashes.

By early June, Rebel forces were close enough to Helena to

Brig. Gen. John S. Marmaduke, CSA. (Library of Congress, Washington, D.C.)

exchange fire with Union pickets, but they made no attack on the city. For a brief time the westerners—boys from Iowa, Kansas, and Missouri—stationed at Helena were more interested in a different kind of "enemy." They encountered for the first time a division of easterners: the strange race known as "Yankees." No actual violence erupted between them, but the insults flew back and forth so fast that the general in charge threatened to land the Yankees on the other side of the river if the easterners and the westerners didn't behave. This encounter highlighted the country's regional differences, with tension between east and west, although not as pronounced as that between north and south.

The real enemy, of course, was somewhere out there in a kind of no-man's-land beyond the Union picket lines. Inconclusive intelligence reports of an impending Rebel attack were relayed from higher headquarters, and Maj. Gen. Benjamin Prentiss, commander of the Union forces at Helena, decided to take no chances. He put the men to work strengthening the city's already formidable defenses, so that new spider holes—what a later generation called foxholes—ringed the artillery batteries positioned on four hills covering approaches to the city from the north, west, and south. The river was to the east, where a powerful gunboat, the *Tyler*, was anchored. Prentiss also sent out work parties armed with axes to cut down trees to block all the roads leading into the city.

All together Prentiss had 4,129 troops under his command. In addition to the 36th, he had four other Iowa regiments as well as the 43rd Indiana (which would fight alongside the 36th in a tragic battle the following year).

Finally, beginning on June 28, Prentiss ordered reveille to be sounded at 2:30 A.M. each morning. A veteran of the fighting at Shiloh, where Union forces were still in their beds when they were overrun in a surprise attack, he took no chances on being caught asleep.

The reports of an impending attack on Helena were true. A Rebel army with a sizable contingent of mounted infantry was on the march toward the city with a force of 7,646 men, nearly twice the size of the Helena garrison. As the Confederate soldiers' horses clopped down the country roads toward Helena, the farm families that lined the way cheered them on. The cheers were heartening, but the neglected fields in the once-prosperous area were a sad sight for the soldiers, many of whom were Arkansas farm boys themselves.

The leader of the Confederate forces was Lt. Gen. Theophilus H. Holmes. Among Rebel commanders, Holmes ranked near the bottom in competence. One of his own soldiers said of him: "Poor old creature—I wish he was some where else, for I do not think him a fit subject to command an army."

What he lacked in competence, however, Holmes made up in ambition. His plan was to strike Helena at break of day on the Fourth of July and quickly capture the city, putting him in a position to harass or even stop Union traffic along the river. The attack was also supposed to help lessen Federal pressure on the defenders at Vicksburg. He told his troops that their assault would be part of a make-or-break effort by Confederate forces all across the divided nation.

In the hours after midnight, the Confederates left their camps after a brief rest and moved toward the city on five roads converging from the south, west, and north. Feeling their way through the darkness, they stumbled into the trees that Prentiss's men had felled to block the way. These obstacles were so unexpected that they had neglected to bring along axes. Their only choice was to leave their horses behind and grope their way on foot into an attacking position. A quarter of the force was left to hold the horses while the artillerymen struggled to find a way to move their weapons forward.

Holmes had ordered the attack to begin at first light. This would give his men perhaps an hour or more to fight before the summer sun rose in the east and shone directly in their eyes. But one commander didn't understand the orders: He thought he was supposed to attack at sunup rather than at first light. So while two other columns rushed forward, his men waited for the sun to peek over the horizon. The result was that the Union guns were able to concentrate on the two other columns with devastating effect.

The 36th Iowa was assigned to defend the approaches to the city from the north, along the Old St. Francis Road. Their enemy here was General Marmaduke. But Marmaduke, relying on local guides, got lost and had to wait until daybreak to figure out where he was. Like the other attacking units, he found his way blocked by fallen trees. He and his dismounted men then struggled on foot toward the northern approaches to the city.

There they were stopped by the defensive line manned by soldiers of the 33rd and 36th Iowa regiments. Twice Marmaduke sent messengers asking Brig. Gen. Marsh Walker, who commanded a neighboring unit, to attack the troops blocking his way. Twice Walker ignored him.

In the center of the line, the Confederate forces managed to take one Union battery on Graveyard Hill, west of the town, but the Federal men spiked their artillery pieces before they retreated. No sooner had the Rebels taken the useless guns than they became the target for the *Tyler*, the gunship lying just offshore. Her guns fired one of the conflict's most feared artillery shells—an eight-inch round whose fuse caused it to explode 12 to 15 seconds after it hit. It was estimated after the battle that as many as 600 of the Confederate attackers had been killed by the *Tyler's* guns alone.

On the south end of town, the forces of Confederate Brig. Gen. James Fagan bore some of the heaviest fighting of the day; in several cases they overcame Federal picket lines with bayonet charges. But they were brought to a stop by concentrated rifle and artillery fire. The attackers found themselves in a no-win situation: If they continued the attack, they would be mowed down. If they retreated or tried to surrender, their own army's sharpshooters, stationed behind their ranks, would shoot them.

By 11 A.M., it was obvious to Holmes that a continued attack was futile. Marmaduke received the order to retreat and was able to disengage successfully. But he was so angry at Walker for not coming to his aid earlier that he didn't tell Walker about the order to withdraw. Not until Walker's men saw the Union soldiers, freed by Marmaduke's departure, moving toward them did they hurry to their horses and ride away.

By noon, the battle was over. Of Holmes's 7,646 men, he had lost 169 killed, 659 wounded, and 36 missing. Losses among the 4,129 Union troops were much lower: 57 killed, 146 wounded, and 36 missing. Although they had not been in the area of the heaviest fighting, the men of the 36th Iowa had participated in a decisive victory, driving off Marmaduke with relative ease.

Prentiss, the Union commander, had done just about everything right, while Holmes and his subordinates had done just the opposite. But now it was Prentiss who made a big mistake: He waited on alert for several days, expecting another attack. He did not realize how badly the enemy had been beaten.

Just walking over the battlefield, Prentiss should have sensed how devastating were the losses that the attackers had suffered. Burial details of the 36th and the other regiments went out the day after the battle, and even that soon the bodies had already turned black under the summer sun and were covered with flies and maggots. The stench was almost unendurable. As quickly as they could, the soldiers got the bodies underground, burying as many as 40 in a single large grave.

If Prentiss had pursued the battered enemy forces, he might have ended the Rebel domination of much of southern Arkansas. As a result of this failure, however, Marmaduke, Fagan, and their surviving men got away to fight another day. The 36th Iowa would meet them again under much less favorable circumstances.

The defenders of Helena were busy on the day of the battle and afterward, but they had much to celebrate in the following days. The surrender of Vicksburg, the defeat of General Lee and his army at Gettysburg, and of course their own decisive victory had all taken place on the same day, July 4.

To many, it seemed that the war should now come to an end. Sherman thought so. "But," he later wrote, "the rebel leaders were mad, and seemed determined that their people should drink of the very lowest dregs of the cup of war, which they themselves had prepared."

It was then that Sherman began developing the concept of "total war" for which he later became famous. In September 1863 he wrote to an aide to Grant: "I would make this war as severe as possible, and show no symptoms of tiring till the south begs for mercy. . . . The south had done her worst, and now is the time for us to pile on our blows thick and fast."

But Sherman also saw how the seizure of Vicksburg had changed the war. "After the fall of Vicksburg," he wrote in his memoirs, ". . . the Mississippi River was wholly in the possession of the Union forces, and formed a perfect line of separation in the territories of our opponents. Thenceforth, they could not cross it save by stealth, and the military affairs on its west bank became unimportant."

However, it was to this "unimportant" theater of the war that the 36th Iowa would soon be dispatched to meet its bloody fate.

Chapter Five

"The Tennessee Quick-Step"

When Andrew Brayman left his regiment and boarded a crowded steamer for the trip upriver on January 25, 1863, he had been suffering for more than a month with what the soldiers then called "the Tennessee Quick-Step." Soldiers of a later generation would call it the "GIs" or, more bluntly, the "GI shits."

Weakened by loss of fluids, he was miserable. By the winter of 1862–63, the army had a number of specially fitted-out steamers serving as hospital ships on the Mississippi. On the way downstream, the ships were comfortable and nicely provisioned. But on the way back up the river, they were jammed with sick and wounded men, who were packed together on the cabin floor and decks. The fresh vegetables and fruit with which the ships had set sail down the river were long gone.

As Andrew sailed painfully northward, he was surrounded not only by the sick from Helena—already notorious for its pall of sickness and disease—but by ailing men from other units along the river, as well as the wounded survivors of Sherman's failed assault on Vicksburg.

Whether it is called the Tennessee Quick-Step or the GIs, diarrhea can be a matter for rather coarse humor. (Tourists today call it "Montezuma's Revenge.") But for those afflicted, it is anything but a laughing matter. For Civil War doctors, it was the most rampant and most puzzling ailment they confronted, a more serious drain on army strength than any other cause, including battlefield casualties. An average of 73.8 percent of the Union troops were afflicted with diarrhea or dysentery each year, and 48,000 of them died during the war— not counting those who died after they had been discharged and sent home, too ill to remain in service.

The doctors made a rough distinction between diarrhea and dysentery, the latter being the more serious of the two. *Diarrhea* was the word used for looseness of the bowels. *Dysentery* was used when there was blood in the stool. Doctors today recognize two types of dysentery—bacillary dysentery, which was believed to have been brought to this country in slave ships from Africa, and amoebic dysentery, which was imported from the West Indies.

What the Civil War soldiers suffered from is not clear, however. Loose bowels are a symptom of a number of diseases, so it is likely that many soldiers who were diagnosed with diarrhea, as Andrew was, actually were suffering from some other underlying cause.

Andrew's encounter with army medicine began with a visit to the regimental "hospital"—a white wall-tent, almost square, 14 by 15 feet —rising to a peak at the center of 11 feet, with sides four feet high. There an assistant surgeon quickly diagnosed his case and gave him medicine, which didn't help. Andrew was in and out of the regimental hospital four times in December and January before finally being deemed sick enough to be sent up the river to a larger hospital.

In St. Louis he became a patient at the Jefferson Barracks General Hospital, one of nearly 200 large military hospitals that were built by the Union during the war. It was what was termed a "pavilion" hospital, with long wards radiating off a central corridor. Each of the wards was half a block—150 feet—long and 25 feet wide. Down each side, spaced four feet apart, were metal beds with lengthwise wooden slats.

Before the war Andrew and his farm boy friends had never seen a building anywhere near as large as the general hospital in St. Louis. In fact, they had never seen a hospital. Only the desperately poor who had no one to care for them went to what was called a hospital—usually to die. Everyone else was cared for at home. Surgical procedures were rare. When they were performed, it was usually in the patient's home or in a hotel room.

The war, with its sudden, enormous casualties, had found the Union army totally unprepared. It had only 98 surgeons—a term used for all physicians, few of whom had ever seen the inside of a living human body. It had no hospitals and no ambulance service. After the early battles, wounded men sometimes lay on the field of battle for days before being laid on straw on the floor of an army wagon and trundled to a makeshift treatment center. Many of them, of course, didn't survive this obstacle course.

Under Alexander Hammond, an assistant surgeon and ten-year veteran of the peacetime army who was elevated to the post of surgeon general, the army embarked on a massive hospital-building program. By the end of the war, there were 204 hospitals with 136,894 beds. The largest were capable of caring for as many as 5,000 sick or wounded soldiers. The medical corps also took over the ambulance system—after a bureaucratic battle with the quartermaster corps. At first there were two types of ambulance: a two-wheel version for the more seriously wounded and a four-wheel version for other patients. The two-wheeler was so uncomfortable—the soldiers called it the "avalanche"—that it was abandoned, and for the rest of the war all the ambulances had four wheels.

If Andrew expected to lie back and enjoy his recuperation, he had a rude awakening the first morning after his arrival. He was, he quickly discovered, still very much in the army. In many wards the patients who could get out of their beds were put to work scrubbing down the floors, although this routine was omitted in some wards, where officials feared the dampness might be harmful to the patients.

As soon as the ward was in order, the men remained by their beds. As an assistant surgeon arrived at the door of the ward on his rounds, the wardmaster—usually a convalescent soldier responsible for the nursing and cleaning in each ward—shouted "Attention!" All of the men who were able to were standing at the foot of their beds. They snapped to attention and saluted and then stood rigidly until given the order to be "at ease." Thoughtless officers sometimes left them standing at attention much longer than was necessary.

Civil War soldiers did not wear dog tags. But each patient in the hospital wore a tag, attached to a cord around his neck, giving his name, rank, and unit. At the foot of his bed were two cards. One indicated by its color the diet he was supposed to receive. The other recorded the diagnosis and treatment. Quickly the surgeon moved down the long ward, checking each patient's condition and issuing new orders as needed.

Once a week, usually on Sunday, the patients were treated to the spectacle of a full-scale inspection by the surgeon-in-charge. At Jefferson Barracks it was John F. Randolph, a regular army officer. He was accompanied by his medical staff, all in full-dress uniform. While the patients may not have fully appreciated the spectacle, the visit of the surgeon-in-charge at least meant that they had all received clean bedding and clothing.

The wards were arranged so that there were two beds between windows. Early in the war doctors believed that bad or miasmic air was the cause of many ailments. They therefore kept the windows and doors closed. When it was noted that patients who were confined to tents recovered much more rapidly than those inside buildings, the policy was changed to encourage open windows, and the new hospitals were designed to permit a proper air flow through the wards.

Doctors still did not understand, however, how disease is transmitted. They didn't know that anopheles mosquitoes are responsible for the spread of malaria. They didn't realize that the contaminated water that the soldiers drank was responsible for typhoid fever and a variety of intestinal disorders. They didn't realize that flies were carrying diseases from latrines and garbage dumps to the soldiers' food.

They did know, however, that uncovered garbage, dead animals, and open latrine pits all cause unpleasant odors, and they reasoned that the odors themselves were causing the spread of disease. The steps they took to control odors helped to prevent the spread of disease. In the hospital wards, for example, odors were controlled by spraying bromine in the air, which helped to kill airborne bacteria.

In many regiments discipline was lax, and this contributed to the spread of disease. When a regiment set up camp, latrine pits—or "sinks," as they were called—were routinely dug, but they were usually primitive affairs consisting of an open pit and a long horizontal pole for the soldiers to sit on while they did their business. The ordure in the pit was supposed to be covered quickly with dirt but often wasn't. The result was that the latrines quickly became so offensive that many soldiers met the call of nature in the area surrounding the camp, providing the flies with hundreds or thousands of sources for infection.

The situation in the hospitals was better, but in many cases not much better. The source of water was often contaminated. Some of the newer hospitals were equipped with toilets, but they flushed only when someone carried a bucket of water and dumped it in. In other hospitals the soldiers used long troughs that were supposed to be cleaned continually by a flow of water. But often the water was turned on only when the trough was nearly full.

Soldiers who arrived in a hospital to be treated for symptoms such as diarrhea were probably the fortunate ones. For those with wounds or injuries, a hospital was a perilous place.

Doctors did not know that disease can be transmitted from one person to another by dirty hands or instruments. The accepted method for probing a wound was for the surgeon to stick his finger into the hole. Then he would go on to the next patient, perhaps wiping his bloody hand on a dirty rag as he did so. Surgical instruments were washed off but were not boiled or otherwise sterilized. Bandages taken from cadavers were sometimes rinsed out and then applied to another patient's wounds.

Almost every wound became infected. In fact, the doctors thought that a period when a wound exuded pus was a normal part of the healing process.

Many a soldier suffered through this "healing process," pleased that he was on the road to recovery. Then he would see a little black spot, about the size of a quarter, on his wounded arm or leg. Each day the black spot would spread until soon the whole limb was a putrid mass, and in many cases death was not long in coming.

This devastating condition was what the doctors called "hospital gangrene"—and it seemed to spread with the prevailing breeze through a ward and even into other wards downwind. It was not the same as more familiar forms of gangrene, which came from contact with contaminated soil or from blood poisoning. Doctors today don't really know what "hospital gangrene" was, because it disappeared after the introduction, a few years after the war, of antiseptic procedures.

While the soldiers, such as Andrew, who did not have open wounds were spared this form of infection, they shared with all the other patients—and with the army generally—the perils of an awful diet that was almost always poorly cooked. The normal ration consisted of salt pork, beans, hardtack, and coffee. In some cases the ration was supplemented by desiccated vegetables. This meant the vegetables had been completely dried out, a process that preserved them but also leached out most of their food value. The soldiers called them "desecrated" vegetables.

In the early days of the war, the soldiers did their own cooking—frying almost everything and boiling the rest. As the war progressed, company and regimental kitchens were established, but even then much of the cooking was done by ordinary soldiers pressed into the job without training. One surgeon, noting the almost indigestible result of this process, complained of "death from the frying pan."

The poor food and improper preparation were undoubtedly responsible for many of the intestinal disorders that plagued the army throughout the war. In some cases the lack of fresh fruits and vegetables led to scurvy, a disease now known to be caused by a lack of vitamin C. Scurvy causes anemia, general weakness, deterioration of the gums, and bleeding from the nose and mouth. While outbreaks of fullblown scurvy were relatively rare and limited to units that had been forced to subsist on the army ration alone for extended periods, many more soldiers suffered from weakness and intestinal disorders as a result of a shortage of vitamins—incipient scurvy.

Unfortunately for those suffering from such ailments, the hospital diet was not much better than that in the regiments. And with many of the cooks drawn from the ranks of convalescent soldiers, the cooking was often not much better either.

Depending on his condition, a patient would receive a full diet, a half diet, or a low diet. The typical full diet provided coffee, cold meat, and bread for breakfast, pork and beans and bread pudding for dinner, and tea with milk and bread and butter for supper. The half diet consisted of coffee and bread and butter for breakfast, mutton soup and meat, boiled potatoes, and bread for dinner, and the same supper as that provided on the full diet. The low diet offered coffee or tea and bread or toast with butter for breakfast, farina gruel and bread for dinner, and tea or cocoa and bread or toast with butter for supper.

Special—and sometimes bizarre—diets were prescribed for some ailments. A man suffering from a stomach ailment, for example, might be fed hotcakes, cheese, and molasses candy.

The defects in the diets of hospital patients were widely recognized. Surgeons in charge of the hospitals, for example, were expected to use the money they saved from their 18-cents-a-day ration allowance on the half or low diets to buy fruits, jellies, and other treats for their patients.

Members of the U.S. Sanitary Commission, which was organized early in the war to improve the care of sick and wounded soldiers, provided delicacies for the seriously sick in many hospitals. Mothers, wives, and sisters visited the hospitals to care for and provide a more adequate diet for their sons, husbands, and brothers.

Iowa soldiers were the special beneficiaries of the work of Annie Turner Wittenmyer, a Keokuk widow. Alarmed by the conditions she encountered when she visited her youngest brother, who was sick with typhoid fever and dysentery in a hospital in Sedalia, Missouri, she became executive secretary of the Soldiers Aid Society and was appointed sanitary agent for Iowa. Her major contribution to the welfare of sick and wounded soldiers was to establish the Diet Kitchen concept, in which special food was provided, along with experienced cooks to prepare it. By the end of the war, more than 2 million special rations from the Diet Kitchens were being served in Union hospitals each month.

While good food and clean water would, by themselves, have gone a long way toward curing many of the soldiers who were suffering from intestinal disorders, the attending physicians did their best to treat the men with the medicines then available. By today's standards, however, the quality of the medical personnel, their understanding of the maladies they were dealing with, and the medicines they used all left a great deal to be desired.

Training for a would-be doctor was provided in a two-year course. It consisted almost entirely of a series of lectures in the first year and a repetition of the lectures in the second year.

While there were a number of medical schools in the country at the beginning of the Civil War, there were no schools for nurses. When the war brought thousands of wounded and ailing men into the new army hospitals, convalescing soldiers and male civilian volunteers were pressed into service as nurses. As the demand for nursing care grew, many women volunteered. Dorothea Dix, who had made her name as the founder of asylums for the insane, was assigned to enroll nurses. The formidable Miss Dix had strict standards: Women must be over 30, they must be plain if not outright homely, and they must avoid jewelry and attractive clothing. And—she insisted—they had to be Protestant. No Catholics need apply.

With neither formal training as nurses nor experience in army discipline, many of the nurses soon came into conflict with the army doctors, unhappy with the nurses' reluctance to take orders. The doctors were much happier when Catholic sisters volunteered as nurses. Although they were all referred to as Sisters of Charity, they also came from three other Catholic orders: Sisters of St. Joseph, Sisters of Mercy, and Sisters of the Holy Cross. While they also lacked training in medicine, they at least had plenty of experience with discipline. Despite the conflicts between civilian nurses and doctors, the Civil War opened up a broad new career field for women in the nation's hospitals.

The medicines employed by Civil War surgeons ranged from doses so small as to be ineffective to drugs so powerful as to be dangerous or even fatal. What a doctor prescribed often depended on his personal medical philosophy. Those favoring homeopathic cures, for example, treated patients with tiny doses of whatever was supposed to have caused the ailment. When this theory was explained to Abraham Lincoln, he is reported to have remarked that it was like "trying to fertilize a field with a fart."

Many doctors in the years before the war—and during the war—relied very heavily on alcohol, opium in various forms, and medicines containing mercury. One of their favorites for a variety of ailments was calomel—mercurous chloride—a tasteless white powder that caused a patient to salivate prodigious amounts, as much as a quart in 24 hours. Calomel and mercury in other forms contributed to mercury poisoning, weakening the patient and causing his teeth to fall out. In the worst cases the patient's gums and cheeks became a rotting mass.

Surgeon General Hammond was personally convinced that calomel and tartar emetic, another mercury-based drug, did no good and were probably harmful. He issued an order banning their use in May 1863, at the time Andrew Brayman was in the hospital. "No doubt can exist," Hammond said, "that more harm has resulted from the misuse of both of these agents, in the treatment of disease, than benefit from their administration."

Many army doctors violently disagreed and were horrified at being denied use of two of their favorite medications. The result was a "calomel war" within the army medical establishment.

Hammond was the loser. He was court-martialed on a technicality and forced out of the army while many doctors continued to use the mercury-based drugs, disregarding the surgeon general's orders.

Since doctors didn't know what was causing their hospital beds to fill with patients suffering from the Tennessee Quick-Step, they were equally at a loss to know what to prescribe. Some of their prescriptions seem bizarre indeed. Many patients were given Epsom salts or castor oil in the morning as a laxative and some form of opium in the evening. Some surgeons prescribed doses of quinine, which probably did more good in many cases than the other so-called remedies, since loose bowels may have been a symptom of malaria, especially among soldiers who had been stationed in the South.

The favorite remedy for almost any ailment was alcohol, which was administered in small but frequent doses. Proud doctors reported that they had kept one 16-year-old alive by dosing him with 36 ounces of brandy a day. From what is known today about the effects of alcohol, it probably didn't do much for the soldiers' health, but it must certainly have made their wards mellow places with a kind of neverending happy hour.

Hospital life was, for most of the soldiers, rather boring. One of their major diversions was reading illustrated magazines such as *Harper's Weekly* and *Leslie's Weekly*, the nineteenth-century equivalent of television as a source of news and entertainment. These magazines were filled with news of the war, supplementing information provided by the big-city daily newspapers and the local weeklies sent from home. Religious organizations provided a steady flow of Bibles, tracts, and religious books and magazines. The nation also supported a thriving pornographic industry, centered in New York, that turned out publications that looked, at a glance, just like the pocket Bibles handed out by the religious groups.

Soldiers well along in their recuperation even occupied themselves by finding part-time jobs in such cities as Keokuk, helping to make up for the war-caused labor shortage.

During his illness and long convalescence, Andrew Brayman spent time in two big army hospitals—Jefferson Barracks at St. Louis, and Keokuk General, closer to his home in Iowa. At both hospitals those with intestinal disorders filled hundreds of beds.

At Jefferson Barracks, which had 1,700 beds, 6,225 soldiers were admitted for treatment of diarrhea and dysentery between April 30, 1862, and November 21, 1865. At Keokuk General, with 1,350 beds, there were 1,169 admissions for those two ailments between April 1862 and September 1865.

The impact of these diseases on the army can be seen in the figures for deaths and discharges. At Jefferson Barracks the death rate among those admitted for treatment of diarrhea and dysentery was nearly 15 percent, and another 21 percent were discharged. At Keokuk more than 9 percent died and nearly 5 percent were discharged for disability.

While death from disease was a constant, severe drain on Union Army manpower, it was less of a problem than it had been in other armies in earlier years. When Britain sent the first contingent of 25,000 troops to the Crimea in the war with Russia in 1854, they died by the thousands from cholera, various fevers, intestinal disorders, and scurvy. Only 7,000 were alive a year later. Even in peacetime years in the first half of the nineteenth century, the French army sometimes had a disease mortality rate higher than the Union Army's death rate from all causes during the war. In relative terms, then, the American Civil War was a healthy one.

An obvious question is why many of the ailing or wounded soldiers were not simply sent home to be cared for by their loving families, to receive the treatment they would have received if they had been sick or injured in civilian life. Actually, that is the way many officers were cared for. If an officer was too sick or too badly wounded to remain with his regiment and be nursed back to health by his orderly, he was sent home to recuperate. Only a few officers, who had no home to go to, were admitted to the army hospitals, which were filled almost entirely with enlisted men.

As a matter of fact, the army feared, with some justification, that if thousands of soldiers were permitted to go home, many of them, both draftees and volunteers who had experienced the reality of battle, would never return. After the Battle of Vicksburg, General Grant was so fearful that his army might simply melt away that he resisted sending his sick and wounded men even as far north as the big hospitals in Memphis and St. Louis.

It is probably a credit more to Andrew Brayman's health when he entered the army than to any treatment he received that he was finally discharged from Keokuk General, where he had spent five months, on September 29, 1863, and pronounced fit to journey down the Mississippi and up the Arkansas to rejoin his colleagues in the 36th Iowa in Little Rock.

Chapter Six

Reunion in Little Rock

When Andrew Brayman arrived in Little Rock and walked into the campsite of Company I, he was immediately surrounded by old comrades who slapped him on the back and filled him in on their adventures in the eight months that he had been off in the hospital.

Looking around at his old friends, Andrew was struck by the changes in them. When he left in January, they had been little more than green recruits, still farm boys dressed as soldiers. Now he could see the difference. They were lean and tough, harder looking, many of them twirling debonair mustaches. Months of adversity and the introduction to combat had changed them. They were now veterans with a solid year of service behind them.

Eagerly they told of the Yazoo Pass Expedition. They were still bitter and disappointed that they had been ordered to turn around without making an attempt to take the Confederate fort that stood between them and Vicksburg. If only they had been allowed to attack the fort and continue their march, they assured Andrew, the 36th Iowa would have shared in the glory of silencing the Vicksburg guns and opening the Mississippi to Union traffic.

They did tell proudly of their share of the glory in throwing back the Confederate assault on Helena. Although their victory was not as crucial to the outcome of the war as the two other victories of that same Fourth of July—Vicksburg and Gettysburg—it still ranked as one of three victories celebrated throughout the North.

Andrew had of course heard of the Yazoo Pass Expedition and the Battle of Helena. The real news was the regiment's latest adventure— the march from Helena and the capture of Little Rock. Details of that campaign were still fresh in everyone's memory, and Andrew was given a full account.

On August 11 the 36th had set out from Helena, leading a two-division force, strengthened by cavalry and artillery units, under the command of General Steele—the same general who had participated in the disastrous attempt to take the Chickasaw Bluffs behind Vicksburg in December. Orders from Grant gave Steele responsibility for all of Arkansas north of the Arkansas River. In addition to the 7,000 men moving out of Helena, Steele also had in his command another 6,000 cavalrymen under Brig. Gen. John W. Davidson, who came clopping down from their base in Missouri. The two forces were to meet at Clarendon, about 55 miles east of Little Rock, and then aim their combined force toward the capital.

Davidson arrived first at Clarendon on August 15 and took the lead, moving out immediately toward Little Rock.

Before the war Little Rock had been a kind of cultural center in the wilderness, hundreds of miles from any other sizable city. Many of its citizens had come from the Northeast, and in contrast to the residents of many other frontier communities, almost all of them were literate. They waited eagerly for the bundles of magazines and newspapers that arrived aboard riverboats and stagecoaches. With an 1860 population of only 3,727 white residents and 1,100 slaves (free blacks were not permitted to live in the city), Little Rock was the largest and most important city in the state. Many of its residents strongly supported the Union, and the state's decision to leave the Union and join the Confederacy was bitterly debated.

The issue came to a vote twice in the statehouse, which stood on the bank of the Arkansas River at the edge of the downtown area. Even then the statehouse was an historic structure. The central portion of the building is built in the style of a Greek temple, with four classic Doric pillars. But the two wings spreading out on each side give the whole structure the appearance of a Southern mansion. Shortly after the building was constructed in 1836, half a dozen members of prominent families, on a wager, rode their horses up the spiral stairways. On another occasion the speaker of the Arkansas house of representatives stabbed another legislator to death in the building's lobby. When the city's soldiers returned from the Mexican War, they brought with them a silk flag that they had carried into battle and returned it to the women who had made it. Then they all joined in a festive fancy dress ball.

On the first occasion when the issue of secession was debated, the vote went against leaving the Union. But by the time a second vote was taken on May 6, 1861, sentiment had turned. Hundreds of residents of the city, among them many rural folk who had recently migrated there, gathered in and around the building as the legislature met to consider the motion to secede.

The vote was 65 in favor to 5 against. When an attempt to make the vote unanimous followed, one man, named Isaac Murphy, held out. As he cast his "no" vote, a woman in the balcony threw a bouquet of flowers that landed at his feet.

Clearly the event that turned the tide toward secession had been Washington's telegraphed demand for an Arkansas regiment of 780 men to help suppress "the rebellion." While many in Arkansas did not want to leave the Union, they were even more reluctant to fight against their neighbors in the seceding Southern states.

Governor Henry Rector sent an angry reply:

> In answer to your requisition for troops from Arkansas to subjugate the Southern States, I have to say that none will be furnished. The demand is only adding insult to injury. The people of this commonwealth are free men, not slaves, and will defend to the last extremity their honor, lives and property against Northern mendacity and usurpation.

In the early months of the war, Little Rock changed rapidly. Young men volunteered in newly formed regiments and hurried off to fight in far-off Virginia. Many of the city's residents, still opposed to secession, moved back to the northeastern cities from which they had emigrated. Their place was taken by less-well-educated farm families, fleeing the bands of jayhawkers and bushwhackers who, as part of their own private war, terrorized the countryside.

For the first two years of the war Little Rock served as headquarters for Confederate forces. It was not a pleasant time for the residents. Early on, the city became a hospital center, as sick and wounded sol-

Downtown Little Rock at the time of the Civil War. (Arkansas Historical Commission.)

diers from the battles of Pea Ridge, Prairie Grove, Shiloh, and other bloody conflicts streamed into Little Rock for care. Although every effort was made to bury amputated limbs and the bodies of those who died as quickly as possible, sections of the city still reeked with the smell of rotting flesh.

For several years running the harvest in rural Arkansas had been poor, and with the disruption of normal trade, food was so scarce and expensive that many city residents survived on a near-starvation diet. Cloth was almost unobtainable. When wounded soldiers died, their bandages were washed and reused, spreading infection throughout the wards.

Only a few streets along the waterfront were paved; the others were dirt. As the war progressed, maintenance ceased. The result was clouds of dust during dry weather and rivers of mud, pockmarked by huge potholes, when it rained. On one occasion a wagon loaded with bodies on its way to the cemetery became stuck in such a hole and remained there until the following day, when it was finally tugged free.

As word of Union successes reached the city, Confederate morale plummeted. Once-proud Southern officers were seen staggering drunkenly down the streets.

Almost immediately after the Confederate defeat at Helena and the fall of Vicksburg, Lt. Gen. Edmund Kirby Smith, commander of

Markham and Main Streets, Little Rock, at the time of the Civil War. (Arkansas State Archives, Little Rock.)

the Confederacy's Trans-Mississippi Department, headquartered in Shreveport, Louisiana, recognized the potential threat to Little Rock. He also decided he could do little about it. He sent a message to General Holmes, who had led the disastrous attack on Helena, telling him that he could not spare any additional troops to help defend the city.

Publicly, Kirby Smith gave a mixed message to the people of Arkansas. On August 10 he issued a statement indicating that he was in Little Rock and promising to do all in his power to defend the state. But he also advised the residents to burn their cotton so it would not fall into enemy hands. Whether or not the people of Arkansas believed that Smith was in Little Rock to defend them, rumors that he was there were enough to scare General Steele. He asked for—and received—another brigade of 2,000 men as reinforcements. Thus, Kirby Smith's promise to defend the city had the perverse effect of adding to the force advancing on the capital.

The fact is that Little Rock was probably not defendable. When General Holmes took sick, he was replaced by one of his division commanders, Brig. Gen. Sterling Price. He immediately set soldiers to work building a three-mile-long defensive line on the north side of the Arkansas River, across from the city itself. But General Price, too, realized it would be difficult—probably impossible—to defend the city and prevent its capture by the Union forces.

Brig. Gen. Sterling Price, CSA. (Library of Congress, Washington, D.C.)

His problem was that the Arkansas River, which would normally provide a barrier to invaders from the north or east, became so low in September that it could be crossed at a dozen points. Price's only realistic hope for turning back Steele's army was to catch it trying to cross the river and inflict such a stunning defeat that Steele would pull back. Price knew that that was a long shot. He prepared for its failure with a plan to abandon Little Rock and move his army south to Arkadelphia. It was not the kind of plan that brings lasting glory to a military leader, but Price had learned well the lesson of Vicksburg, where General Pemberton had bravely defended the city instead of abandoning it and thus had lost his entire army when the city fell. Price wanted to hold Little Rock, but even more, he wanted to save his army.

The task of trying to inflict a crippling defeat on the advancing Union forces fell to the two Rebel generals that the 36th Iowa had faced two months earlier in the defense of the northern approaches to Helena. Since their Helena defeat, the two generals, Walker and Marmaduke, had been engaged in a feud, fueled by army gossip over who was to blame for the loss.

As the big Union army moved toward Little Rock, Marmaduke, with 1,300 cavalrymen and two cannons, fought a series of delaying actions. But he was no match for Davidson's 6,000 cavalrymen and 16 artillery pieces. The 36th Iowa marched just behind the cavalry, in the van of Steele's infantry forces, but as Marmaduke fell back toward Little Rock, they were not called into action.

In the city itself, considerable confusion prevailed about what was happening a few miles away. On August 22 the *Arkansas State Gazette* reported that the Union army had pulled back to Clarendon. A week later it called on every citizen who could fire a gun to help defend the city. Few volunteered—a measure of the citizens' lukewarm support for the Confederacy.

On August 25 Price made a fateful decision: He ordered his two feuding generals, Walker and Marmaduke, to combine their forces at a stream called Bayou Matou, which blocks the eastern approach to Little Rock, and hold out there as long as possible. Walker was placed in command, but he could not hold the line. Under pressure from the Union forces, the Rebel cavalry fell back to a new defensive position on the Arkansas River southeast of the city.

When Walker had first heard reports that Marmaduke was blaming him for failing to support him at Helena, he had shrugged off the rumor. But as the rumors persisted, he finally confronted Marmaduke and demanded an apology. Marmaduke refused, denying the remarks attributed to him. Hence the feud between the two generals. On September 5 Walker challenged Marmaduke to a duel.

Both men were West Pointers, but both were also hot-blooded cavalrymen: Walker from Texas, Marmaduke from Missouri. Marmaduke accepted the challenge. Despite the presence of a powerful enemy force on their front, the standoff was scheduled for the following day.

Word of the planned duel reached Price about midnight. Price sent orders for both men to remain at their own headquarters. Walker didn't get the word. Marmaduke received the order but ignored it. At dawn the two generals who were charged with defending Little Rock against the most immediate threat met, accompanied by their seconds, at a farm seven miles below Little Rock on the north side of the river. Union guns were so close they could be clearly heard. The two men faced off only 15 paces apart, turned, and fired. Walker fell, mortally wounded.

Price, furious at this irresponsible behavior in the face of the enemy, ordered the arrest of Marmaduke and the seconds who had served both men. But there was a war on. Marmaduke's officers pleaded his case, and Price relented. Not only was the arrest order suspended, but Marmaduke was put in charge of the entire cavalry force —his and Walker's old command. He never was prosecuted for the death of his rival general.

Three days later Marmaduke fought a delaying action near what is today Little Rock Municipal Airport. Walker's brigade refused to come to his aid, and he was forced to fall back.

Whether the duel contributed directly to the fall of Little Rock is doubtful—the city would probably have fallen in any event. But the news that one general had killed another was certainly no boost for Confederate morale.

The fall of the city should properly be credited to Steele's well-conceived moves against the capital. Steele had boldly violated one of the basic rules of combat and astutely divided his force. He sent Davidson with his cavalry to cross the Arkansas River over a pontoon bridge east of the city. This put Davidson in a position to advance toward the city from the southeast. Meanwhile, Steele moved the rest of his force along the north side of the river toward the Confederate defenses. Price, squeezed from both sides and afraid his line of retreat toward Arkadelphia might be blocked, pulled his infantry, artillery, and cavalry back across the river on pontoon bridges, burned the bridges, and prepared to retreat.

By the morning of September 10, the Union forces under Steele's personal command were installed in the deserted Confederate positions on the north side of the river. Artillery pieces were pulled into position and aimed down each of the city's north-south streets running back from the river.

As Steele studied the situation through his field glasses, he saw a lone man hoist a white flag near the river's edge at the end of Ferry Street. The man, Steele later learned, was James A. Henry, one of the city's aldermen. The night before, the city council had met and voted to surrender. But when Henry got up the next morning, he was the only alderman left in town. So he ran up the white flag by himself.

A short time later a band of armed men ordered him to pull it down. As soon as they left, he ran it up again and nailed it to the flagpole.

Steele watched this little episode while his artillerymen stood by, awaiting the order to begin firing on the city. Fortunately, Steele figured out what was happening and held off on the barrage. He soon took a skiff across the river to accept the city's surrender from Mayor C. P. Bertrand. Meanwhile, Davidson dashed into the city from the southeast and captured the armory before it could be destroyed by the retreating enemy.

The Union victory at Little Rock added significantly to the impact of the capture of Vicksburg by further weakening and isolating the Confederate forces west of the Mississippi. No longer could they hope to use northern Arkansas as a base of operations against Missouri, and no longer could they use northern Arkansas, Missouri, and the Indian Territory as recruiting grounds.

The cost for this significant victory was remarkably small—on both sides. Steele reported only 137 casualties for the entire campaign: 18 killed, 118 wounded, and one missing. The Confederates reported 64 casualties: 12 killed, 34 wounded, and 18 captured or missing. Steele thought a more accurate Confederate count would total 1,000, mostly in captured or deserted troops. Certainly in the days after the occupation of Little Rock, the Rebels suffered a large number of desertions, including many men who took the oath to the Union and joined Steele's army.

When Andrew arrived in Little Rock, he took a stroll downtown. The Union army, he saw, had already begun to transform the city. One of Steele's first orders had been to feed the residents from army stores. His order not only brought many families back from the brink of starvation but spread a feeling of goodwill toward the occupying army. The army also took over the makeshift hospitals—schools and business buildings—that had been run by Catholic Sisters of Mercy and women volunteers and immediately improved the level of care for the patients.

As Andrew passed the intersection of Main and Markham streets in the center of town, he watched as wagon after wagon dumped gravel to fill the potholes and provide a smooth surface for the streets.

He was surprised at the number of blacks in the city—far more than one would see back in Centerville or Ottumwa or Keokuk, Iowa. Many plantation owners had fled south, taking as many as 150,000 slaves with them across the border to Texas. Slaveholders who had not fled

Federal troops enter Little Rock, September 10, 1863. (Arkansas Historical Commission.)

tried to hide their slaves as the Union army moved across Arkansas. But the slaves didn't stay hidden. By the time the army reached Little Rock, it carried in its wake thousands of fleeing slaves.

Hundreds of the former slaves volunteered as soldiers and were hastily organized into units with white officers. The unit designation for the black regiments was followed by the letters "A.D.," for African Descent. The white soldiers referred to them as African Devils. Joining the army provided the freed slaves with some money, although less than what white soldiers received, plus the assurance of food, clothing, and shelter. But the black units were given the worst campsites, rocky and far from water. The black soldiers were eager to fight for their freedom, but their officers complained that they were often assigned to heavy physical labor rather than the drill that would turn them into capable soldiers. Members of the 36th Iowa even took up a collection to buy tin plates and cups for a black regiment.

Many of the blacks who did not join the army were put to work loading and unloading ships or repairing roads. Under a law passed by Congress in 1862, they were paid ten dollars a month, of which three dollars could be in the form of clothing. Other blacks, who had learned skills on the plantations, hired themselves out, usually with a white sponsor or protector.

Andrew found his fellow members of Company I and the entire regiment busy cutting pine trees and building themselves cabins—fitting many of them with fireplaces and chimneys—for shelter through the winter. The building of huts was an army tradition dating back to the Revolutionary War. The only difference between the huts at Valley Forge and those at Little Rock was that the Civil War soldiers tied their small canvas tents—shelter halves—over the roofs to help keep the water out. From a distance the camp of wooden shelters had the appearance of a tent city. As Andrew looked over the regiment's camp, on high ground swept by fresh breezes and with an abundant supply of good water from a nearby spring, he marveled at the change from the miasmic camp they had occupied along the river in Helena.

The saddest stories his friends had to tell him were of the sickness that had plagued them in Helena and of the many deaths there and on the long, hard, monthlong march to Little Rock. Helena had a reputation in the regiment, as one of the soldiers put it, as "a pest house of every disease." Andrew already knew about that from personal experience.

When the regiment was preparing to leave Helena, their commander, Colonel Kittredge, had been temporarily promoted to command a brigade. His deputy, Lieutenant Colonel Drake, had been away on sick leave. Thus, to select a regimental commander, General Steele was forced, because of the ravages of disease, to reach down three levels of officers. One of the popular young company officers, Capt. Martin Varner, was commander of Company A and thus the senior captain. He was put in charge of the entire 36th Iowa.

On the march Varner had roused his men each day at 4:30 A.M., planning to move as far as he could in the early morning, before the full heat and humidity of the Arkansas summer were felt. But day after day the regiment was forced to stand aside while wagon trains, carrying ammunition and supplies for General Davidson's cavalrymen, rumbled toward the front. When they finally got on the road at 9:30 or 10 o'clock, the men soon began to drop by the wayside. On the second day out, they managed to make 15 or 16 miles, but on the following

day they covered only seven or eight miles, and many of the men collapsed and had to be carried into camp.

By the time the regiment reached Clarendon on August 15, only
150 men were still on their feet. Scores had been overcome by illness
and the heat and had been left lying beside the road. Over the next
few days, the stragglers were brought into camp or made their way
themselves. But there were still only about 260 officers and men—in a
regiment that had numbered more than 900 when it was sworn into
Federal duty less than a year before.

Drake returned from leave on August 23 and took command of the
regiment for the march to Devall's Bluff, on the White River, ten miles
north of Clarendon and 45 miles east of Little Rock. The march was
not hard, but many of the men were so sick with diarrhea and malaria
that they were barely able to march. So many were ill, in fact, that a
hospital area was established at Devall's Bluff and plans were made to
send the men to an army hospital, probably in Memphis.

On September 1 the 36th Iowa marched off toward Little Rock.
Varner had relinquished command of the unit only a few days before;
he was left behind, feeling terribly ill. Around him, men were dying so
fast that the survivors were hard-pressed to give their dead comrades a
decent burial. On September 3 three steamers arrived, and three days
later Varner and many of the other sick men boarded the ships for the
trip down the White River to Helena and then up the Mississippi
toward Memphis, St. Louis, and perhaps even home to Iowa. Varner
was so sick that afternoon, he thought he would die.

Like many of the sick men, Varner clung to the hope that, if he
could somehow just get back home, his family could nurse him back to
health. But he didn't make it. He died—of what his friends considered
typhoid fever—before the boat reached St. Louis. He had $52 in his
pockets, and his friends used the money to buy a metal burial case so
the body could be shipped on to Iowa.

The bodies of a few soldiers—mostly officers—were returned to
their families for burial. The reality of war was brought home to the
people of Ottumwa, Iowa, for example, after the Union victory at Fort
Donelson in February 1862, when the body of a young lieutenant was
laid out in the family living room so his wife and children could give
him a proper farewell. But most of those killed in battle were hastily
buried where they fell or, in many cases, simply left to decay or to be
ravaged by wild animals.

To the surviving members of the 36th Iowa, it seemed that every steamer arriving in Little Rock carrying eagerly awaited mail from home also brought word of the deaths of fellow soldiers who had taken sick on the march to Little Rock.

As he had approached Little Rock, Steele, in an urgent request for reinforcements, noted that 1,000 of his men were unfit for duty and complained: "This is the poorest command that I have ever seen, except the cavalry." Steele was certainly exaggerating in order to add force to his request for more troops, but the condition of the army was clearly a major concern to Steele and his regimental officers.

Colonel Kittredge, now back in command of the regiment, concentrated on trying to get his men into good physical condition for the trials that might lie ahead. His efforts—and the location of the camp on high ground near the city—paid off. On December 9 surgeon Joseph B. Smith, the medical director of the army, inspected the regimental camp and concluded: "The camp of the 36th Regiment Iowa Infantry is now a model of order, cleanliness and comfort. In a division where all surgeons do their duty, it may well be a source of pride to have acquired the pre-eminence."

In early December, at the time of the medical director's visit, the weather seemed to the Iowans to be unseasonably warm and pleasant. And then winter arrived. On January 1, 1864, the jet stream—whose existence, of course, would not be known for many years—dipped southward, bringing with it a mass of arctic air. High winds swept across the camp, whipping the soldiers' huts with sheets of hail. Then came snow, piling in drifts two feet high. The Arkansas River froze solid—the first time that had happened in 11 years. Even for boys from Iowa, who were used to fierce prairie winters, this was a storm to be reckoned with.

For days the bad weather continued, with cold winds, rain, sleet, and snow. January 5 dawned bright and clear, but the cold continued, covering the ground with a sheet of glare ice. Horses and mules skidded ludicrously. When they fell, there was no way to get them back on their feet, and many were left to die.

One more severe storm swept through the camp at the end of February, leaving two inches of sleet and snow on the ground and icicles more than two feet long. And then suddenly spring was in the air, with warm weather and soft breezes. Andrew joined the soldiers gathered along the banks of the Arkansas to watch the roaring torrent, swollen with water from rapidly melting snow, as it coursed by the city.

With the warmer weather came rumors of an impending move, and anticipation stirred throughout the camp. But one dark episode in the depths of the winter would linger in the minds of Andrew and the other men of the 36th as long as they lived—which, for many of them, would not be long.

Chapter Seven

The Hanging of David Dodd

On December 30, 1863, word flashed through Little Rock that a suspected Confederate spy had been captured while trying to sneak through the Union picket line, just outside of town, into Rebel territory.

The arrest of David Dodd immediately caused a sensation, not only among the soldiers but among many local residents who had known him and his family for years.

Dodd was far from fitting the stereotype of a cloak-and-dagger espionage agent. A tall dark-haired boy, barely 17 years old, he was well known in town and in recent days had been living openly in Little Rock, dating local girls. In fact, two nights before his capture, he had taken Mary Swindle, one of his girlfriends, to a dance.

Early on the morning after the dance, Dodd mounted his mule and rode out of town, planning to join his parents in Camden, Arkansas, which was then in Rebel control. In his pocket he had a pass from the Union army's adjutant general permitting him to pass through the Union picket lines. He stopped at the last guardpost on the road leading toward Hot Springs. The army sentinel, Pvt. Daniel Olderburg, told Dodd he was then entering enemy-controlled territory. He took Dodd's pass and tore it up so it could not be used again.

Dodd stayed that night in Rebel territory at the rural home of his uncle, about 18 miles from Little Rock. The next morning, instead of continuing on down the road toward Hot Springs, he took a shortcut across the countryside, planning to visit a friend and trade his mule for a horse. His shortcut, however, took him back through a corner of Union territory—right into the path of a Union cavalry patrol.

Dodd explained that he had surrendered his pass the evening before. To prove it, he accompanied the Union troopers back to the guardpost. But Olderburg was off duty. The sentinel at the checkpoint knew nothing about Dodd or his pass. The cavalrymen took Dodd on to their headquarters to be questioned by an officer. Up to this point, Dodd was just a kid who had been riding his mule where he shouldn't have been. There was no reason to suspect he was a spy or for him to fear that he was in deep trouble.

The trouble began when he surrendered a little notebook he carried in his pocket. It contained some routine diary-type entries. But several pages were different: They were filled with dots and dashes. Dodd explained that he had worked at a telegraph office in Little Rock and was simply practicing his Morse code. One of the officers knew enough Morse code to decipher a few lines referring to guns. They called in Captain Robert C. Clowrey, assistant superintendent of the Union military telegraph and later president of the Western Union Telegraph Company.

Clowrey quickly decoded the dots and dashes. What he read was a detailed description of the defenses of Little Rock.

Dodd was arrested, accused of espionage, and held for trial by a military commission that had been created earlier in the year. He did not have to wait long for his trial.

The court assembled the very next morning, December 31. Presiding over the five-man military commission was Brig. Gen. John M. Thayer, a 43-year-old lawyer and Indian fighter. The judge advocate, acting as prosecutor, was Capt. B. F. Rice of the Third Minnesota Volunteer Infantry Regiment. Rice read the formal charge accusing Dodd of entering Union lines, gathering military information, obtaining a Federal pass, and attempting to travel into enemy territory. It also charged that he "did otherwise lurk, and act as a spy."

Dodd pleaded not guilty.

When court reconvened at 9 A.M. on New Year's Day, Dodd was represented by two prominent local lawyers, T.D.W Yonley and William M. Fishback, later a governor of Arkansas.

They presented a written plea in which Dodd agreed to take the oath of allegiance to the Union and thus take advantage of a proclamation of amnesty issued by Abraham Lincoln three weeks earlier, which offered a pardon to all Confederates except government offi-

David O. Dodd, hanged as a spy in Little Rock, January 8, 1864. (Arkansas Historical Commission.)

cials and Rebel officers. The court deliberated and then decided that the amnesty did not apply to spies.

On the following morning, Rice, the prosecutor, presented his case. Dodd's lawyers listened in dismay as one witness after another drew the net tighter and tighter around their client. The clincher was the testimony from Captain Clowrey. Holding the notebook found in Dodd's possession, he decoded the dots and dashes: "3rd Ohio battery has 4 guns—brass. 4th Ohio battery has 6 guns—brass. . . . Three brigades of Cavalry in a Division. Three regiments in a brigade, brigade commanded by Davidson. . . ."

Everyone in the courtroom was roughly familiar with the size and disposition of the city's defenses. No one doubted that Dodd's encoded notes were an accurate description, down to the last cannon. Even though the Confederates had until recently occupied the city, knowledge of the strength and disposition of Union forces would have been useful in an attack or raid.

Yonley and Fishback called a number of prominent citizens to speak favorably of Dodd's character and to testify that they had seen him going openly about the city in the days before his arrest, not lurking or acting like a spy. Dodd had lived and worked in Little Rock earlier but left with his family in mid-December to move to Camden. His father then sent the boy back to Little Rock on December 22 to finish up his business for him. It was at the conclusion of this errand that David had been captured.

The defense attorneys decided not to put Dodd himself on the stand. Instead, they submitted a written statement in his behalf. It argued that he wasn't a spy. But it also contended that, if he was a spy, he had been drawn into it by older accomplices. The lawyers tried their best to overcome the compelling case against their client with a flurry of flowery words. Quoting Dodd, they wrote:

> I have just entered upon the threshold of life; and in the light of its green fields and inviting flowers, I have not had either the time or the inclination to dream of treason and of stratagem. . . . Proud of the name of American—my budding sympathies were unfolding themselves in the light of Constitutional Liberty—The young tendrils of mind were entwining about the majestic columns of the Temple of Freedom. . . . Above all, Oh My Judges, will you hear the words of my mother prophetic of my own emotions. She has rejoiced that I was a minor, and unable to bear arms against the flag of the Union.

The members of the military commission were unswayed by the appeal, but they still anguished over their verdict. Given the evidence, they could not in good conscience find him not guilty. But under a law enacted by Congress the previous year, the penalty for espionage was death—and they had little stomach for sending a 17-year-old to the gallows. It was not hard to think of the boy before them as a son or brother. But they found a guilty verdict inescapable.

Dodd was convicted on January 3, and Steele immediately set the date for his execution five days hence, between 10 A.M. and 4 P.M. on January 8.

A number of prominent citizens visited Steele to plead with him to spare the boy's life. Dodd himself met with Steele and, according to some accounts, told him that General Fagan, whose units had borne some of the heaviest fighting in the Battle of Helena, had personally sent him on his spy mission.

It is doubtful that Steele had very much leeway under the law to cancel the hanging. But even if he could have found a loophole, he may also have wanted to let the people of Little Rock know how tough he could be. In the three months since his army had occupied the city, he had been a compassionate and even rather popular conquerer, caring for the sick, feeding the hungry, and repairing the streets. He may have begun to worry that some were taking advantage of his leniency—and some were.

After the war one woman related how she had gone to see Steele personally to ask for a permit to cross the picket lines to visit her husband, who was in the Confederate army. She found Steele "a quiet, kind man," who not only made out the permit but offered to provide an escort outside the Federal lines. And then, she said, she and her niece hid $6,000 in gold in special pockets under their voluminous hoopskirts and smuggled it across the lines.

Whatever the choices available to him and whatever his motives, Steele was not swayed by the appeals for mercy. He decreed that the execution would go ahead as scheduled.

On the morning of the hanging, a work detail arrived at St. John's Masonic College—a school Dodd had himself attended and which had been converted into a military hospital—and erected a rough wooden scaffolding on the parade ground. The structure consisted of two upright timbers and a crossbar with a new rope hanging from it. There was no platform and no trapdoor, as in a conventional gallows.

Hours before the hanging was to take place, troops of the 36th regiment and other units formed up in their assembly areas, carrying their rifles and bayonets. After inspection by their officers, they marched to the college grounds. The infantrymen formed three sides of a square. The fourth side was filled in by cavalrymen, five ranks deep. The soldiers filled the entire space around the gallows, but thousands of civilians streamed to the area, eager for a glimpse of the prisoner and his execution. The Arkansas River was still frozen solid in that bitter January weather, and many civilians walked across the river to witness the hanging. As many as 6,000 people gathered—nearly double the city's peacetime population. They climbed the walls of the college building and filled the branches of every nearby tree. From a vantage point in a nearby building, one man carefully arranged a telescope on a tripod to give himself a close-up view of the spectacle.

A hush fell over the crowd a few minutes before 3 P.M. as an army ambulance labored up the hill to the site. In the back of the wagon was a rough wooden coffin. And on the coffin sat David Dodd. On the way to the execution site, the wagon had passed the home of Mary Swindle, the girl Dodd had danced with a few nights before. Another girl with whom he had associated during his visit to Little Rock had quietly left town, fearful that she might be implicated.

The wagon was driven right in under the gallows. Lieutenant Dekay, assistant provost marshal and chief of military police, acted as executioner, while Capt. S. S. McNaughton, the provost marshal general, stood by, presiding over the ceremony. Dekay lowered the tailgate and tied it in a horizontal position with a piece of cord. Then he ordered Dodd to stand on the tailgate while the rope was fitted around his neck and his hands were bound behind his back.

Dodd appeared calm—more so than the soldiers charged with carrying out the execution. When Dekay found he had no blindfold, which was required by army regulations, Dodd volunteered the handkerchief in his pocket. Dodd's frame of mind was expressed in a letter he wrote to his family on the morning of his execution:

> Military Prison
> Little Rock   Jan 8th   10 o'clock am 1864
>
> My Dear Parents and Sisters
> I was arrested as a Spy and tried and was Sentenced to be
> hung today at 3 oclock   the time is fast approaching but
> thank God I am prepared to die   I expect to meet you all
> in heaven   I will soon be out of this world of sorrow and
> trouble   I would like to see you all before I die but let Gods
> will be done not ours   I pray to God to give you strength
> to bear your troubles while in this world   I hope God will
> receive you all in heaven   Mother I know it will be hard
> for you to give up your only son but you must remember it
> is Gods will   Good by   God will give you strength to
> bear your troubles   I pray that we may meet in heaven
> Good by   God will bless you all   your Son and brother
>
> David O Dodd

The condemned boy had expected to be comforted to the end by his spiritual adviser, Rev. Dr. R. G. Colburn of the First Methodist

Episcopal Church South. But Colburn took ill and left just before the hanging. How sick he actually was is questionable. There is reason to believe that he was simply afraid—afraid that he might be implicated with Dodd and end up following him to the gallows. A few days earlier Colburn's church had been taken over by the army, and Chaplain Hare of the 36th Iowa had been put in charge of it.

Lt. Benjamin F. Pearson, a deeply religious officer and friend of Hare's, had attended Colburn's church a few weeks earlier, listened to his sermon, and concluded that he was a "perfect Rebel." When Colburn backed out at the last minute, Pearson was outraged: "Colburn left the spy in the very hour of his greatest need . . . Some think he is more guilty than the spy that was caught."

In Colburn's place, a military chaplain was recruited to comfort Dodd in his final moments.

The reverend fell to his knees beside the tailgate and launched into what seemed to the soldiers and spectators to be an interminable prayer. Dodd stood quietly, but those in charge of the execution fidgeted, anxious to have their onerous duty over with. Finally the minister ended his communion with the Lord and rose to his feet.

Dekay reached out with a knife and quickly cut the cord holding the tailgate in place. Dodd dropped toward the ground. The new rope stretched. His toes touched the earth, and he began to writhe at the end of the rope.

In the front row of the troops, one soldier collapsed, the clatter of his equipment breaking the silence that had descended over the multitude.

Quickly one of the soldiers in the execution detail scrambled to the top of the scaffold and pulled up on the rope to hasten the boy's death. After eight minutes the body hung lifeless, and a surgeon stepped forward to pronounce him dead.

Whether Dodd slowly strangled to death or whether he was actually killed by the initial drop is in question. A surgeon who examined the body afterward said he died of a "disrupted spine." But Andrew Brayman and the other soldiers who witnessed the event had no doubts that they had seen a horribly bungled execution. Leander Stillwell, a private in the 61st Illinois Infantry and one of those present, later described the Dodd execution as "unspeakably cruel and cold-blooded."

"On one side," Stillwell recalled,

> were thousands of men with weapons in their hands, coolly looking on; on the other was one, lone unfortunate boy. My

conscience has never troubled me for anything I may have done on the firing line, in time of battle. There were the other fellows in plain sight, shooting, and doing all in their power to kill us. It was my duty to shoot at them, aim low, and kill some of them, if possible, and I did the best I could, and have no remorse whatever. But whenever my memory recalls the choking to death of that boy, (for that is what was done), I feel bad, and don't like to write or think about it.

Despite their revulsion at the method of the execution, few disagreed with the rule that spies—male spies, at least—deserved execution. The feeling among the soldiers was that a man's duty was to shoulder a weapon and fight openly for the cause he believed in. Women, on the other hand, were not expected to fight, and those who put their lives in jeopardy by acting as spies tended to be respected and even treated as heroines.

Dodd was an exception to this rule. Perhaps because of his youth and the poignant circumstances of his capture and execution, he became a folk hero in Arkansas and is remembered as such even to this day. He was buried in Little Rock's Mt. Holly Cemetery. In 1913, half a century after his death, admirers erected an eight-foot marble spire over his grave with the inscription: "Here lie the remains of David O. Dodd. Born in Lavaca County, Texas, Nov. 10, 1846, died Jan. 8, 1864." A low marble curb outlining the grave carries a marble scroll with the words: "Boy Martyr of the Confederacy."

Others executed by the Union army in Little Rock were not mourned and were quickly forgotten except by close friends and relatives.

On March 18, shortly before the 36th Iowa left the city, two men were hanged at the state penitentiary in Little Rock. Unlike Dodd, whose name was known to everyone, the soldiers knew little about these men. One was Jeremiah Earnest, who was 52 years old, considered himself a captain, and was the father of a soldier in the Union Fourth Arkansas Cavalry. The other was Thomas Jefferson Miller, a 47-year-old schoolteacher and an active member of the Methodist Episcopal Church.

The two men were accused of being members of a guerrilla band—the northerners knew such groups as bushwhackers, the southerners as jayhawkers—that had dragged several Union supporters from their farm homes and hanged them in the presence of their wives and children.

One regiment—the 61st Illinois—was mustered to serve as a guard during the execution. Chaplain Hare of the 36th Iowa was called on to accompany the condemned men to the scaffold. He conferred briefly with them and then sang "Rock of Ages." As he finished, the colonel in charge of the execution gave the signal, and the two men dropped through the trapdoor of the gallows.

Given the hostile attitude toward bushwhackers, they were probably fortunate to have been brought to Little Rock and tried before being hanged. Often guerrillas, when captured, were hanged or shot on the spot, sometimes after a brief drumhead court, many times without any trial at all.

Such rough justice was clearly condoned by high-ranking Union officials. Secretary of War Edwin M. Stanton was succinct: "Let them swing." And Gen. H. W. Halleck, for a time the top Union commander, said: "Let them be tried immediately by a drumhead court, and punished by death."

The guerrilla bands ranged from semimilitary units with a link to one of the armies to outright brigands. They were a particular problem in Arkansas because there was no police force to protect isolated farm families, and neither army was in a position to provide such protection. To discourage the guerrillas, the Union army resorted to harsh treatment of those captured.

Late in 1863, when guerrillas persisted in cutting the telegraph lines to Fort Smith, on the western border between Arkansas and the Indian Territory, Brig. Gen. John McNeil, the Union commander at Fort Smith, issued a draconian order: Every time a wire was cut, a bushwhacker prisoner would be hanged from the telegraph pole nearest to the cut; and the home of every Confederate sympathizer within ten miles of the cut in the line would be burned.

Early in 1864, when General Thayer, who had presided at Dodd's trial, took over at Fort Smith, he issued an order to his men "to hunt down and hang or shoot every guerrilla caught in the vicinity where the mails were captured or the telegraph lines were cut."

Such severe measures may have reduced guerrilla depredations throughout Arkansas, particularly in the northern area nominally under Union control. But they certainly did not halt them. For all practical purposes, most of Arkansas was a giant no-man's-land. In March 1864 the 36th Iowa was one of the regiments preparing to venture into that quagmire.

Part Two

More Men Needed

PAGE 82: *Andrew Brayman. A lock of his hair was enclosed in the frame of this picture.* (Authors' collection.)

Chapter Eight

Another Son Goes to War

For Mary and Lewis Brayman, 1863 was a time of worry and anxiety. They worried about Andrew, sick so long in the big impersonal army hospitals. Mary ached to have her son home, where he could receive good food and proper care. At least as long as he remained in the hospital, he wouldn't be exposed to combat. But from what they heard, the hospitals were often deadlier than the battlefields.

They worried, too, about Barney. Although still just a boy in his parents' eyes, he thought of little except the time when he would be able to follow Andrew into military service.

The family's anxiety was relieved, although certainly not removed, by the wave of euphoria that swept over the North after the great victories at Gettysburg and Vicksburg in the summer of 1863. Many Northerners seized on the good news to convince themselves that the war would soon come to an end.

Among politicians and some of the more astute generals, however, there was a more realistic assessment: the war could—some said "must"—be ended before the presidential election of November 1864. Even in the midst of a civil war—or perhaps *especially* in the midst of a civil war—political considerations were at least as important as military strategy.

This hope that the war would soon be brought to an end rested largely on the cooperation of the South: The South's politicians and its generals should understand, it was thought, that they were doomed to defeat militarily and should quit before there was further bloodshed and destruction of property.

But Southern leaders saw the situation quite differently: If they could hold out through 1863 and well into the presidential election year of 1864, the North's will and political ability to continue the war would collapse, Lincoln and the Republicans would be swept from office, and the South would succeed in its goal of establishing a separate nation on the North American continent.

To a remarkable degree, the situation was similar to that faced by the United States and North Vietnam a hundred years later, during the war in Southeast Asia. The goal of the United States was to use its immense superiority in technology to hurt the enemy so badly that they would call it quits. The North Vietnamese goal was to endure until the United States lost its will to continue the fight. In the end, the North Vietnamese proved more willing to suffer punishment than the United States proved willing to inflict it.

In 1863 it would not have been at all clear to a neutral observer that the North would be able to muster the political will to continue to bleed the South longer than the South was willing to continue to suffer.

While Abraham Lincoln and other Northern leaders were hoping for a speedy military collapse of the South, they prepared for more war—and this meant not only increasing war production but recruiting more men, men by the hundreds of thousands. As the war had gone on, it had become apparent that the Union could not rely on a continuing supply of volunteers to fill its regiments. The draft was instituted in the spring of 1863, when Congress passed the Enrollment Act on March 3. It was the first true draft in the nation's history, and it was a clumsy, unfair system.

Every man between the ages of 20 and 45 years of age was subject to being called up. But in an effort to avoid draft resistance, the law was riddled with loopholes. A man could avoid service by paying a "commutation" fee of $300. Or he could hire a substitute to take his place in the army. Brokers quickly set up shop providing substitutes— many of whom took the money and whatever bonus was offered and then skedaddled, only to sign up somewhere else and repeat the bounty-jumping process.

A few thousand men evaded the draft by moving to Canada, and even more headed for the gold fields out west. Early in 1864 Governor

W. M. Stone, who had just succeeded Samuel Kirkwood as governor of Iowa, became so alarmed at the drain on the state's manpower that he ordered the posting of guards at the state's western borders to detain able-bodied men heading west.

One result of the draft—and a source of much of the opposition to it—was the fact that it pulled poor men into the army while permitting those with money to escape service—in what was called the "rich man's war, poor man's fight." The draft was, in that regard, much like the draft during the Vietnam War, when liberal college deferments permitted those who could afford it to stay in school while poorer boys were shipped off to the jungles of Southeast Asia.

Paradoxically, the Confederacy, formed from states that had left the Union to assert their sovereignty as states, created a draft system that was both fairer and more efficient than the system in the North. Unfortunately for the South, however, its draft was better at getting men into the service than the Confederate army was at keeping them there. Throughout the war the Confederacy was plagued by a high desertion rate. It was bad enough that many men simply went home. What was worse was that thousands took the oath of allegiance and joined the Union forces.

By the middle of 1863, it was obvious that the South had more or less exhausted its manpower resources. In January 1864 Irish-born Maj. Gen. Patrick Cleburne, one of the South's most brilliant young generals, proposed the only plausible solution to the South's manpower problems: arm the slaves and promise them freedom in return for service in the army.

"As between the loss of independence and the loss of slavery," Cleburne told a group of fellow generals, "we assume that every patriot will freely give up the latter—give up the Negro slave rather than be a slave himself." Although many of the generals agreed, his proposal was rejected as politically unrealistic, and he was ordered to keep it secret. Doubtless many Southerners would have considered armed blacks more dangerous than a Union victory.

The North, for its part, did enlist thousands of men of African descent into separate regiments. And it had a much larger pool of whites of fighting age from which to draw. It even signed up a few "graybeard regiments" of men in their fifties and sixties. These advantages, however, were undermined by the fact that the enlistments of thousands of the Union soldiers were due to expire in 1864.

Most of the states had organized entire regiments—like the 36th

Iowa—which were then mustered into Federal service as units, rather than providing individual soldiers as "fillers" for existing regiments. Since each regiment required its full complement of officers appointed by the state governor, this system was a rich source of patronage jobs. But it also presented problems for the Union war effort. For one, each new regiment had to learn the arts of war without the guidance of a large core of veterans, and thus the regiments tended to decrease in size as battlefield losses and sickness took their toll. Another problem was that since all the men had been mustered in at the same time, they were all free to go home at the same time.

Of the Union Army's 946 infantry regiments, the enlistments of 455 would end in the spring and summer of 1864. Of the 158 artillery batteries, the enlistments of 81 were also due to end. And time was running out for half the cavalry regiments. Hefty bonuses, a generous leave policy, and other inducements were prepared to encourage reenlistment, but no one could be sure whether most of the men would sign up for another tour of duty as veteran volunteers or simply go home.

Thus the draft was seen as a necessity, not only to increase the size of the Union Army but to replace the uncertain number of soldiers who might soon be leaving their regiments.

The institution of the draft was greeted with massive resistance in some parts of the country. In some cases, men refused to register or failed to report for duty when called. Even worse, antidraft riots broke out in Chicago, Milwaukee, New York, and Portsmouth, New Hampshire. The riots were among the most violent in the nation's history, far more destructive than the antiwar rallies of the Vietnam War era.

The worst rioting occurred in New York City.

Early on Monday, July 5, 1863, just as the smoke was settling over the Gettysburg battlefield in southern Pennsylvania, columns of slum dwellers marched north up the city's west side, then crossed over Central Park to assemble at a vacant lot on the east side, near what was, then as now, one of the city's most affluent areas. Then they marched south again, assembling at the enrollment office at 677 Third Avenue, between Forty-sixth and Forty-seventh Streets, where the names of draftees were being pulled from a large lottery drum. The marchers went into the building, smashed the hated drum, pushed aside the police, and destroyed furniture. With them they had brought several containers of turpentine. It was sprinkled around and ignited, and soon the building was a pyre of flame.

On Broadway near the southern tip of Manhattan, a disciplined police offensive stopped and routed the mob. But the rioters scattered and continued their depradations, hunting down and beating or killing Negroes. By the reasoning of the antidraft rioters, there would have been no war if not for the abolitionists and their concern for the welfare of the slaves.

It was not until Thursday, in the fourth day of the disturbance, that it was finally brought under control, with the arrival of Federal troops fresh from the battle at Gettysburg.

While the rioters were mostly Irish immigrant slum-dwellers—both men and women—resistance to the war and the draft had certainly been encouraged by prominent members of the white, Anglo-Saxon Protestant establishment.

In a speech to a July Fourth gathering on the day before the riots, Governor Horatio Seymour, a conservative Democrat who had been elected by a large margin, denounced the draft: "One out of about two-and-a-half of our citizens is destined to be brought over into Messrs. Lincoln and Company's charnel house."

In words that later took on added significance, he declared: "Remember this: that the bloody, treasonable and revolutionary doctrine of public necessity can be proclaimed by a mob as well as a government."

Even after the full scale of the antidraft violence became apparent, several of the city's anti-administration newspapers took the side of the rioters. The *World* editorialized: "[T]he masses of the people of New York . . . have been stung by the madness and irritated by the chicanery of the administration." The *Daily News* even went so far as to condemn the police response to the riot.

Resistance to the draft was not limited to New York, but the violence that shook that city became a symbol of the intense opposition in the North, not only to the draft but to the war itself and the Lincoln administration.

In Iowa, Governor Kirkwood had two major concerns in the summer and fall of 1863.

While most Iowans supported the Union and the war and prided themselves on their state's contribution to the war effort, those who had doubts or even supported the Southern cause became bolder as the war, with its horrifying casualties, dragged on. Those who spoke openly against the war, or advocated a compromise that would permit the South to return to the Union, or who favored the western states joining the Confederacy, were called Copperheads. But there were many other Iowans, organized in secret cells of the Knights of the Golden Circle, who stockpiled arms and prepared for armed resistance.

By one estimate, the Knights had cells in every township in the state and a membership of as many as 42,000 men. The members took a secret oath to support the Constitution of the United States, to resist the draft, and to do all in their power "to unite the states of the North-west with the Southern Confederacy."

Early in 1863 Governor Kirkwood wrote to a supporter: "I am, very reluctantly, compelled to believe there is danger of an outbreak in our own state in favor of the rebellion, unless measures be taken to prevent it. I am now taking the necessary steps to have a volunteer Company of *undoubtedly* loyal men organized and armed in each one of the second tier of counties from our south line."

In another letter in March, Kirkwood told a supporter of his concerns: "It would be a terrible thing to have civil war with all its horrors in our state, and if it comes I intend it shall be terribly atoned for by those who bring it upon us."

Kirkwood's fears were almost realized in August 1863, when open conflict broke out between opponents of the war and the draft, led by a minister named George C. Tally, and the residents of South English, a quiet little town in Keokuk County. The conflict, variously known as the Tally War or the Skunk River War, was brought under control only after Kirkwood dispatched 11 home guard companies to the scene of the conflict, brought in six companies of the Seventh Iowa Cavalry, and hurried to the scene himself.

The other major concern weighing on Kirkwood's mind was the draft. He hoped that Iowa could fulfill its quota by enlisting volunteers and so be spared the draft. This would not only uphold Iowa's "honor" as a supporter of the Union and the war, but it would also remove a major target of the Copperheads and others opposed to the war.

It was in these circumstances that organization of the Eighth Iowa Cavalry was authorized by the U.S. War Department on April 6, 1863. Governor Kirkwood chose Joseph B. Dorr to organize the regiment and to serve as its colonel.

Before the war, Dorr had been editor of the Dubuque *Herald*, a Democratic newspaper—but of the Stephen Douglas persuasion. Douglas, one of two Democrats who had faced Abraham Lincoln in the 1860 presidential election, was the leader of the Democratic faction that opposed dividing the nation.

Although Dorr lacked military experience before the war, in the early days of the conflict he had received a commission as quartermaster of the Twelfth Iowa Infantry. During the Battle of Shiloh, he had received honorable mention for gallantry, even though his job as quartermaster did not require him to become involved in the action.

In taking on the job of organizing a regiment, Dorr had definite—and unconventional—ideas about what kind of a regiment it should be. Instead of a cavalry unit, he asked permission to put together a regiment of "mounted infantry" or "mounted riflemen"—a concept popular in the South but rare in the North.

In a fervent letter to Kirkwood, he gave his reasons for wanting to lead mounted infantry rather than cavalry:

> A regiment of mounted riflemen or mounted infantry can be recruited in less time than a regiment of cavalry for the reason that it is an entirely new organization in the West—that the opinion prevails that it will be less likely to be broken up to furnish body guards, couriers, orderlies, etc.—that the enlisted men are not encumbered with arms, useless most of the time—that it will attract many experienced marksmen from the frontier who have confidence in their proficiency with the rifle but who object to enlisting in the infantry. . . . That the regiment when raised can be made proficient in tactics in much less time than a cavalry regiment.

While the distinction between cavalrymen riding horses and infantrymen doing the same thing may seem insignificant to the layperson, there were important differences in practice.

The cavalryman is armed with a saber, a short-range carbine, and a relatively small-caliber pistol. He is trained to fight mounted, in slashing saber charges. The mounted infantryman, on the other hand, is unencumbered by a saber but instead carries a more powerful infantry rifle. He is trained to gallop from one spot to another, dismount, and go into battle as a foot soldier.

In practice, few saber-wielding cavalry charges were made during the war. On a number of occasions lightly armed Union cavalrymen were ordered to fight dismounted, but only until they could be relieved by more heavily armed foot soldiers, who moved up through the ranks, jeering the cavalrymen as they fell back to the rear.

In the South mounted infantry had proved to be important as what would now be called a "force multiplier." Mounting infantrymen on horses gave them a mobility that permitted relatively small Confederate forces to move rapidly and concentrate quickly to gain the advantage over larger but slower Union forces.

Dorr's request for permission to create a military unit "new in the West" apparently was not seriously considered and was rejected out of hand. Tradition and bureaucratic inertia won out, as they so often do. The army wanted a cavalry regiment, and that was what it got.

Whether the young men of Iowa thought they were enlisting as cavalrymen or mounted rifles, they came marching in by squads and companies to Camp Roberts on the outskirts of Davenport in the late summer of 1863. While the push of the draft may have inspired some of them, most were attracted by the opportunity to serve in a dashing, elite mounted unit. In all 22 companies, totaling more than 2,000 men, reported for duty.

Young Edward Barney Brayman was one of those who volunteered—just about a year after his brother had marched off to war and despite the knowledge that Andrew had spent much of that year in army hospitals. The boys' father, Louis, was thus left without either of his sons to help on the farm. He gave up farming and established a small hotel and rooming house in Bellair.

Barney signed up on August 22, 1863, in Centerville, as a private in Company H of the Eighth Cavalry. His enlistment papers say he was 17 years old. But having been born on January 8 or 9, 1847, he was only 16. At five feet, eight and a half inches tall, he was almost exactly the same height as the average Civil War soldier. Like his brother, he had blue eyes, light hair, and a fair complexion, darkened by the farm boy's constant exposure to the sun.

As soon as the volunteers arrived at Camp Roberts, the weeding-out process began. The number of volunteers was almost twice as large as that needed to fill out a cavalry regiment.

Several volunteers were rejected because they were too young. Others were sent home because they were ill or in poor physical condition. Earlier in the war many men who were unfit for duty had nonetheless slipped through a cursory physical examination. In one case, a surgeon stood by and watched men march by in the rain, screening out a few as they hobbled along. But by the time the men of the Eighth Cavalry reported for duty, competent doctors were on hand to weed out those who would only cause problems in training or on the battlefield.

Barney Brayman. (Roger Davis, Keokuk, Iowa.)

Of those remaining, 500 were shifted over to the Ninth Cavalry and another 100 to the Fourth Iowa Battery of artillery. That left 1,234 men, among them Barney Brayman, to fill out the 12 companies of the new regiment. Dorr, who had his pick of the recruits, felt "the organization of the regiment was perfected under the most favorable conditions."

Barney Brayman and the other recruits were quickly sorted out into companies, and the companies assigned to battalions. Barney remained with others from Appanoose County in Company H, which had been organized and was headed by Capt. M. M. Walden, a Centerville schoolteacher who had also organized the county's first volunteer infantry company in 1861. After participating in the Battle of Shiloh, he became ill and returned home, where he remained until reentering the service in 1863.

Shortly after their arrival in camp, the recruits were lined up and herded past a quartermaster window, where an unsympathetic sergeant handed out clothes without regard to size. When the boys complained, they were assured that the clothes would "average up all right."

The same procedure was followed in issuing horses. Often the smallest man got the biggest horse and vice versa. Here too they were assured that the horses would "average up," and after some judicious swapping, they did.

The new troopers also received a special issue of cavalry equipment: a saber and metal scabbard, pistol, carbine, haversack and nosebag, poncho, spurs, cartridge box, and canteen. Equipping a cavalry regiment—from nosebag to the horse itself—cost the government about a quarter of a million dollars.

When the troopers received their weapons, they looked them over with the expert eye of boys who had grown up with their own firearms. The strange looks of the carbine intrigued them. The Cosmopolitan, manufactured in Ohio, was the only carbine purchased for the Union Army that was made west of the Allegheny Mountains. It had a distinctive look with an S-shaped external hammer and a stock that did not extend forward to give added support to the barrel. A relatively small weapon, and thus suitable for use on horseback, it was just over a yard long, weighed a little over six pounds, and fired a .52-caliber bullet.

It did not take the troopers of the Eighth Cavalry long to learn that their Cosmopolitan carbine left something to be desired. It was not very accurate, and it tended to break with the least stress. Even worse, after a few shots it leaked fire around the cartridge chamber. Their low opinion of their new weapon was confirmed later by the chief ordnance officer of the Department of West Virginia, who condemned it as "a very worthless weapon . . . thrust upon the Ordnance Department by political influence of contractors."

Only 9,000 Cosmopolitan carbines were issued—compared with 95,000 of the more popular and technically superior Spencer carbines. Unfortunately for the Eighth Cavalry, they were one of the few units with the inferior Cosmopolitan.

Although many cavalry units were issued navy revolvers—smaller and lighter than the army issue—the troopers of the Eighth Cavalry received bulky .44- and .45-caliber army pistols. In contrast to the carbines, the revolvers were serviceable and reliable weapons.

For farm boys, used to the quiet of their rural homes and accustomed to being awakened by the call of a rooster, the first morning in camp let them know how much their life had changed. The first sound they heard was the wake-up call—reveille—blown by the regimental bugler and echoed down the line by the company buglers. In Company H the call was played by W. V. Wilcox. He was shorter and younger than the rest of the recruits, who called him "Billy the Bugler."

Annoying as the bugles may have seemed at first, their almost constant sound was an important part of life in the cavalry. Whereas the infantry often used drums to communicate orders, the cavalry used the piercing notes of the bugle to cut through the thundering of horses' hooves and pass instructions instantly to each soldier. In all, the troops had to learn and react to more than 40 different bugle calls.

The various bugle calls overlay the entire day of a cavalry regiment: reveille, stable call, breakfast call, sick call, police call (ordering a cleanup of the camp), guard mount, water call, drill call, dinner call, stable call, and supper call.

At sundown came retreat call, following the usual dress parade. When taps was finally sounded, the troopers were happy to collapse on their cots.

Colonel Dorr was fortunate in having a number of veterans of early service as both commissioned and noncommissioned officers in the regiment. But despite the eagerness of the new recruits, their efforts to prepare for service were seriously hampered. The regiment was sworn into Federal service on September 30, but it was not issued horses until October 15—after it had already been ordered to leave its training camp and hurry to the scene of conflict in Tennessee. And even when the recruits received fine horses, they still were not issued saddles.

Alarmed, N. B. Baker, the state adjutant general who was the link between the state and the Iowa regiments in Federal service, wrote to Governor Kirkwood on October 14: "The 8th Cavalry are ordered away tomorrow—to Louisville. They are not fully mounted—officers not paid—and no drill on horseback—no cavalry exercise—use of carbine to accustom horses to stand fire, etc."

Baker followed up with a telegram to Maj. Gen. William S. Rosecrans, the commander of the Department of the Cumberland. On October 28, after the Eighth Cavalry had already left Davenport, he received a reply from Rosecrans's adjutant that seemed, on first reading, to be reassuring. He told Baker the regiment would be held at Louisville, Kentucky, to be paid and then added:

"When the regiment reaches here [Chattanooga] it will be placed on duty which will permit them to drill and become well acquainted with their duties as soldiers, before being called into active field service, unless some exigency should occur which would make their service necessary at the front."

That last clause was hardly reassuring, especially since Baker knew

Rosecrans, whose forces had been defeated at the great Battle of Chickamauga, expected renewed heavy combat and perhaps a battle for Chattanooga itself.

The move from Camp Roberts at Davenport was an exciting event. The regiment had some 1,250 officers and men, 1,225 horses, 84 mules, 14 army wagons, and an ambulance for each of the 12 companies. It took most of the day to load the horses and equipment aboard three long freight trains. It was not until late afternoon that the men boarded two additional trains, cramming themselves into small passenger coaches where there was little room to move about, let alone exercise.

Before their departure, the cooks made up three days' rations, and the troopers carried the food in oilcloth haversacks. As they quickly discovered, the oilcloth tainted the rations, making them inedible.

Late the next day the trains pulled into Michigan City, Indiana. There all the horses were unloaded, fed, watered, and then loaded back onto the boxcars. That night, the trains resumed the journey, stopping to water and feed the horses the next morning in Indianapolis before going on to arrive at Jeffersonville, Indiana, just across the Ohio River from Louisville, Kentucky, at 3 o'clock the next morning. The men were tired, hungry, and stiff from the long ride in their crowded coaches.

In Jeffersonville they got the two things they needed before they could even begin to think of themselves as true cavalrymen: shoes for their horses and saddles. Then, with bugles blaring orders, they made their first attempts at mounted drill.

It is one thing to ride a horse—at which almost all of the troopers were adept. It is quite another to perform intricate maneuvers, such as the right or left wheel by company, one of the most difficult evolutions in the cavalry drill. The first drills quickly disintegrated into a milling mass of neighing horses and confused would-be cavalrymen.

Despite the confusion, the troopers worked hard. They fully expected to go into action within the next few weeks. On November 4, after only 13 days in training, they were ordered to march south to Nashville.

Chapter Nine

Cavalrymen
at Last

Early on the morning of November 4, 1863, Barney and the other members of the Eighth Iowa Cavalry cinched up their new saddles on their freshly shod horses, strapped their bedrolls and carbines into place, and formed up in columns on the road to Nashville and the war.

Their horses were overburdened with equipment they didn't really need and would soon throw away. But for the first time they had the look and feel of true cavalrymen rather than farm boys clumsily playing soldier. And for the first time they were entering a war zone, where the possibility of ambush by guerrillas or even a clash with enemy cavalry was real. The troopers were ordered to be on the alert, and an advance guard was sent out to protect the column from a surprise attack.

Marching along with the Iowans were two sections of the First Kansas artillery battery and about a hundred heavily laden army wagons. The entire train stretched out for more than two miles.

Colonel Dorr carefully shepherded his unit's strength, making the 220-mile trek from Louisville to Nashville in six days by easy stages, averaging a little over 35 miles a day. They passed the mouth of the Salt River and marched through Elizabethtown, Bowling Green, and Franklin, Kentucky—following roughly the route of today's Interstate 65.

As the Iowans approached Nashville on November 10, they stared in awe at the largest city they had ever seen, a vast, bustling metropolis of 80,000, with the tents of thousands of troops circling the city and extending in all directions. The smoke of army campfires hovered in the cool autumn air. Long before the troopers reached their camp-site on the north edge of the city, not far from the dilapidated state capitol building, the acrid odor of the smoke, mixing with the other smells given off by tens of thousands of men and animals, assailed their nostrils.

Up until this point in the war, the Union had received almost all the benefit to transportation from the network of rivers that flow into the Mississippi and then on down through the heart of the South. Where the South held a fort on a river—as it did at Fort Henry and Fort Donelson and Vicksburg—its goal was to prevent Federal use of the river as a means to penetrate more deeply into the South rather than to use it for their own purposes. As each fort or strong position fell, the Union's watery highway into the South opened wider, culminating in the fall of Vicksburg and the opening of the Mississippi, effectively cutting the Confederacy into two distinct parts.

Steamboats operating on the river system gave the Union forces marvelous flexibility. They did not require an established port or even a dock. In thousands of places along the rivers, they could simply tie up along the levee and discharge or pick up troops and supplies.

But in the autumn of 1863, having crossed most of the major rivers, the Union was approaching the end of this easy, flexible system of transport. From now on it would have to rely on the railroads to move men and supplies. And whenever troops ventured away from the inflexible steel rails, they would have to rely on animal-drawn wagon trains.

Nashville, on the Cumberland River, was the great staging area for the next phase of the war. In February 1862 the Confederate forces had abandoned the city without a fight after blowing up the arsenal, removing as many supplies as possible, and demolishing a railroad drawbridge and a 700-foot-long wire suspension bridge—both sources of great pride to the city's residents. The Union had occupied it ever since.

The dimensions of the Union buildup in Nashville were readily apparent to the Iowans. Steamboats belching smoke lined the city's waterfront, disgorging 2,000 to 3,000 tons of freight a day. As many as

500 teams of horses or mules labored through the streets hauling supplies to hastily built but sturdy warehouses, up to a quarter of a mile
long. Corrals and stables covered scores of acres. The teeming rail
yards looked as though they were home to every locomotive and
freight car west of the Alleghenies—and that was very close to being
the case.

As they walked into town on their few days off, the Iowa farm boys
stared openmouthed at the sights of what, under the impact of thousands of soldiers, might well be described as Sin City, U.S.A.

Even if they didn't venture down to Smokey Row, an area two
blocks wide and four blocks long—the first block south of Spring Street
on Front, Market, College and Cherry Streets—where prostitution
flourished, they could not help noticing the prostitutes riding up and
down the main streets in carriages with often-drunken soldiers—to
the horror of the city's residents. One soldier who had visited brothels
in New York City was impressed by what he saw in Nashville. The city,
he said, "beats all for bad women."

Prostitution, and the venereal diseases that came with it, became a
major concern for the army brass. So many soldiers came down with
various forms of venereal disease that an entire separate hospital was
set aside for treatment. Unfortunately for the afflicted soldiers, there
was little the doctors could do for them, and what the doctors did do
probably caused at least as much harm as the diseases. The favorite
treatments, once again, involved administering large doses of drugs
containing mercury, which added mercury poisoning to the patient's
problems. If the disease caused a man difficulty in urinating, he might
be advised to carry a long pin in his cap, to use to open up the urinary
channel.

In an effort to get the prostitution and disease problem under control, the army rounded up 110 women, put them aboard the steamer
Idaho, a new vessel, and sent them upriver to Cincinnati. But the good
people of Cincinnati refused to let them land. After sitting in midriver
for days, the women became so angry that they went on a rampage and
destroyed the interior of the new ship. The women were eventually
returned to Nashville, where a new tack was tried: Each was licensed
as a prostitute or "kept woman," inspected weekly for disease, and
charged for the privilege of practicing her trade. The army's rate for
disability from venereal disease dropped from 35 percent to 5 percent.
The license fees brought in enough money to pay for the program and
even turn a small profit.

Throughout the war the theater proved a popular form of enter-tainment. In February 1864 John Wilkes Booth, the actor who later shot the president, starred in 13 different plays during a two-week engagement in Nashville. Unfortunately, there were occasions when drunken soldiers disrupted the proceedings.

But while entertainment in various forms flourished, the city's churches fared poorly during what is still called "the occupation." The Methodist Printing House, which had used its facilities to promote the Confederacy, was taken over by the Union Army. The Episcopal church was turned into an arsenal. Most of the other churches closed their doors.

Geographically, Nashville was perfectly situated to serve as a major supply base. But politically, it was far from perfect. In one of those strange twists of war, the Federal armies gained control of western Ten-nessee, whose sympathies were largely, if not unanimously, Southern. The Confederacy, on the other hand, was dominant in eastern Ten-nessee, where the people strongly favored the Union. The result was that the countryside around Nashville was filled with small guerrilla bands, and the city itself was a major source of goods smuggled to the Southern armies.

To deal with the problem of spies and trading with the enemy, the army established its own detective force under a man named William Truesdail, who had been both a merchant and a railroad contractor. By employing undercover agents, Truesdail managed to catch a number of suspected spies. At the same time he set himself up in business, mak-ing a large profit on everything from the sale of beef to control of the soldiers' mail.

As soon as the Eighth Iowa settled in its camp outside Nashville, Colonel Dorr sent a wire to Maj. Gen. George H. Thomas, who had just relieved General Rosecrans as commander of the Army of the Cumberland, in Chattanooga. Thomas had earned the title "rock of Chickamauga" by his stubborn defense during the battle south of Chattanooga beginning on September 19, in which the Union had been defeated. Although Thomas had broken the Confederate siege of his forces at Chattanooga a few days before the Eighth Cavalry arrived in Nashville, the Rebels still held the high ground around Chat-tanooga. They not only blocked Thomas from moving to the south or east but also posed a grave threat to Union control of eastern Tennessee.

Although there was already talk in Washington of putting Grant in charge of all the Union armies, he was still in command of the armies in the West in the late fall of 1863, with his headquarters in Chattanooga. He was eager to strike southward into the heartland of the Confederacy as soon as possible. But his situation was hardly conducive to a major offensive. The Confederate army that had defeated the Union at Chickamauga—but then failed to follow up with the capture of Chattanooga—was still in place in northern Georgia. Rebel Lt. Gen. James Longstreet, who had hurried by rail from Virginia in the eastern theater of operations to Georgia in the western theater with 20,000 men to turn the tide at Chickamauga, was still in the west. Grant didn't realize that Longstreet's force had shrunk to only 12,000 hungry, ill-clad men; he still considered it a major threat to eastern Tennessee.

The Union armies at Chattanooga and Knoxville were partially besieged. Despite the brimming warehouses a short distance away at Nashville, the soldiers were on half rations and in no position to spearhead an offensive.

Dorr, familiar with the military situation, fully expected to be ordered south to what he thought of as "the front" as soon as he and his men arrived in Nashville. But Sherman, with 20,000 veteran troops, was already on his way from Memphis to Chattanooga and would arrive there on November 23. So instead of receiving the expected order to hurry south, Dorr was ordered to march his regiment west along the line of the new Nashville and North Western Railroad as far as the Tennessee River. There he was to track down and eliminate the guerrilla bands that infested the area.

Probably fortunately for their morale and physical well-being, the troopers of the Eighth Iowa spent only two and a half weeks camped near the fleshpots of Nashville. On December 1, in company with the Kansas artillerymen, they marched west. Barney and his colleagues in Company H were dropped off, along with the three other companies of the third battalion, to patrol the area near Section 31 on the railroad line. The railroad was already finished and running up to this point, about 25 miles west of Nashville.

The men set up large tents capable of holding a dozen men each. If they had been more experienced and had proper tools, they would have set to work quickly building wooden huts and erecting wooden stables for their horses. Although the tents were comfortable at first, they proved inadequate shelter later, when the weather turned bitterly cold.

Dorr continued on with the rest of his force to the Tennessee River and set up his headquarters in the little town of Waverly, six miles east of the river. From that vantage point, with a total of something less than 1,500 cavalrymen and artillerymen under his command, he was to suppress the area's guerrilla bands. Dorr's assignment was an awesome one: He had to cover an area stretching 70 miles west from Nashville to the Tennessee and 100 miles from Fort Donelson in the north to the town of Clifton in the south—an expanse of 7,000 square miles, roughly the size of Massachusetts. The troopers found pleasant fertile valleys with large plantations in some areas. But much of the territory was a heavily wooded, ravine-laced wilderness.

The residents were openly hostile to the Union troops. Many of the men were Confederate soldiers home on furlough or had recently served in the Confederate army and still considered themselves fighters for the Southern cause. Residents of Humphreys County, of which Waverly was the county seat, boasted that only one Union man had lived in the county—and he had been killed.

For the troopers of the Eighth Cavalry, the assignment to spend the winter scouring the backwoods of western Tennessee for enemies of the Union was probably an ideal transition from their lives at home and in the training camps to their future role on the fringes of a larger army.

While infantrymen almost always march as part of a main force and eventually find themselves lined up against the enemy at "the front," cavalrymen most often operate in much smaller units on the flanks of an army, or even at some distance from other military units. The infantryman is trained for the iron discipline of a mass advance against enemy guns. The cavalryman requires self-discipline, self-reliance, and the initiative to move rapidly on the fringes of the larger military operation.

The hills of western Tennessee provided an almost perfect training ground for such operations, without exposing the inexperienced men to undue hazard.

When they first moved out cautiously along the route of the new railroad, the soldiers heard ominous reports from the unsympathetic residents. A certain Colonel Hawkins, they were warned, was active in the area and was capable of concentrating a force large enough to drive the Iowans back to Nashville—if not to wipe them out entirely. As the men of the Eighth Cavalry gained experience, however, they learned that that was just wishful thinking on the part of the residents.

Hawkins operated with units of as few as ten men and seemed unable to muster more than fifty at one time.

Typically the Confederate guerrillas concentrated together long enough to carry out an operation—whether it be an act of vengeance against a suspect farmer or the ambush of a Union railroad or wagon train—and then melted back into the landscape over familiar trails and byways.

Particularly troubling to the troopers, the bushwhackers would sometimes creep up and shoot at a lone guard on picket duty. Such incidents were pointless because the guerrillas made no attempt to follow up with an attack on the camp. The Iowans called them "attempted murders."

Although the bushwhackers occasionally fired upon pickets guarding camps of white soldiers, they focused most of their harassing fire on a regiment of black soldiers whose camp was at Section 49 on the railroad, adjoining the camp of the second battalion of the Eighth Iowa. After some initial mutual wariness, the two Union regiments got along well. The Iowans weren't sure what to expect, but they were impressed by the clean uniforms and the soldierly conduct of the African-American troops, who alternated between guard duty for their own camp and work on the railroad.

The white soldiers were dismayed, however, by the high mortality rate among the black soldiers. A few of their pickets were killed, but many more were felled by measles and pneumonia. Almost every day the sound of a final salute, fired by a burial party, would ring over the camp.

The Iowans, on the other hand, remained almost unbelievably healthy. One member of the unit later said he couldn't even recall anyone sick enough to be sent to a hospital. Dorr boasted that the sanitary conditions of his command were excellent, making it "probably the healthiest regiment in the service."

Tennessee, although bitterly divided, had seceded from the Union and was thus enemy territory. In the huge area for which Dorr was responsible, he was given extraordinary power—in charge of both military and civil affairs. His word was the law. He later explained his draconian but successful policy this way:

"Instead of administering the oath of allegiance to the citizens, I adopted the policy of placing them under bonds with sureties, and found this had a wonderful influence towards quieting the country. Repentant rebels have a much greater fear of losing their property than of violating an oath, which, indeed, most of them consider compulsory."

Despite orders against foraging, the cavalrymen did not hesitate, when supplies ran short, to help themselves to food from the farms or plantations they passed. Since the area had never before been occupied by organized units of either North or South, "we got along very well," as one soldier put it.

Gradually, the Eighth Iowa successfully imposed its will on the vast area between Nashville and the Tennessee River. The calvarymen captured Hawkins himself and many of his men, secured the rail line, and pacified the area.

The enemy bushwhackers actually proved less of a challenge to the troopers than the terrible storms of that winter—brought on by the same frigid air mass that covered Little Rock and much of the nation's central section.

When reveille sounded on the first day of 1864, those who had managed to sleep through the night were appalled when they stuck their noses out of their tents into the arctic morning. The pickets on duty during the night were almost frozen. The horses, tied to trees or to a long picket line, had suffered terribly. Saddles were coated thickly with ice. Halter straps were icy and stiff as iron.

While everyone huddled around large fires for warmth, the men of Company I heard the bugle sound "boots and saddles." They were ordered to mount and go in search of a few miserable bushwhackers who, they all hoped, had already frozen to death. Their route took them down a road that crisscrossed back and forth over a stream called Piney Creek. The men and horses were soon coated with huge chunks of ice. The soldiers couldn't dismount and walk for warmth because of the frequent necessity to cross the creek, which was belly deep on the horses.

They finally found shelter at a large plantation and built fires to thaw themselves, dry out their clothes, and get their equipment back in usable condition. After a brief, bloodless encounter with a small group of bushwhackers, they returned to camp two days later. But several of the soldiers had suffered such severe frostbite in their feet that they could no longer serve in the military.

By the first of February, with much-improved weather, the men of the Eighth Cavalry were growing almost comfortable in the degree of control they had over their vast area of responsibility. In January they had scoured the country up the Tennessee River as far as Fort Henry.

Other detachments made wide sweeps through the area, rounding up a number of prisoners, horses, and weapons. Then on the first of February came alarming news: The Confederate Brig. Gen. Philip D. Roddey, with a large force of cavalry, had crossed the Tennessee River at Florence, Alabama, and was headed north to raid the area that the Eighth Cavalry was in the process of pacifying.

Colonel Dorr put the entire regiment on the alert and sent Company A galloping south to see what Roddey was up to. And then as quickly as he had come, the Rebel general turned and crossed back over the river to the south. It was not, however, the Eighth Cavalry's last time to be concerned about Roddey. They would meet him again later, under surprising and much less favorable circumstances deep in Georgia.

On March 13, 1864, after more than three months' work in western Tennessee, the Eighth Cavalry turned over its responsibility to another unit and marched back to Nashville, arriving there on March 17. After its winter of seasoning in the wilderness, the Eighth Cavalry was, as Dorr put it, "about to enter upon an active and vigorous campaign against the regularly organized forces of the rebel army, in which it was, for the first time, to operate in conjunction with other cavalry regiments."

During the Eighth Cavalry's season in the wilderness, the military situation had become much more favorable for the Union. The Confederates had been pushed back from Chattanooga, and that city had become a second major staging area for the Union Army as it poised for a move across the border into Georgia.

As the army moved away from reliance on the rivers, Chattanooga was of particular importance because it was the point where north-south and east-west railroad lines of the same gauge crossed. In much of the continent, the gauge, or distance between the rails, varied slightly, depending on the whim of the entrepreneurs who built the lines; where rails of two different gauges met, freight would have to be unloaded from the cars of one train and loaded onto another. A rail center like Chattanooga, where freight could be switched and sent on its way without having to be transferred, was of priceless value to an army on the move.

The Confederate forces, however, had cut the lines that linked Chattanooga with its two major sources of supplies: Memphis and

Nashville. Instead of running straight southeast from Nashville to Chattanooga, the Nashville and Chattanooga Railroad dipped down into northern Alabama, where it joined the line connecting Chattanooga with Memphis. By cutting the bridge at Bridgeport, Alabama, 29 miles from Chattanooga, the Rebels had broken the city's links to both Nashville and Memphis.

Under orders from the War Department, Col. David McCallum, who had been superintendent of the New York and Erie before the war, hurried west with 285 picked men in December. By mid-January they had rebuilt the bridge at Bridgeport and opened the stretch from there to Chattanooga.

Perhaps more important than all the North's physical preparations for renewed warfare was the fact that, on the first day of spring in 1864, it finally had a master plan for fighting and winning the war.

Details of the plan were pinned down at the Burnet House, a rooming house in Cincinnati, where Grant and Sherman spent the afternoon of March 20 together. On March 12 Grant had been placed in charge of all the Union armies and was preparing to depart for Washington. On March 18, in turn, he had placed Sherman in charge of all the forces in the west, as commander of the Military Division of the Mississippi. When they emerged from their Cincinnati meeting, they had agreed on a combined spring offensive: Grant would attack Lee in the east; Sherman would strike south toward Atlanta in the west; both would keep up constant pressure so that the enemy forces would never be free to concentrate themselves against either of the Union armies, as had happened when Longstreet was shifted the year before, tipping the balance at Chickamauga.

When he arrived in Nashville after his meeting with Grant and with a grand strategy firmly in mind, Sherman recognized rail transportation as his biggest immediate problem. The mathematics were sobering. His staff calculated that, to stockpile supplies for his army—consisting of 100,000 men and 35,000 animals—he would need 130 cars to deliver ten tons each to Chattanooga each day before and during the campaign.

Sherman took personal charge of the rail problem. He ordered that soldiers march and cattle be driven instead of riding the rails. General Thomas had been providing food for the starving people of eastern Tennessee; Sherman cut them off and persisted even after Lincoln, who was concerned about abandoning a core of Union supporters, made a personal appeal. All military units within 35 miles of Nashville were ordered to use wagons to obtain their supplies.

But Sherman's chief of transportation told him that even that wasn't enough. By the time he arrived on the scene, they had 60 serviceable locomotives and about 600 cars of all types. He insisted they needed at least a hundred locomotives and a thousand rail cars. "I then instructed and authorized him," Sherman recalled later, "to hold on to all trains that arrived at Nashville from Louisville, and to allow none to go back until he had secured enough to fill the requirements of our problem."

Months later, deep in Georgia, Sherman was amused to see cars with the names of almost every railroad north of the Ohio River. "How those railroad companies ever recovered their property, or settled their transportation accounts, I have never heard, but to this fact, as much as to any other single fact, I attribute the perfect success which afterward attended our campaigns," Sherman wrote.

Having issued the appropriate orders, Sherman left details of the buildup to his chief quartermaster, Lt. Col. James L. Donaldson. His instructions to Donaldson were to the point: "If you don't have my army supplied, and keep it supplied, we'll eat your mules up, sir—eat your mules up!"

The Eighth Cavalry, one cog in this gigantic war machine, prepared, along with hundreds of other units, for the great march south. But first there was the matter of a little sideshow across the Mississippi—a diversion inspired by politics and greed in which the 36th Iowa Volunteer Infantry—and Barney's brother, Andrew Brayman, would be tragically involved.

Part Three

Sideshow in the West

PAGE 108: *Maj. Gen. Nathaniel P. Banks*. (Library of Congress, Washington, D.C.)

Chapter Ten

Thinking the Unthinkable

Sitting in his headquarters in Shreveport, Louisiana, Confederate General Kirby Smith had a hard time believing the news his spies and scouts kept bringing to him of a massive Union attack across the Mississippi and up the Red River into the heart of Louisiana.

"I still think that the enemy cannot be so infatuated as to occupy a large force in this department when every man should be employed east of the river, where the result of the campaign this summer must be decisive of our future for our weal or woe," he wrote on March 13 to his chief subordinate, Maj. Gen. Richard Taylor.

Taylor, the son of Zachary Taylor, hero of the U.S. war with Mexico in 1848 and later president of the United States, was closer to the action, and he had no doubts such an assault was under way.

Both men were right: Such an attack was unthinkable and it was happening.

As Kirby Smith correctly understood, the Union had no business committing a large force to combat west of the Mississippi. At best, such an operation would be a sideshow, drawing needed manpower and guns away from the decisive battles soon to be fought east of the Mississippi. But the performance was on, and it was on a grand scale.

On March 7 a cavalry unit of 5,000 men left New Orleans and began the long march toward Alexandria, Louisiana. Three days later 10,000 veterans—among them eight Iowa regiments and an army unit known as the Mississippi Marine Brigade—marched down to the docks at Vicksburg and crowded into every available space on 21 big army transport vessels. They sailed down the Mississippi, then, with their big paddle wheels churning the muddy water, they turned up the Red River, heading northwest toward Alexandria.

As they did so, they were joined by another 22 naval vessels—13 ironclads, four ships with lighter tin armor, and five other armed vessels. Adding together the army transports, the naval fighting ships, and a handful of quartermaster vessels, the Union force totaled some 60 vessels bristling with an awesome 210 guns.

On March 15, after a weeklong delay caused by torrential rains, another 15,000 infantry- and artillerymen from the command headquartered at New Orleans began the march toward Alexandria. Their arrival on March 25—a week late—completed the largest buildup of military power that had ever been seen west of the Mississippi: 30,000 men with 90 guns, in addition to the firepower provided by the naval flotilla.

But that was not all: On March 23 General Steele marched south from Little Rock with 6,800 fighting men, including Andrew Brayman's 36th Iowa Infantry. At the same time General Thayer marched east from Fort Smith with another 3,600 troops, planning to meet Steele. The total force of 10,400 men was swelled further by several thousand teamsters and other support personnel who weren't expected to fight but who still had to be fed. The force under Steele was to form the other arm of the giant pincer closing in on Shreveport, near the Texas border in the northwestern corner of Louisiana.

Anyone looking for a reasonable military rationale for this vast, ill-conceived undertaking will search in vain. Militarily the expedition made little if any sense. It was impelled, instead, by political considerations and by the powerful economics of the cotton trade.

Politics and cotton of course were important forces that had helped break the nation apart and led eventually to war. But the genesis of the Red River expedition, as it came to be known, can be linked specifically to a theory that had been born among abolitionists and cotton mill owners in New England in the early days of the war. German settlers in central Texas, they noted, were successfully growing and selling cotton with their own labor, without relying on slaves. Perhaps, the theorists proposed, if more free men entered the cotton trade, as growers and sellers, they could undermine and eventually destroy the slave-based economy of the rest of the South. They urged that Texas

Maj. Gen. Edmund Kirby Smith, CSA. (Library of Congress, Washington, D.C.)

be taken from the Confederacy and then colonized by, as *The New York Times* put it, "industrious, practical, enterprising, liberty-loving men."

In the fall of 1862, Maj. Gen. Nathaniel P. Banks set up shop in New York and began recruiting volunteers from throughout New England to seize Texas and then to grow cotton.

Banks was a dubious choice for a dubious mission. A professional politician, he had served as speaker of the U.S. House of Representatives and as a three-term governor of Massachusetts. He was an impressive orator, a skilled politician, and an honest man whose ambitions did not stop short of the White House. When the war began, he was one of a small group of prominent politicians who hurried to the colors, receiving commissions as generals. Banks's early date of rank thus meant that he outranked many professional soldiers, including Generals Grant and Sherman.

He proved physically brave himself, but he had neither the military training nor the experience that would qualify him to command men in battle.

The men Banks recruited were formally enlisted as soldiers, and the plan was for them to sail from New York and make an amphibious landing in Texas. But they thought of themselves as colonizers, not soldiers, and most of them, by training and temperament, were as poorly suited to serve in an expeditionary army to seize enemy-held territory half a continent away as their general was to lead them.

Before he departed in December, Banks received secret orders. Instead of sailing to Texas, he was ordered to proceed to New Orleans and apply himself to helping to open the Mississippi to Union traffic. This of course was many months before the fall of Vicksburg opened the river and divided the Confederacy. Banks was also informed that he would replace Maj. Gen. Benjamin Butler as commander of the Department of the Gulf.

Butler, another Massachusetts politician, had been a despotic military governor of occupied New Orleans, and the people were delighted to see him go. Like other Southern cities, New Orleans suffered a yellow fever epidemic almost every summer. During his tenure Butler had hired a quarantine officer at a generous salary and cleaned up all sources of odors. While the Union was there, the city did not suffer from yellow fever. But the people attributed their freedom from disease to divine intervention. The Lord, they reasoned, would not send Ben Butler and yellow fever to afflict them at the same time.

Butler was even less a general than Banks. Lincoln considered him incompetent to do his part in opening the Mississippi. Replacing him with another Massachusetts politican was a way of finessing an awkward political problem.

When Banks directed his flotilla up the Mississippi to New Orleans instead of sailing on directly to the invasion of Texas, almost everyone was surprised. His soldiers were surprised. General Butler was surprised. And the cotton speculators who had crowded, uninvited, onto one of Banks's vessels were surprised and outraged.

Traders in cotton already infested the area, suffering from the same kind of contagious fever that had driven men to the California goldfields in 1849. Because of the war thousands of spindles were idle in the mills of New England, and the price of cotton was soaring. The mill owners were so hungry for cotton that a supplier could make a fortune with a single transaction—and such transactions often involved a direct sale of cotton by a Southerner to the enemy.

Within two weeks of his arrival, Banks received a message from two of the speculators—one of them General Butler's brother. If they were allowed to continue their "commercial program" with the same support they had received from Butler, they promised Banks, they would "place at your disposal $100,000."

Banks, to his credit, didn't take the bribe. He wrote to his wife about the offer: "It was no temptation for me. I thank God every night that I have no desire for dishonest gains."

It says something about the atmosphere in New Orleans at the time, however, that Banks merely turned down the offer and didn't follow up by arresting the two men and having them shot.

Actually, trade across enemy lines was not only tolerated but officially sanctioned. A number of merchants received written authorization from Lincoln himself to conduct such trade. His motives were twofold: to obtain cotton to keep the mills of New England busy and to retain the support for himself and his party of the men who were enriching themselves in the trade. He also apparently believed that, since cotton would be traded for arms in any event, it was better for the North to attempt to control the trade. In a letter to one of his generals in 1864, Lincoln wrote that "it becomes immensely important to us to get the cotton away from him. Better give him guns for it, than let him, as now, get both guns and ammunition."

Having been diverted from his Texas adventure, Banks seemed strangely confused about what he was supposed to do in Louisiana. Instead of trying to move up the Mississippi and help open it to Union traffic, he sent his troops on a series of forays into the central part of the state, gathering up cotton and livestock. General Halleck, then the top army commander in Washington, was mightily displeased. He wrote an angry note to Banks:

"The *opening of the Mississippi River* has been continually presented as the *first* and *most important* object to be attained. Operations up the Red River, toward Texas, or toward Alabama, are only of secondary importance, to be undertaken *after* we get possession of the river."

Banks finally moved up the Mississippi and besieged Port Hudson, a less important Confederate strongpoint on the Mississippi than Vicksburg. When Vicksburg fell, Port Hudson also fell, opening the river entirely.

With the river open, Banks turned his attention once again toward Texas. But while Halleck, now that the Mississippi was in Union control, seemed almost obsessed with making a move up the Red River to

Shreveport and then into northeastern Texas, Banks focused his
attention on the Texas coast. In September, in an attempted landing
at the Sabine Pass, where the Sabine River, which divides Louisiana
from Texas, enters the gulf, an amphibious force was thrown back.
Banks also made a halfhearted cross-country effort later that month
but got only as far as Opelousas, in the middle of Louisiana.

Banks did manage to make landings in November all along
the Texas coast: at Brazos Santiago, Brownsville, Rio Grande City,
Aransas Pass, and Matagorda Island. A Union governor was even
installed at Brownsville, and the Stars and Stripes, as Banks proudly
reported, flew over Texas—mostly, however, over isolated patches of
sand. Banks thought he had done what he was supposed to do and
turned his attention to the east—toward the capture of the important
port at Mobile, Alabama.

Letters of congratulation arrived from both Lincoln and his secretary of war, who seemed satisfied with what Banks had done.

In 1863 a major move into Texas had seemed to Lincoln and his
civilian advisers to be a matter of some urgency as a way to send a message to the French, who were then in the process of conquering Mexico, that Texas was off-limits. By early 1864, however, the French
threat had receded, and Lincoln felt no urgency about moving Union
forces into Texas. But Halleck continued to act as though the early
conquest of Texas were a high priority—and he remained infatuated
with the prospect of moving into northeastern Texas by way of the
Red River. In a letter in early January to Grant—who favored using
the available forces to take Mobile—Halleck wrote:

> As a military measure simply, it [a move up the Red
> River] presented less advantages than a movement on
> Mobile and the Alabama River. . . . But however this may
> have been, it was deemed necessary as a matter of political or
> State policy, connected with our foreign relations, and espe-
> cially with France and Mexico, that our troops should
> occupy and hold at least a portion of Texas. . . . Keep in mind
> the fact that General Banks' operations in Texas, either on
> the Gulf coast or by the Louisiana frontier, must be contin-
> ued during the winter, it is to be considered whether it will
> not be better to direct our efforts, for the present, to the
> entire breaking up of the rebel forces west of the Mississippi,

rather than to divide them by also operating against Mobile and Alabama.

By January, Banks had gotten Halleck's message. He became a strong supporter of the Red River route to Texas.

At this point, one man had the high-level contacts and the military prestige to head off this diversion of Union troops west of the Mississippi. That was General Sherman. After all, it was Sherman who, in the aftermath of Vicksburg, had concluded that military affairs on the west bank of the Mississippi had become unimportant.

But Sherman, driven by restlessness for action more than by good military sense, became an enthusiastic backer of the Red River plan. He saw it as part of a bigger effort to create a *cordon sanitaire* around the Confederacy, driving Rebel forces away from the Mississippi on both sides of the river. Andrew Brayman and the 36th Iowa, still in Little Rock, were to play their role west of the Mississippi.

Early in 1864 Sherman personally led a daring raid from Vicksburg directly across the state of Mississippi to a major Confederate supply base and transportation junction in the little town of Meridian. On their way across Mississippi, the raiders lived off the land, giving the residents a taste of the kind of total war Sherman would inflict on a broader swath of the South in his march to the sea.

When the troops arrived in Meridian, they were as thoroughly destructive as any biblical plague. Not a building was left standing. The rails were torn up for miles in all directions, then heated, bent out of shape, and left in tangled heaps. The raid fell far short of Sherman's expectations, however. The Rebel leaders in Meridian had gotten word of Sherman's coming and had cleaned out most military supplies, along with their troops, before his arrival.

Sherman and his men had headed back to Vicksburg, confident they had inflicted a great deal of long-term damage. But the Southerners brought in a newly invented device to straighten out the bent rails. In those days trains ran on narrow wooden beams that were capped with relatively lightweight metal rails. Unlike today's long, heavy sections of steel, these rails were flimsy enough to be torn up and bent, but they were also light enough to be twisted back into shape with the new machine. With the help of the new device, the lines through Meridian were soon back in operation.

Sherman desperately wanted to lead the Red River expedition.

And Grant, even though he opposed the operation, wanted Sherman to lead it because he felt that Sherman would do it right and return the troops quickly for duties east of the Mississippi. They agreed, however, that Sherman had more important things to do. Instead of going with the operation himself, he committed the 10,000 men from Vicksburg and sent them off under the command of Brig. Gen. A. J. Smith, a career army man, with the firm understanding that they would be returned in 30 days.

It was Banks, the political general, however, who headed the expedition on both land and sea. This is not to say that he was in any realistic sense in *command* of the operation.

He had, for one thing, only the most tenuous control over Admiral Porter, a fiercely independent-minded military genius who had built and commanded a formidable brown-water navy that sailed the inland sea formed by the Mississippi and its tributaries. Porter would command the vast flotilla as it sailed up the Red River, and he was not the type to take orders from anyone.

Banks had a similarly loose command over Sherman's infantry and the Mississippi Marine Brigade under General Smith, moving independently from Vicksburg. And some of the regiments under Smith were a notoriously unruly lot, at least as interested in pillage and burning as they were in fighting.

If Banks had only a loose handle on the military forces nominally under his command, he had much less control over the cotton speculators who joined the expedition. To them the expedition was not at all about conquering Texas but instead about obtaining the cotton that was stockpiled at plantations throughout Louisiana. Even Banks and Porter seemed, on occasion, to share this view of the operation.

When word got around, early in 1864, that Porter was rounding up ships for a foray up the Red River, Samuel Casey, a former member of Congress and a prominent cotton speculator, feared that Porter would get the cotton he hoped to gather in. He wired Lincoln: "Do not let Admiral Porter send an expedition up Red River until you hear from me again. If he should he will defeat all my plans."

For a cotton speculator to intervene so directly in plans for a military operation seems bizarre, to say the least. But his demand should be seen in the light of an extraordinary document Lincoln signed on December 14, 1863:

"All Military and Naval commanders please give to the Hon. Samuel Casey, of Kentucky . . . protection and safe conduct from Cairo to Red River, and up said river, it's [sic] tributaries, till he shall pass beyond our Military lines, and also give him such protection and safe conduct, on his return to our lines, back to Cairo with any cargoes he may bring; and on his safe return from beyond our lines, with said boats and tows, allow him to repeat once or twice if he shall desire."

Banks himself authorized one of the speculators to send an agent to Shreveport to negotiate with General Kirby Smith for the purchase of cotton.

As Banks and his troops set out, it appeared to the speculators that there would be profits aplenty along the way. To some extent, the expedition became a race to see who could get the cotton first.

As his armada sailed northwestward, Porter's sailors fanned out into the surrounding areas, marking bales of cotton with a bold "USN." Many of the bales had already been claimed by the Southern army and were marked "CSA." The joke in the fleet was that the initials "CSAUSN" stood for "Cotton Stealing Association of the United States Navy."

General Smith's troops were in a surly mood. On the way toward Shreveport, the army had captured a Confederate strongpoint known as Fort deRusy. Smith ordered the fort destroyed. In the process, during the middle of the night, an ammunition magazine near where the troops were sleeping was blown up. Two men were killed and several wounded. When Smith rode by a few days later, his men hissed him.

Despite the distractions caused by the lust for cotton and the loose military command structure, when Banks arrived in Alexandria on March 25 the prospects for a successful move on Shreveport and then on into Texas seemed highly promising. Porter's navy ships and the army transports filled the waters along the city's waterfront, and thousands of soldiers were prepared to march on the enemy.

Military commanders seem almost instinctively to overestimate the size of the enemy force facing them. Banks, the politician-general, was no exception. If he had known how small the force facing him really was, he would have considered his prospects even brighter.

The force facing him was a motley collection of military units totaling less than half the numbers of the Federal forces. Moreover, their leaders, Kirby Smith and Taylor, barely tolerated—if they did not actively hate—each other.

While Banks prepared to move out of Alexandria toward Shreveport, a reluctant General Steele was beginning his move south from Little Rock in the general direction of Shreveport.

Chapter Eleven

Fight for Elkins' Ferry

As the veterans of the 36th Iowa shouldered their packs and fell in on the road leading from Little Rock to Arkadelphia on the morning of March 23, 1864, there was a spring in their steps. A warm sun shone down out of a bright blue springtime sky, and the regimental band played a sprightly version of "Yankee Doodle Dandy." The long winter had left them in robust good health, weary of garrison duty, and restless for action.

With them in the long column marched friends of past battles and comrades in future combat, including the men of the 43rd Indiana. Up and down the long column there was a sense of excitement about the adventures, and perhaps action and "glory," that lay ahead.

But if the young soldiers could have shared the thoughts of the old soldier who was leading their parade, the sun would have shone less brightly and the spring would have vanished from their step.

For months, General Steele had been fighting as hard as he could to avoid this march—this mission impossible. His adjutant's files were full of messages back and forth between himself and Halleck, Grant, Sherman, Banks. His arguments were not always consistent, but their message was always the same: He should remain in Little Rock and maintain other bases in central Arkansas, to protect both Arkansas and Missouri and keep them both in Union hands. The best he could offer would be a "demonstration" to draw Rebel troops away from Banks's forces.

Brig. Gen. Frederick Steele, commander of Camden expedition. (Library of Congress, Washington, D.C.)

In some of his messages, Steele portrayed the enemy as so weak that they would "run to Texas" or desert when Banks advanced. In others he worried that the enemy forces were so strong that they would overrun Little Rock and Pine Bluff if he moved south, as Sherman and Banks wanted him to do.

One of Steele's major arguments was that he had to remain in central Arkansas to ensure the outcome of a forthcoming election, by protecting citizens on their way to the polls and by safeguarding the ballot boxes. In his worries about the election, he showed himself more aware than many other generals that this was a political, not just a military, war.

As early as December he wrote to a superior in St. Louis: "Last year the people of Arkansas were induced to commit themselves to the cause of the Union, and were afterward abandoned to the mercy of the Rebels. I hope that no plan may be adopted which will give these people (the majority of whom are loyal to the United States) good reason to complain that they have been twice deceived by the promises of federal commanders."

Steele also worried that many of his men were on leave and had not yet returned from home.

Sherman was not impressed by these arguments. On March 6 he sent a message to Steele: "Must confess I feel uneasy at your assertion you can only move with 7,000 infantry and that you prefer to wait until after the election. . . . If we have to modify military plans for civil elections, we had better go home."

On the following day, Steele wrote to Banks. He told him of reports that the Rebels were trying to break up the elections and again complained that his veteran troops had not returned. Then he added: "The streams are all high now, and the roads through the bottoms bad, but in addition to the cavalry force mentioned in my last letter, I will endeavor to send a column of infantry and some light guns on the road to Arkadelphia and Washington."

On March 10 Steele wrote to both Grant and Sherman. To Grant, he complained that Banks and Sherman were mistaken about the force he had available:

> I have been intending to write you for a long time, but you do not appear to have any local habitation. The forces under Banks will make Kirby Smith [the Rebel commander in Shreveport] run without a battle. From what I can learn through people returning to their homes within my lines, Kirby and all his friends are prepared to leave for parts unknown. I shall move by way of Washington with all my available force to cooperate with Banks. I cannot spare from the line of the Arkansas [river] more than about 7,000 of all arms.

On the same day, Steele sent a message to Sherman in which he said:

> You and General Banks are laboring under a mistake in regard to the strength of my command and I think in regard to other matters in Arkansas. . . . The force you send, joined to Banks' 17,000, can drive all the troops in Kirby Smith's department into the Gulf. I would be glad to take a contract to do it, if I had the command.

Steele acknowledged that he had 16,517 men available. But he insisted he could spare only 7,000 for a Red River expedition and warned: "The country between here and Red River has been nearly exhausted of supplies by both armies, and it will be very difficult to obtain forage and impossible to subsist even 7,000 troops."

On March 12 Steele, fearful that he had lost the argument with Sherman, tried to go over Sherman's head in a message to Halleck in Washington:

> General Banks, with 17,000 and 10,000 of Sherman's, will be at Alexandria on the 17th instant. This is more than an equal for everything Kirby Smith can bring against them. Smith will run. By holding the line of the Arkansas secure I can soon free this state of armed Rebels. Sherman insists upon my moving upon Shreveport to cooperate with the above-mentioned force with all my effective force. I have prepared to do so, against my own judgment and that of the best-informed people here. The roads are most if not quite impracticable; the country is destitute of provision on the route we should be obliged to take. . . . I can move with about 7,000, including the frontier. . . . Please give me your opinion immediately, as I shall march tomorrow or next day.

The "frontier" he referred to was the force under General Thayer at Fort Smith.

By that time, Steele was pretty well resigned to making the march with a large force. His men had already made sure the horses and mules were properly shod and the wagons were all repaired. On March 12 he issued this order:

> The troops will go in light marching order. Each man will carry in his knapsack, his blanket, poncho, one shirt, one pair of stockings, two days' rations in his haversack, and 40 rounds of ammunition. One wagon will be allowed to each regiment for transportation of cooking utensils, etc., and one wagon for brigade headquarters.

On the very day Steele sent his message to Halleck appealing against Sherman's orders to march toward Shreveport, Grant was named general-in-chief, replacing Halleck. Perhaps if more time had been available, Grant would have listened sympathetically to Steele. Grant had never been an enthusiast for the Red River expedition and had only reluctantly agreed to permit Sherman to send 10,000 of his men to support Banks. But by March 12 the troops from Banks's command and those from Sherman's base in Vicksburg, as well as Porter's ships, were already on the move. Grant's orders to Steele were explicit:

> Move your force in full co-operation with General N.P. Banks' attack on Shreveport. A mere demonstration will not be sufficient. Now that a large force has gone up Red river it is necessary that Shreveport and the Red river should come into our possession.

Even if there had been no enemy forces between him and Shreveport, Steele had a difficult assignment. His plan was to march south with 6,800 troops from Little Rock. At the same time General Thayer would leave Fort Smith, on the border between Arkansas and the Indian Territory to the west, with 3,600 troops and join up with Steele near Arkadelphia. Teamsters and other support units added several thousand to the number to be fed.

The distance from Little Rock to Shreveport was somewhat more than 200 miles. Army quartermasters routinely calculated that a sizable force could not be supported by animal-drawn wagons over a distance of more than 100 miles. At any greater distance, the animals would have to haul so much food for themselves that there would be no room to carry supplies for the army.

When Steele's men camped for the first night, they were told the inescapable news: Starting immediately, they would be on half rations—at best—of everything except coffee for the rest of the march. As Steele had accurately warned his superiors, his men and animals would have to try to live off a sparsely populated countryside that had already been stripped of food and fodder by armies of both sides.

The direct route from Arkadelphia would take Steele almost due south toward Shreveport. As he marched southward, he would quickly move from the mountains that dominate northern and western Arkansas to the upper Mississippi delta region, rolling countryside laced with streams flowing south and east toward the Mississippi. Across the army's path lay the Ouachita and Little Missouri rivers and all of their little tributaries swollen by the springtime runoff.

That direct route would take Steele between the two major centers of population in southern Arkansas. To the west was the town of Washington, a major trading center that the Confederates had made the capital of Arkansas after Steele had driven them from Little Rock. It was only after the war that the railroad through southern Arkansas had shifted commerce to the new city of Hope and left Washington to wither away. To the east lay the city of Camden, strategically located on bluffs overlooking the Ouachita, which was open and navigable all the way to the Mississippi. With a population of 15,000, it was the second-largest city in the state and a fortified Rebel strongpoint.

At his headquarters in Shreveport, Kirby Smith faced a difficult choice: Should he concentrate all of his forces against either Banks or Steele, or should he violate the textbook rule and divide his force, opposing each arm of the pincer with an outnumbered force?

The Confederate general decided, correctly, that Banks, plus Porter's flotilla, posed the larger and more immediate threat. Steele had a smaller force and was farther away. Kirby Smith divided his force. He pulled the infantry units stationed at Camden south to join the infantry preparing to meet Banks. To slow Steele's advance, he relied on a light force of mounted infantry and mounted artillery under the command of Sterling Price, now a major general, headquartered at Camden.

Loosely under Price's command were the mounted divisions of Brig. Gen. James Fagan and John Marmaduke—the same Rebel leaders the 36th Iowa had met at Helena and Little Rock—supported by four batteries of horse artillery. Hurrying to the scene was a third mounted division from the Indian Territory under Brig. Gen. Samuel B. Maxey, plus another battery of horse artillery. Because they rode hard and moved fast and remained far from headquarters, the mounted troops tended to consider orders from Price as advice or suggestions rather than commands to be obeyed without question. But because they were highly mobile and independent-minded, the mounted troops posed exactly the kind of challenge that Steele would find most difficult to deal with, harassing his bigger Union force, delaying it, but avoiding a pitched battle.

The Confederates faced a dilemma, however: They weren't sure where Steele was headed. They suspected he intended to attack their state capital at Washington. If Steele took Washington, it would have both a military and political impact. But Steele might also turn east and attempt to take Camden.

If the Confederate horsemen made a stand at either Camden or Washington, they would probably be badly beaten by the Union infantry. If they didn't fight for either city, they would lose their slim claim to control a portion of Arkansas.

A third possibility was that Steele might simply brush past the light Rebel units and hurry on toward Shreveport. After all, it was by just such a clever maneuver that Steele had slipped past the Rebels and forced them to abandon Little Rock.

As Steele's troops marched southward, they passed through a pleasant countryside. For much of their route, they were shaded by forests of loblolly and shortleaf pine, their steps cushioned by the duff formed by years of dead needles. The forests were far more open than today's forests, since fires set by the Indians, settlers, or nature regularly cleansed the forest floor of undergrowth and small hardwood trees, permitting the pines to grow to towering heights.

But there were also groves of hardwoods, especially along the streams. Although they couldn't call all of them by name, the soldiers saw some 20 species of oak plus hickory, sweet gum, beech, rum birch, bald cypress, tupelo gum, willow, American holly, some walnut, and possibly some cottonwood. Around farmhouses and along the creeks flowering trees—apple, peach, hawthorn, wild plum, and dogwood—were just coming into bloom.

The forests were full of game. There were many deer—though not so many as today—and so many bears that Arkansas was known as the bear state. But the sounds and smells of the marching army kept the wildlife well back out of sight.

On the second day they reached the abandoned village of Rockport and the first significant water barrier on their line of march. It was a pleasant surprise. They found the Ouachita River at Rockport a clear, sparkling stream tumbling over a gravel bed. They deployed their pontoon bridge for the wagons, but the river was shallow enough at a number of points to be easily forded.

On the third day they entered the town of Arkadelphia, which had just been abandoned by the Rebel forces who had moved there after fleeing from Little Rock the previous September. Although it was only about 60 miles south of Little Rock, Arkadelphia was already feeling the effects of spring. The grass, trees, and bushes all appeared greener and more luxuriant than they had a few days before in Little Rock.

With hunger already beginning to gnaw at their bellies, the soldiers fanned out through the community looking for food. They found little. In those days families routinely filled their basements in the fall with smoked and sugar-cured hams, potatoes, apples, and other fruits and vegetables to tide them through the winter. A properly constructed cellar acted like a large refrigerator, safely preserving food for months. But Arkadelphia, like much of Arkansas, was suffering from the disruption caused by war. Most of the food that the people had laid away after the previous year's harvest had already been consumed. Perhaps frustrated by their unsuccessful search for food, a small group of soldiers went on a rampage through a young ladies' seminary and smashed the girls' piano.

Despite the lack of food for his army, Steele remained at Arkadelphia for a week, waiting for Thayer's troops—a mixed force of frontier troops and two black regiments—to arrive from Fort Smith.

Finally Steele decided he had to move even though he didn't know where Thayer was or when he would arrive. Steele worried that the missing force might have been attacked by the Rebels. But Thayer was actually simply creeping along on his cross-country march from Fort Smith, slowed by a huge train of decrepit wagons.

From Arkadelphia, a day's march took Steele's troops to the vicinity of the tiny towns of Okolona and Antoine, high ground from which the men could look down over gently rolling country toward the Little Missouri River. By this time, hunger was taking its toll on the effectiveness of the army. As they marched, the soldiers lightened their loads by throwing away some of the 40 bullets that weighed down their packs. At campsites a few of the soldiers got rid of additional weight by hammering their bayonets into the ground. If the sergeant asked, they would simply say the weapon had been lost, and there wasn't much he could do about it.

Throwing away bullets may have seemed to make sense to the hungry soldiers. After all, they had been gone from Little Rock for more than a week with little sign of the enemy. Perhaps Steele's intelligence was right and the Rebels had skedaddled without a fight.

If the troops could somehow have gotten an overall view of the military situation in south-central Arkansas, however, they would have been hoarding bullets and sharpening their bayonets rather than lightening their loads.

No sooner had the last of Steele's men lost sight of Arkadelphia on the morning of April 1 than Rebel mounted infantry began nibbling at their rear guard. The Confederate horsemen were no match for Steele's big army. But suddenly a highly mobile force was not only behind Steele but between him and Thayer. Other Rebel units were also on the move, both behind and in front of Steele's army.

Rebel General Price was about to put his strategy into action. Without heavy infantry units, which were still occupied with facing Banks in Louisiana, Price could not afford a set-piece battle with Steele. What he could do was to harass Steele's army, making hit-and-run attacks, taking up fortified positions and then melting away as soon as the Union soldiers spread out in preparation for a fight. Every day they succeeded in delaying Steele meant that his soldiers and his animals would get hungrier and weaker. Then if the Rebel infantry could defeat Banks and march north, Steele would be in serious trouble.

As Steele's men prepared to march down from the highlands near Okolona toward the Little Missouri on April 2, tension grew all along the column. If the enemy intended to try to block their way, the crossing of the Little Missouri would be an ideal place to do it.

Steele was worried. As the bulk of his army marched toward the river, prepared to camp on the north bank, he ordered the second brigade of the third division to hurry ahead, cross the river, and try to make contact with the enemy.

Col. William E. McLean, the brigade commander, ordered his men to the river in a forced march. At Elkins' Ferry on the night of April 2, the men forded the river after dark to camp on the south bank between the river and a small tributary known as Hickory Creek. In his force were McLean's own 43rd Indiana Infantry under the command of Maj. W. W. Norris; the 36th Iowa, under Colonel Kittredge; a battery of the Second Missouri Light Artillery under Lt. Charles Peetz; and a squadron of cavalry acting as advance pickets.

The next afternoon McLean ordered Lieutenant Colonel Drake, the second in command of the 36th Iowa, to take three companies from his own regiment and three from the 43rd Indiana and move up to the picket line to see if he could learn what the Rebels were up to. Andrew Brayman's Company I, along with the remainder of the regiment, remained behind in reserve.

Drake found the cavalry pickets, about a hundred of them, in an old orchard about a mile and a quarter from the ford. Rebel sharpshooters were busy trying to drive the cavalrymen from the shelter of the trees. Drake crept forward from tree to tree until he could see the enemy positions. He immediately sent a note back to McLean warning him that the enemy, with artillery, was present in force and appeared to be preparing for an attack the next morning. He told McLean he would deploy his six companies of infantry and urged him to send Lieutenant Peetz forward with his artillery.

At dawn the next morning, the Rebel forces, in a long line spread across the open field in front of the orchard, advanced, quickly driving the cavalry back out of the shelter of the trees.

Drake ordered his infantrymen to spread out and advance through the orchard. The cavalrymen dismounted and joined the skirmish line.

The two lines of troops were soon engaged in a furious firefight. It was obvious to Drake that his 400 men were badly outnumbered. But the Union men had the advantage of firing from behind the trees in the orchard. Bullets whizzed through the air, cutting branches and slamming into tree trunks. The Rebels, out in the open, began to fall. The weight of numbers took its toll, driving the Union forces back, but only by a few yards.

During a lull in the action, Drake's men were even able to advance to where they had stood when the battle started and retrieve the knapsacks they had left behind.

Back at the ford, Kittredge heard the first shots of the battle and hurried forward with the remainder of the 36th Iowa, including Andrew's Company I. Many of the soldiers were veterans of fighting at Helena and on the march to Little Rock. But for Andrew, who had spent months in the hospital, this was his first contact with the enemy. His heart beat faster and his mouth was dry as he double-timed forward toward the sound of the guns.

Kittredge deployed his seven companies of infantry just in front of the artillery and just behind Drake's skirmishers. Then Kittredge rode forward to confer with Drake.

Just then two mounted Rebel officers were seen galloping past the rear of one of Drake's companies. The Iowans were about to fire when one of the riders waved a white handkerchief. The troops were ordered to hold their fire. One of the officers turned and came forward to surrender, but the other wheeled his horse and galloped away.

As the Rebel officer came forward, he spotted Drake and said: "Hello, Drake, is that you?"

Surprised, Drake answered: "Yes. And who are you?"

"My name is Fackler and I used to sell you goods while a salesman in the wholesale house of Pittman Brothers of St. Louis," he replied. "I am General Marmaduke's aide-de-camp and it was Marmaduke who has just so narrowly escaped."

It was from Fackler that Drake and Kittredge learned they were facing Marmaduke's entire division of some 3,000 men.

Kittredge returned to his unit and was in the process of deploying them on both sides of a road that ran through the battlefield when Colonel McLean, the brigade commander, rode up and ordered him to fall back behind the artillery. Kittredge saw the whole line of Drake's skirmishers on the left side of the road running back across an open field. He spread his men in a line behind the artillery on the left of the road and ordered them to lie down.

On the right side of the road, Drake's men fell back slowly even though the enemy had deployed four pieces of artillery on his flanks, raking the woods with solid shot, grapeshot, and shell while the enemy soldiers charged, firing their muskets and, as Drake later put it, "yelling like demons."

The Rebel artillery then turned its attention to Lieutenant Peetz's two guns. Shells rained down in the area, but none of them came close enough to silence the Union guns. To Kittredge, it seemed obvious that the Rebel goal was to knock out or capture the artillery. Peering over a slight rise in the earth, he saw the enemy advancing across an open field.

He ordered his men to stand up and fire. As they joined the battle, Peetz drew his guns back across Hickory Creek. And then, after a few more volleys from the Union troops, the firing ceased on both sides.

As the firing tapered off, Brig. Gen. Samuel A. Rice, a brigade commander and one of Steele's most trusted officers, arrived on the north bank of the Little Missouri with his brigade. Riding forward, he found Drake and asked him where to place his men.

"If we are forced from our present position, we shall fall behind the riverbanks," Drake replied. "Better place your brigade on the opposite bank and you can fire over us."

Just then, a bullet slashed through the top of Rice's fatigue cap, cutting a furrow in the top of his head. Blood streamed down his face.

Years later, Drake recalled his reaction: "I hope, general, you are not seriously hurt, but the top of your cap is gone."

"I feel as though the top of my head is gone, and will go to the rear, but will have my brigade in position," Rice replied. Although "scalped" by the Rebel bullet, Rice was not seriously injured and was able to resume his command.

After seeing Rice off to the rear, Drake aligned his troops with the rest of the regiment, and the men lay down in the field for the night. At dawn, skirmishers advanced cautiously to find that the enemy had left the field during the night.

During the night of April 4 and the morning of the fifth, Steele brought the remainder of his army forward and camped near the river. The 36th Iowa, with help from the 43rd Indiana, the Missouri artillery, and a hundred cavalrymen, had repulsed a much larger enemy force and held the vital ford for Steele's army.

The battle of Elkins' Ferry cost the Union forces 31 men wounded, 11 of them mortally. Hastily dug graves, found on the battlefield the next morning, indicated the Rebel losses had been far heavier.

Although Steele probably didn't realize it at the time, he had narrowly escaped disaster because of a failure of leadership on the part of the Rebel General Price. Instead of concentrating all his forces at the Little Missouri, Price had left two units to guard the crossing of the Saline River to the west, long after it had become apparent Steele was not taking that route. He thus missed his best chance not just to harass Steele but to stop him cold.

Steele remained at the crossing of the Little Missouri River for several more days. The sunny skies that had blessed their march so far turned gray and threatening. Heavy rain began to fall, with severe thunder and lightning. The river and its tributaries rose, and the roads turned to mush. Steele sent engineers back to lay logs crosswise in the mud to form a bumpy corduroy road for Thayer's wagons, and he deployed his pontoon bridge over the swollen Little Missouri.

On April 9 Thayer's motley assortment of troops and decrepit wagons wended their way across the bridge and joined Steele's army. By the time he arrived, Steele was only a third of the way to Shreveport but his men and animals had consumed enough food to have gotten them all the way if they had traveled without delay. Steele relayed word back to Little Rock with orders to send him enough half rations for 15,000 men as soon as possible.

Then he resumed his off-again, on-again march to the south.

Chapter Twelve

Disaster at Sabine Crossroads

On April 3, the same day that the 36th Iowa and other elements of a small outnumbered Union force secured the crossing at Elkins' Ferry and opened the way for Steele's army, General Banks, in Grand Ecore, Louisiana, made a fateful mistake.

Relying on the word of one man, he sent the bulk of his army off toward Shreveport on what he thought was the only road to that destination. If he had asked almost any native of the area, he would have learned that there was another road, one that would have been far more suitable because it paralleled the Red River instead of moving away from it, as did the one that the army took. His faulty decision left part of his army and Porter's flotilla to travel on the river while the rest of his troops would march several miles away. That meant his infantry would not be able to protect the boats, and the navy guns would be too far away to protect the infantry and cavalry.

Admiral Porter left Grand Ecore, about halfway between Alexandria and Shreveport, on April 7 and started up the river toward Shreveport with eight navy vessels and two dozen transports and quartermaster vessels. Spring rains had not swollen the river as much as normal, so he was forced to leave his larger ships behind.

In Shreveport, General Kirby Smith, the Confederate leader, issued orders to General Taylor, his chief subordinate, that were written with marvelous ambiguity. In effect, they were designed to free Kirby Smith of responsibility for any defeat yet give him enough time to arrive on the scene and claim credit for any victory. But things did not quite turn out that way. Events moved too fast.

On the afternoon of April 8, advance units of Banks's troops came upon Taylor's men at the Sabine Crossroads, near the small town of Mansfield, Louisiana. Banks rode forward to check out the situation. A skilled politician but certainly no general, Banks gave conflicting orders that left his subordinates uncertain about what to do. Taylor, a brilliant tactician, took control of the situation with a slashing attack that caught the strung-out Union forces on the flanks and sent them streaming back through the woods in a panicky retreat.

As Taylor sat on a hillside above the battlefield, smoking a cigar and one leg crossed over his saddle, a messenger arrived from Kirby Smith that ordered him to avoid a battle. Taylor sent the messenger back with a cryptic response: "Too late, sir. The battle is won."

Of 12,000 men on or near the battlefield, Banks lost 113 killed, 581 wounded, and 1,541 missing (many of them dead). He also lost 20 pieces of artillery, 156 wagons, and close to 1,000 horses and mules. Long into the night, the frightened Union soldiers heard the victorious Confederates rummaging through the captured supply wagons and driving off with them to the rear.

On the following day, April 9, the two sides clashed again at Pleasant Hill, a short distance from the site of battle at Sabine Crossroads. This time, A. J. Smith's westerners caught Taylor's troops in the flank and routed them. As the Confederates fled, Banks rode up to Smith, the same general who had been hissed by his troops a few days before, and exclaimed: "God bless you, general. You have saved the army." It was a narrow victory for Banks's troops, but a victory nevertheless.

Banks wanted to gather his forces and forge on toward Shreveport. But even though Pleasant Hill was a Union victory, Banks's subordinates were sickened by the carnage on the battlefield. They urged him to pull back again to Grand Ecore. It was not that they were afraid of the enemy. They were afraid of going into another battle under Banks.

One of his subordinate generals later wrote: "From what I had seen of General Banks' ability to command in the field, I was certain that an operation depending on plenty of troops, rather than upon skill in handling them, was the only one which would have probability of success in his hands."

Banks took the advice of his subordinates and withdrew, turning a tactical victory into a strategic defeat. His departure from the battlefield gave off a strong smell of panic. Wounded soldiers, suffering with the cold of the night and screaming for water, were left on the battlefield to be cared for, as best they could, by the Confederates. A. J. Smith, the man responsible for the victory at Pleasant Hill, begged Banks to permit him to stay behind to care for the wounded. Twice Banks refused his entreaties.

Smith was so disturbed that he talked of putting Banks under arrest and taking command himself. But a colleague reminded him that he was talking mutiny, and he dropped the subject.

Relations between Taylor and Kirby Smith were just about as bad as those between Banks and A. J. Smith. With Banks moving back toward Grand Ecore, Kirby Smith immediately peeled off three infantry divisions and ordered them north to meet Steele. Taylor was furious. He thought Steele was already in so much trouble that he could be left to Price's mounted infantry while he—Taylor—pounced on Banks with the full Rebel force and finished him off. He envisioned not only defeating Banks but capturing the naval flotilla that had accompanied him.

Taylor's state of mind was obvious from a letter he wrote to Kirby Smith a short time later: "The grave errors you have committed in the recent campaign may be repeated if the unhappy consequences are not kept before you. After the desire to serve my country, I have none more ardent than to be relieved from longer serving under your command."

Kirby Smith was adamant. Not only did he reject Taylor's ideas and send the three divisions north, but he hurried north himself to set up a new headquarters in Calhoun, just across the Louisiana line in southern Arkansas.

This left a strange situation in Louisiana. Taylor had only about 8,000 troops. But with them he succeeded in holding the entire Union force of about 25,000 men—all of Banks's troops plus Porter's vessels, which had worked their way back down the river—penned up in Grand Ecore.

On April 19, under orders from Grant to return A. J. Smith's troops to Sherman's army and worried that the unseasonal low water in the river might trap Porter's navy far from the Mississippi, Banks gave up. Not only did he abandon the effort to take Shreveport, but he ordered the entire force to leave central Louisiana to the Confederates.

As the Union troops left Grand Ecore on April 21, they burned the town and, with it, piles of supplies they could not take with them. The burning didn't end there. As they went, A. J. Smith's men burned every structure they encountered, leaving flaming beacons along the way as the army marched on through the night. Cows, hogs, horses, and mules were killed. Even the shacks of slaves were burned.

The commander of the Nineteenth Army Corps was so disturbed by the path of destruction left by the retreating army that he denounced the "indiscriminate marauding and incendiarism, disgraceful to the army of a civilized nation" and offered a $500 reward for evidence to be used in a court-martial of those responsible.

Taylor's troops nipped at the heels of the Union rear guard, forcing them time after time to stop and deploy into battle formation. And then, on April 23, as Banks's army prepared to cross a tributary of the Red River, Taylor, with his outnumbered forces, attempted a bold attack that, had it succeeded, would have destroyed Banks's army and left thousands of the Union men prisoners. But at the last moment one of Taylor's units gave way, permitting the Union force to escape across the river.

Taylor followed the fleeing Federals down the river to Alexandria and bottled them up there as he had at Grand Ecore. Banks remained at Alexandria only long enough to ensure that Porter's boats could be floated down past the rapids before resuming his full-scale retreat out of central Louisiana. He departed from Alexandria in mid-May. Despite strict orders, his troops left the town in flames.

Everyone involved in the Red River expedition had grave doubts from the beginning about Banks's ability to manage such an operation. The march had barely begun when Banks sent an optimistic note to his friend Lincoln, promising to drive the Confederate forces into Texas. Lincoln wrote to a friend: "I am sorry to see this tone of confidence; the next news we shall hear from there will be of a defeat."

And yet Banks remained politically unassailable. When Grant took over as commander-in-chief, he received two letters condemning Banks's performance as a military commander. "His own reports and these letters clearly show all his disasters to be attributable to his own incompetency," Grant wrote. He told Halleck he wanted to fire Banks. But Halleck, wiser in the ways of Washington, warned him:

> I think the President will consent to the order if you
> insist upon General Banks' removal as a military necessity,

but he will do so very reluctantly, as it would give offense to many of his friends, and would probably be opposed by a portion of his cabinet. Moreover, what could be done with Banks? He has many political friends who would probably demand for him a command equal to the one he now has.

In another message in the same vein, Halleck told Grant:

> General Banks is a personal friend of the President, and has strong political supporters in and out of Congress. There will undoubtedly be a very strong opposition to his being removed or superseded, and I think the President will hesitate to act unless he has a definite request from you to do so, as a military necessity. . . . You will perceive that the press in New Orleans and in the Eastern States are already beginning to open in General Banks' favor.

Another officer was eventually placed in command of the military forces in southern Louisiana, without the actual removal of Banks from his job.

Chapter Thirteen

Flight to Camden

When Steele marched south from Little Rock, he left behind his telegraphic link with other parts of the nation. He was thus left in ignorance of Banks's progress toward Shreveport—or lack of it—from March 23 until a messenger with confusing information reached him on April 18.

By that time, Steele and his army were in very serious trouble.

After Thayer joined him on April 9, Steele moved slowly southward on what was called the Old Military Road, which led toward the Confederate capital at Washington. But before the road reached Washington, it intersected with the Washington-Camden road and another road that led south toward Shreveport. Price, the Rebel general, concentrated most of his force in a position from which he could either block the road to Washington if Steele kept on in that direction or continue to harass him if he pressed on toward Shreveport.

On Sunday, April 10, the vanguard of the Union army emerged from the pine forests that had shaded much of their route onto the broad Prairie de Anne.

An unusual geographic feature in southern Arkansas, Prairie de Anne is the result of glacial action that deposited samples of almost every soil type known in Arkansas. It had long been treasured by the Indians, who observed a kind of annual hunting season to take advantage of the game that flourished there while still conserving the animals for future years. The eastern portion of the prairie is now occupied by the small town of Prescott, which was not there during the Civil War, and the battlefield is bisected by Interstate 30.

Covering an area 18 miles long and 15 miles east to west, the grass of the prairie looked, in the 1860s, almost as smooth as a sea of glass. A few widely scattered farm buildings dotted the scene. One soldier wrote: "Like an oasis lies this beautiful prairie in the midst of dense forests and almost impassable swamps, a relief for the eye of the traveller, who for many days has hardly seen anything but rocks crowned by dark pines or gloomy cypress swamps."

When the soldiers looked toward a rise in the land stretching across the prairie, however, what they saw was certainly no "relief for the eye of the traveller." Enemy soldiers were clearly visible at work along a line of huge gum trees, some of them as big as five feet in diameter and more than 150 feet tall, hurriedly erecting a line of log bunkers and earthworks. By seizing the high ground and fortifying their defensive positions, they had made up in some degree for the Union army's advantage in numbers.

Two of the Union brigades began marching onto the prairie shortly after noon, taking up positions on both sides of the road that ran through the prairie. The 36th Iowa was back along the line of march, moving in small detachments to protect the baggage train. As the sounds of skirmishing and artillery fire were heard from up ahead, Andrew and the other members of the regiment were sent forward at double quick time, running a distance of nearly three miles. Late in the afternoon they were posted on the left side of the road.

Along the ridge under the gum trees, concentrated on both sides of the road toward Washington, were some 7,000 Confederate soldiers, roughly half as many as in Steele's army. Even that number exaggerates the size of the Confederate force, because one out of every four mounted infantrymen remained behind the lines holding the horses.

During the late afternoon and on into the night, the two sides engaged in a furious artillery duel. A Confederate report described the duel as "terrible and magnificent. . . . Over all the bursting bombs and the white powder clouds came fast and furious." The Rebel forces gradually pulled back along the road toward Washington, and the firing tapered off about midnight. Despite the heavy gunfire, losses on both sides were small.

That night the Union soldiers lay in the open prairie without shelter or fire. Monday morning dawned bright and clear, a beautiful day. Birds sang cheerfully in the thickets. There were occasional sounds of artillery fire or musketry, but a strange calm seemed to have settled over the battlefield. The soldiers hunted rabbits, played cards, read, or wrote letters.

During the afternoon Union skirmishers probed the Confederate lines. They succeeded in determining the enemy positions but failed to draw them out into the open.

Monday night was miserable for the soldiers, who were lying on their rifles in the open under an almost steady rain. But Tuesday morning dawned clear and pleasant. With a roll of drums and the call of bugles, the entire army was assembled in line of battle beginning at 7 A.M.

Andrew was positioned near the center of the line. Looking to the right and left, he could see the row of soldiers stretching off almost to the horizon in each direction. Flags snapped in the morning breeze. The officers' horses pranced and neighed, waiting for the signal to advance.

Lieutenant Pearson, the diarist in Company G of the 36th Iowa, described the scene in glowing terms:

> When we were all in motion it presented to my view one of the grandest scenes my eyes ever beheld. Truly the scene was grand and sublime, and the cracking of rifles by the lines of skirmishers with an occasional fire from the artillery and the bursting shells added to the sublimity of the surroundings. . . . All in motion, every man of us believing a fight certain and a victory sure were jubilant.
>
> But the rebs took a scare and stampeded from their formidable breast works of timber which were near or quite a mile long, with additional earth works from which they fled in haste without waiting to fire on us from behind them.

Actually, after having succeeded in stalling Steele's advance for at least three days while his troops and animals got hungrier and hungrier, the outnumbered Confederate forces had made a disciplined strategic retreat.

The Union soldiers chased the enemy for about five miles, with small losses on both sides, and as the Union forces gathered for the advance on Washington, the Rebels clearly believed that they were in for a battle.

But instead of continuing on toward Washington or heading for Shreveport, Steele surprised both the enemy and his own troops by suddenly turning his force directly to the east and heading for Camden. This may not have been a spur-of-the-moment reaction to the battlefield situation, however. Before leaving Little Rock, Steele, in a message to Sherman, had referred to a possible stop in Camden. Perhaps he realized from the outset that his half-starved army could not march directly to Shreveport and arrive in fighting condition and that he would need a stopover place along the way.

As soon as Price, the Confederate commander, realized what Steele was up to, he sent his fast-moving mounted infantry and horse artillery to harass the Union column with hit-and-run raids on its rear and flanks. For the weary men in Steele's army, it was a miserable march. Their route took them up and down hills, across swamps, and then, for almost an entire afternoon, over hills of almost pure sand. While they marched toward Camden, General Marmaduke galloped eastward on a road parallel to that taken by Steele's army and beat the Union force to a crossroads at a point called Poison Springs, about 15 miles west of Camden.

Marmaduke was outnumbered and Steele's men forced their way through, taking Camden with little opposition on April 15. To protect the rear of the army as it marched on toward Camden, five companies of the 36th Iowa and a battery of light artillery remained at the crossroads from 2 until 6 P.M. The Iowans then marched on to Camden to camp after midnight outside the fortifications about a mile northwest of the city. The next day they moved down and joined the thousands of other soldiers camped wherever they could find room within the city itself.

Price had, for all practical purposes, abandoned Camden on April 5, about the time Steele was crossing the Little Missouri. He removed or destroyed all the military supplies and left only a small rear guard to cut the pontoon bridge across the Ouachita River if and when the Union army arrived.

It did not take the professional military men on Steele's staff long to figure out why the enemy had abandoned Camden with barely a fight. The city's defenses had been laid out by Brig. Gen. Alexander T. Hawthorn, a Camden lawyer with no background in engineering. He did the best he could, erecting five redoubts where cannons could be positioned to cover both the water and the land approaches to the city. But he failed to connect these strongpoints with trenches, and he failed to clear the areas around the redoubts to prevent enemy soldiers from sneaking up on them. The Federal officers immediately set to work correcting the defects in the city's defenses, but that took time, and in the meantime the city was vulnerable to Confederate attack.

An enemy attack was not Steele's only or even his most urgent worry. He had a huge starving army on his hands, and there was little or no food to be had. In the fall of 1863, the city had been occupied by ragged, threadbare Confederate troops who had helped themselves to whatever food they could find. One resident complained: "Stealing is going on at a bold rate."

Steele moved into the stately tree-shaded home of Col. John T. Chidester on Washington Street. His arrival was a strange experience for the ladies of the house. Until a few days before, they had been playing host to Confederate General Price, who had also claimed the house as his headquarters. Chidester's wife, Leah, was nervous. Her husband, who operated a large stagecoach company covering Georgia, Alabama, and Mississippi and extending to the southwest, was wanted by the Federals, who suspected him of using his coach lines to gather intelligence and transport spies for the Confederacy.

When the Union troops marched into town, Chidester was actually at home. He climbed the stairs to the attic, to a room where his coach drivers slept during stopovers in Camden, and hid in a small space between the wall of the room and the eaves. Before Steele moved in, the Union soldiers made a thorough search of the house. They even fired a couple of pistol bullets into the wall behind which Chidester was hiding. But they neither found him nor hit him, and he remained hidden while Steele and his officers conferred downstairs.

Steele moved into a bright, sunny bedroom on the southeastern corner of the house and took over the adjoining parlor as an office. He asked Mrs. Chidester if his men should remove the carpet to prevent it from being scarred by his officers' spurs, but she told him to leave it where it was. If it was taken up, she said, the men would just cut it up for saddle blankets.

Down the street at the home of Mrs. Virginia Stinson—whose father had built the house occupied by the Chidester family—Union soldiers found some hams in the smokehouse and took them. Mrs. Stinson complained to Steele, and he arranged for an officer to live at her home to protect her.

Other women were not so fortunate. Clara Dunlap, who lived on a farm outside town, said in a letter to her sister that the Union troops at first seemed well mannered. But then, she complained, "they came and took all of our mules, com. meat, sugar, molasses, flour, everything in the world we had to eat. . . . They even took all my soap, candles, coffee, and every hen, chicken, turkey, eggs, etc. on the place except two or three old setting hens that ran off in the woods. . . . Even took my wedding slippers."

The Dunlap family had a dozen slaves, and all of them left except for one woman whom Mrs. Dunlap paid to remain and help with her baby.

Among the troops brought by Thayer from Fort Smith were two regiments of former slaves, commanded by white officers. The black troops were at least as well behaved as the white troops—better, in fact, than the Irishman caught dancing on top of the grand piano in one woman's home. But the mere sight of black men in uniform, armed with rifles, stirred a deep sense of dread in the breasts of many Camden citizens.

Virginia Stinson later recalled: "Only one thing stirred my Southern blood to heat, was when a negro regiment passed my home going to fight our own dear men. . . . How fierce they did look, it was then that I gave vent to my feelings."

During the army's stay in Camden, Steele's subordinates stopped devising schemes to defeat the enemy and instead began to worry about how to extricate the army from its present predicament. Among themselves, some of them harbored grave misgivings about the whole expedition. They wondered if Steele knew what he was doing. Brig. Gen. Frederick Salomon, who commanded the division in which Andrew Brayman served, had a very low opinion of his boss, although he was discreet enough to keep word from getting back to Steele. The 38-year-old Salomon was born in Prussia and had served in the Prussian army as a lieutenant before moving to Wisconsin in 1849. He told one aide that Steele, a West Pointer, "don't know anything about Arkansas, where he is or what he thinks of doing.

"Damn those regulars," he added. "They map out battles on paper, draw their salaries and smoke cigars. The worse of it is they always keep clear of the firing line, which bars the good luck of getting them shot out of the way."

If Steele was spared the grumbling of his subordinates, he was getting plenty of unvarnished bad news from his quartermaster, Capt. C. A. Henry. Unlike a modern army, which can simply wait for supplies if its tanks run out of gas, a Civil War army had to feed its horses and mules or they would sicken and die. A few days after their arrival in Camden, Henry put his concerns in writing:

> I would, general, most respectfully represent that we have only half forage for the animals of this command for one day, and in view of the alarming scarcity of forage along the line

of the Ouachita, I beg leave to suggest that all the worthless
animals attached to this command be collected and turned
out to graze in the canebrakes within our lines under charge
of a suitable guard. There are now over 10,000 animals
attached to this command for which it will be impossible to
provide forage after the next two or three days. I believe that
over 2,000 worthless horses and mules could be collected
and thus relieve us from the necessity of procuring forage
for them.

Steele was trying desperately to scrounge food for his animals and
men from a countryside already stripped nearly bare. Confederate
troops had not only gathered up all the food they could find but had
also burned most of the mills in the area surrounding Camden. On
April 17 he sent a wagon train to the west, where a supply of corn was
reported to be hidden. The next day he sent Andrew's regiment, the
36th Iowa, under the command of Lieutenant Colonel Drake, six
miles southeast to process corn at Britton's Mill.

In both cases Steele was afraid to send too large a force, despite the
enemy horsemen roaming the area, for fear of leaving Camden without sufficient defense against a Confederate attack. The result in one
case was a narrow escape. The other expedition ended in an appalling
disaster.

Chapter Fourteen

Massacre at Poison Springs

On the morning of April 17, the day before the 36th Iowa was sent to Britton's Mill, 198 wagons, guarded by a long column of foot soldiers, cavalry, and artillery moved slowly west out of Camden into a coun-tryside where the enemy's horsemen roamed at will. Their goal was to bring back 5,000 bushels of corn that the soldiers had spotted, but had not been able to carry, on their march toward Camden. The wagon train would have to travel about 16 miles west from Camden, past the point at Poison Springs where the 36th Iowa had remained to protect the rear of the retreating army a few days earlier.

In the line were one of the two regiments of black soldiers whose presence had stirred the animosity of the people of Camden—the First Kansas Colored Infantry. Also in the column were troopers from three Kansas cavalry units and two guns of the Second Indiana Battery. In all they numbered 695 fighting men, plus the teamsters. They were joined the next day by reinforcements: the Eighteenth Iowa Infantry, 90 more Kansas cavalrymen, and two mountain howitzers. That swelled the number of soldiers in the force foraging west of Camden to 1,160.

In charge of the expedition was Col. James M. Williams, the white commander of the colored infantry regiment. Williams, who had been a lawyer before the war, had already distinguished himself in several battles in Indian Territory.

As the column began its move on the morning of April 17, the familiar sounds of a large moving army camp blended together: the clang of the blacksmith's hammer, the shouted orders of sergeants, the tramp of marching men, the anxious tones of conversation as the men speculated about their future. They had been on half rations for nearly a month, and then the half rations had been cut in half. They prayed that the column would bring back food or that a rumored train of supply wagons from Pine Bluff would soon appear.

Late that afternoon, back in Camden, Lieutenant Colonel Drake received orders to take out a separate column of 40 wagons to process corn for the hungry army. His goal was one of the few mills in the area that had not been destroyed by the Confederate forces. It was the James M. Britton steam mill, six miles southeast of Camden. The distance Drake had to travel was shorter than that to be covered by the column under Colonel Williams that had gone off to the east that morning. But, to protect the wagon train, Drake was given only one regiment—the 36th Iowa—and a squadron of 20 cavalrymen, a tiny force compared with the enemy units known to be in the vicinity.

As the men fell in at 7 o'clock on April 18, the grumbling up and down the line went well beyond the normal griping in any army. Officers as well as men complained openly at being sent out with such a small force into such a dangerous situation. One officer, a veteran of a number of engagements, said he had never heard of anything like it. Still, the men marched as ordered, struggling over two swollen streams and through a swamp. A bridge over the swamp had been burned by the enemy.

The column reached Britton's Mill about 9 o'clock. Guards were posted, and then the remainder of the men were put to work: One group cut and gathered wood to power the mill's steam engine, another shucked the corn, and a third ran the mill, grinding the corn into meal for the army. Drake rode in a circle about two miles out from the mill to size up the military situation. All along the circuit, he and the cavalrymen accompanying him came in contact with Rebel scouts. He became convinced that much of the enemy army was concentrating in that area for an attack on Camden. He sent a messenger back to Camden for General Salomon, the division commander, with a warning of the threat to the city and to his own force.

During the afternoon, as the soldiers worked their way through several thousand bushels of corn, they heard a prolonged rumble of artillery fire in the distance. Drake, it seemed, was wrong in his conclusion that the bulk of the enemy force was massing nearby for an attack on Camden. From the sound of the cannon fire, it was obvious that a sizable engagement was under way somewhere off to the west. They had no way to know what was going on, and there was nothing they could do about it. They continued to grind the corn long into the night.

Finally, about midnight, an aide to General Salomon, escorted by a squadron of cavalry, galloped into the camp at Britton's Mill. Without even waiting for Drake to read his orders, the aide shouted excitedly that they were to hurry back to Camden as soon as possible. The Iowans loaded up the wagons and made their way back to town. The march had taken two hours in the morning sunlight. But it took the weary, hungry soldiers the rest of the night to retrace their steps. They arrived just as the sun was coming up.

The camp was astir with a strange buzz of excitement. As the soldiers marched down the street, they saw other men who would normally be going about their routine duties at this hour of the morning standing in knots talking excitedly.

As soon as they were dismissed, Andrew joined one of the groups to hear the news: The cannon fire they had heard the afternoon before was the sound of a terrible battle in which Colonel Williams's column had been set upon by a much larger Rebel force. The survivors had managed to reach Camden about 11 o'clock the night before. But many men were dead, wounded, or missing. The wagon train carrying the precious food had been either captured or destroyed.

And that, Andrew and the others of his regiment thought, might well have been our fate if the winds of war had been blowing from a slightly different direction.

The men of the 36th Iowa were too tired to spend much time talking. They had been marching or working hard for a good 24 hours. They spread out their blankets and went to sleep.

When they awoke later in the day, a more coherent picture of what had happened to the other wagon train was beginning to take shape, although it would not be until after the war that the full dimensions of the horror at Poison Springs became known. This is what had happened:

Williams's men marched 18 miles west on the Washington road and set up camp. Then Williams sent part of his wagon train another six miles west in search of corn. They returned about midnight, most of the wagons loaded with corn.

At muster the next morning, April 18, Williams listed 100 of his black soldiers as "unfit for duty," worn down by the lack of food and the long march. At sunrise the column headed back toward Camden. They had gone about four miles when they met the reinforcements Steele had sent to help them: 375 men of the Eighteenth Iowa, 90 horsemen from the Second, Sixth, and Fourteenth Kansas Cavalry, and the two mountain howitzers—another 465 men.

Although Williams thus had a total of 1,160 men under his command, many of the cavalrymen had, as Williams later complained, "in violation of orders, straggled from their commands." They were off marauding through the scattered farm homes in the area, helping themselves to everything from smoked hams to silverware. Thus when Williams's advance units ran into a few enemy pickets about a mile down the road from where the reinforcements had joined them, he had barely 1,000 men available. The pickets fell back about a mile and joined a more formidable line of skirmishers at Poison Springs.

Williams knew he was in trouble. An enemy force—he had no way of knowing how big—stood between him and safety in Camden. He ordered the wagons to park as close together as possible and then deployed his own regiment—the former slaves of the First Kansas Colored Infantry—in an L-shaped formation to guard the front and flank of the wagon train. Having passed through the same spot the previous day, Williams knew that the area on the right side of the road sloped slightly upward to the south. To the left, or north, the terrain dropped off sharply into a ravine and, beyond that, a swamp, limiting his freedom to maneuver.

At the front of the column, Williams placed the Fourteenth Kansas Cavalry on the left flank and the Second and Sixth Kansas Cavalry on the right flank of his colored infantry. He sent word to the commander of the Eighteenth Iowa Infantry to deploy his troops, plus the cavalry and guns he had brought out as reinforcements, to guard the rear of the train.

Williams then ordered the two guns of the Second Indiana Battery to open fire. The sound of the guns would be a signal to foraging parties that had been sent out early to hurry back. Williams also expected the Rebels, if they had cannons in their force, to return the fire. This would give him an idea of what he was up against.

With the enemy between him and Camden, Williams's decision to put the colored infantry at the front of the wagon train placed the black soldiers in the most vulnerable position. They would take the brunt of a clash with the enemy, while the white Iowa infantry was stationed in what might be a safer position to the rear of the train.

Far from intending to sacrifice his black infantry, however, Williams had made a prudent decision, placing his best troops and those he knew best where he needed them most. Unlike most other black units, which were shortchanged in training and equipment and used primarily as cheap labor, the First Kansas Colored was a first-rate infantry unit that had already distinguished itself in combat.

The Rebel response to Williams's opening artillery barrage was disappointing. Instead of return fire that would tell him how many guns the enemy had and where they were, all he got was a flurry of shots from the skirmishers' muskets. Williams concluded that the enemy commander was trying to lure him into moving into a more open area to his front. Instead, he sent the cavalry on his right flank forward through the brush that obstructed his view through the forest. Within 400 yards they ran into heavy musket fire, and a number of horses were shot down.

At that moment Williams got the answer to his question about the enemy artillery. One six-gun battery opened from in front. Another three guns began an incessant cross fire from his right flank. With the artillery barrage came a furious infantry attack from his front and right.

Williams ordered his men to load their rifles with buck and ball—a devastating combination of a rifle bullet and buckshot—but to hold their fire. When the enemy infantry came within about 100 yards, Williams gave the order to fire. The enemy soldiers fell back. But Williams was not deceived. In that brief first encounter, it was obvious to him that he could not hope to win this battle. The best he could do would be to hold out long enough for reinforcements to come hurrying out from Camden.

Pacing the tree-shaded porch of the Chidester house back in Camden, General Steele heard the first tentative shots fired by Williams's two cannons. Then a short time later he heard the much more intense fire of the enemy guns. From the sound, it was obvious that Williams had run into a larger and better-armed force and that he was in serious trouble.

Steele paced quietly in deep thought. If he did not send reinforcements immediately, the corn—more valuable then than gold—that Williams had been sent to retrieve would be lost. And there was a good chance that Williams's guns and many of his men would also be lost. Drake and the 36th Iowa were already off on another perilous mission. If the general did send a relief column big enough to make a difference, his remaining force in Camden might be vulnerable to piecemeal destruction. Could this all be part of a plan to force him to divide his army so that Camden itself could be stormed?

The sounds of battle were the second installment of bad news Steele received that day. A messenger he had sent to contact General Banks in Louisiana had just returned with the first firsthand report of the situation there. It was disturbing news. The messenger reported that Banks claimed to have beaten the Confederate forces at Sabine Crossroads (which was a lie) and Pleasant Hill but had then fallen back to Grand Ecore for supplies. Although the message was ambiguous—claiming victory but acknowledging a retreat—its meaning to Steele was ominous. It meant that Banks had let up the pressure on Kirby Smith's troops and that the Confederate general was thus now free to send his infantry to confront Steele.

In earlier messages to Sherman, Steele had made it clear that if Banks "let Kirby Smith go," he would not be able to withstand the combined assault by infantry and mounted infantry that the Confederates could then concentrate against him.

The message from Banks confirmed Steele's worst fears. In fact, Kirby Smith had already detached his infantry and sent it north to face Steele. He himself was only a few miles away, preparing to take over the attack on Steele.

While Steele pondered, the whole camp listened to the distant thunder of battle. The privates could read the sounds almost as well as the generals could: Williams's foraging party was in serious trouble. The sounds were of special concern to the soldiers of the Second Kansas Colored Infantry. They knew that their sister regiment would be in the thick of the battle.

Steele listened a while longer and then made his decision: There would be no relief column. Williams and his men were on their own.

Williams's black troops stood their ground against the first attack, and after about fifteen minutes the Rebel soldiers fell back. No sooner had they pulled back, however, than two fresh Rebel regiments renewed the attack with flags flying. They came on relentlessly, cheering so loudly they drowned out the sound of the muskets. After another quarter of an hour, they too fell back. But by then half of Williams's soldiers were down, either dead or wounded, and three companies had lost all their officers. To Williams, it was obvious from the way the enemy commanders kept throwing fresh units into the battle that he was badly outnumbered. He decided to pull the remaining troops back along the line of the wagon train and join them with the Eighteenth Iowa, which was itself under sharp attack.

This was no casual meeting engagement, in which Williams had stumbled on an enemy unit on the move. General Price, the Confederate commander, had learned of Williams's foraging expedition almost as soon as he left Camden on the morning of April 17. He had ordered General Marmaduke to gather all the forces he could lay his hands on and lie in wait for Williams as he retraced his route toward Camden.

What Williams faced with his thousand men was a powerful force of mounted infantry and artillery—3,600 men and twelve cannons—representing a cross section of the Confederacy's military power west of the Mississippi. There were 786 Missourians from Marmaduke's own division and 1,500 Arkansans in brigades under Brig. Gens. William L. Cabell and William A. Crawford. Of particular interest in this battle was a division brought in from the Indian Territory by Brig. Gen. Samuel B. Maxey: 655 Texans in one brigade and 680 Choctaw Indians in the other.

When the Texans spotted the colors of the First Kansas Colored, something like an electric shock went up and down the line. As the first black combat unit in the Union Army, the First Kansas was well known to every Confederate soldier west of the Mississippi. But it had a special meaning for the Texans. They had met the black infantry before, and they carried a bitter memory of that encounter. On July 17, 1863, less than a year earlier, the 29th Texas Cavalry—one of the units under Maxey's command—had been defeated by the First Kansas in a battle at Honey Springs in Indian Territory. The blacks twice shot down the Texans' standard-bearers and then put them to rout. That defeat at the hands of former slaves still rankled.

As they spotted their old foes, now badly outnumbered, the Texans shouted: "You First Kansas Niggers now buck to the Twenty-ninth Texas!"

The Choctaws, in their buckskins and feathers, also had a special hatred for the black troops—perhaps a manifestation of the perverse tendency of oppressed peoples to take out their anger on each other.

The combination of the Texans, the Choctaws, and the black sol-diers was an explosive mixture that turned what was shaping up as a glorious victory for the Confederate forces into one of the most shame-ful episodes in American history.

As the Union forces fell back, the Texans and the Indians followed, shouting gleefully and killing the wounded blacks and any whom they could capture.

Williams, fighting a disciplined but increasingly desperate rear-guard action, assembled as many men as he could from his command in a swamp off to the north of the battlefield and then took them on a long end run around the enemy forces and back to Camden. Some of the blacks, trying desperately to drag their wounded friends away with them, threw away their rifles. Their officers later explained that most of the weapons had been sunk in the swamp so they could not be gath-ered up by the enemy.

The blacks who could not get away were massacred. Those who fell into the hands of the Indians were scalped—before or after they were shot or knifed to death.

The Texans were heard tramping across the battlefield chanting. One would shout: "Where is the First Kansas Nigger now?" The others would respond in unison: "All cut to pieces and gone to hell."

One Southern lieutenant wrote in his journal: "The havoc among the Negroes had been tremendous—over a small portion of the field we saw at least 40 dead bodies lying in all conceivable attitudes, some scalped & nearly all stripped by the bloodthirsty Choctaws."

Another soldier wrote: "You ought to see Indians fight Negroes—kill and scalp them. . . . Let me tell you, I never expected to see as many dead Negroes again. They were so thick you could walk on them."

General Cabell noted in his official report: "The number of killed of the enemy was very great, especially among the negroes. You could track our troops by the dead bodies lying on the ground."

What happened at Poison Springs went well beyond the kind of sense-less slaughter that sometimes occurs in the heat of combat.

After the Federals fled and the Confederates had given up the chase, the victors turned their attention to the corn-filled wagons, preparing to move them away. General Cabell's Arkansans, most of whom had not joined in the massacre, deliberately drove the wagons over the dead and dying blacks, trying to see who could crush the most "nigger heads."

Under the headline "Choctaw Humor," the *Washington Telegraph*, an outspoken Confederate journal in Arkansas, wrote: "After the battle of Poison Springs, the Choctaws buried a Yankee in an ordinary grave. For a headstone they put up a stiff negro buried to the waist. For a footstone another negro reversed, out from the waist to the heels."

The bodies of three white officers of the black regiment were later found on the battlefield. They had been scalped, stripped of their clothes, and laid facedown as a sign of dishonor. The corpses of black soldiers were arrayed in a circle around them.

One measure of the dimensions of the massacre is the casualty figures: Of the 438 black soldiers who started out on the foraging expedition, 117 were killed and 65 were wounded. Normally in a Civil War battle, the numbers of the killed and wounded would have been reversed.

Even official Confederate reports hinted at what had happened. General Price wrote of the battle: "This was a perfect success. Their whole train was captured, all their artillery, and a large number of prisoners. The enemy were completely routed, leaving near 500 dead (mostly negroes) on the field."

General Cabell wrote: "My whole command captured 62 prisoners —58 white troops and 4 negroes."

The Battle of Poison Springs marked the descent of the Civil War to a new level of barbarity. The Emancipation Proclamation, issued on January 1, 1863, and Lincoln's decision—apparently against Grant's misgivings—to field black troops had set off a wave of revulsion in the South. With it came a determination among Confederate soldiers to take the most drastic measures against black troops and their white officers.

John Eakin, the fire-breathing editor of the *Washington* (Arkansas) *Telegraph*, wrote:

> It follows irresistibly that we *cannot* treat negroes taken in arms as prisoners of war without a destruction of the social system for which we contend. In this we must be firm, uncompromising, and unfaltering. We *must* claim the full control of all negroes who may fall into our hands, to punish with death, or any other penalty, or remand to their owners.

> If the enemy retaliate, we must do likewise; and if the *black flag* follows, the blood be upon their heads.

This sentiment never did become official policy. But Confederate General Kirby Smith came close to making it official when, ten months before Poison Springs, he reprimanded a subordinate: "I have been unofficially informed that some of your troops have captured negroes in arms. I hope this may not be so, and that your subordinates who may have been in command of capturing parties may have recognized the propriety of giving no quarter to armed negroes and their officers."

"Give no quarter" was a code phrase for killing prisoners.

The massacre at Poison Springs came only six days after a similar incident at Fort Pillow, Tennessee. On April 12, Maj. Gen. Nathan Bedford Forrest's cavalry attacked the fort, 40 miles north of Memphis on the Mississippi. Although the fort occupied a strategic position on the river, it may have been of more interest to Forrest because the garrison there was busy recruiting blacks for service in the Union Army.

As the attackers swept through the fort, the defenders fell back toward the riverbank. Whether they were attempting to surrender or were continuing to resist remained in question long after the war. But a congressional committee later concluded that Forrest's men deliberately killed a number of the blacks and their white officers, shouting, "No quarter! No quarter! Kill the damned negroes. Shoot them down."

One result of these and similar incidents was to increase both the fear and the spirit of revenge among black troops.

As news of what had happened at Poison Springs sank in, Col. Samuel J. Crawford, commander of the Second Kansas Colored Infantry, called the regiment's white officers together at their camp in Camden. They discussed the massacre, and then each of them solemnly swore that "in future the regiment would take no prisoners so long as the Rebels continued to murder our men." It would not be long before they had the opportunity to put this brutal policy into effect.

In reaction to the Fort Pillow killings, a Negro regiment in Memphis knelt and made a similar pledge. Other black regiments signaled that they would neither seek nor give quarter by going into battle under a black flag.

In Camden General Steele was deeply worried. His mood of near-despair comes through in a message to Sherman on April 22: "We have been bushwhacked, attacked in front and rear and flank. . . . They are just opening with artillery upon my outposts."

He felt increasing concern even for his own personal safety. After shots were fired into the Chidester house, he moved to another home down the street and then to a hotel, fearful of an assassination attempt. He and his officers debated how to make the best of an increasingly bad situation. One possibility was to hold out in Camden and hope enough supplies could be brought in to keep the army alive. Another possibility was to retreat to Little Rock before the enemy's infantry reinforcements could be brought into position.

While the officers debated, a train of 240 wagons made it through to Camden from Pine Bluff, 70 miles to the northeast, on April 20 with enough supplies to permit them to hold out a little longer. This delivery was added to 3,000 bushels of corn that had been found on a rebel ship captured on the Ouachita a few days earlier. But the soldiers of the 33rd Iowa Infantry, who had escorted the supply train, also brought bad news. On April 13 two ships, the *Adams* and the *Chippewa*, en route down the Arkansas from Little Rock to Pine Bluff with provisions for Steele, had collided. The *Adams* sank, and the *Chippewa* was badly damaged.

The very fact that the supply train had made it through safely from Pine Bluff was good news. Steele had sent patrols up and down the Ouachita River to destroy every crossing, hoping to keep the Confederate forces west of the river and thus leave open the route between Camden and Pine Bluff. But on April 22 it was learned that Confederate Brig. Gen. Joseph O. Shelby, one of the enemy's most capable commanders, had managed to cross the river north of Camden with some 2,000 men and was thus in a position to try to block any effort to bring in more supplies.

Despite this disturbing news, Steele decided to send the wagon train back north again—but with an escort strong enough to fight its way through if necessary. The biggest part of the escort he selected was almost the same as the force that had held open the crossing at Elkins' Ferry two and a half weeks earlier: the 36th Iowa and the 43rd Indiana and Lieutenant Peetz's artillery. He also sent the 77th Ohio regiment.

Following along would be 520 members of the First Iowa Cavalry. Even with his army in desperate straits in Camden, Steele felt obliged to send the cavalrymen home on veteran furlough. At least he wouldn't

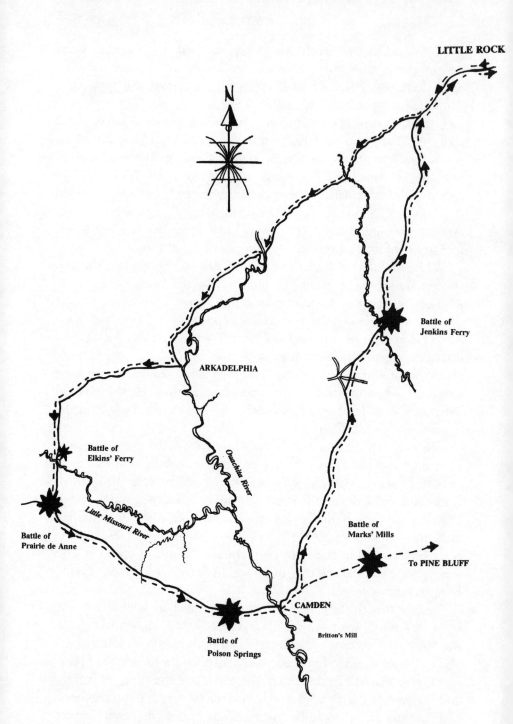

LITTLE ROCK

Battle of
Jenkins Ferry

ARKADELPHIA

Ouachita River

Battle of
Elkins' Ferry

Little Missouri River

Battle of
Prairie de Anne

Battle of
Marks' Mills

To PINE BLUFF

CAMDEN

Britton's Mill

Battle of
Poison Springs

Map of route pursued by Army commanded by Maj. Gen. Frederick Steele from March 25 till May 2, 1864.

have to feed them. But he ordered them to leave their horses behind.

Normally, Colonel McLean of the 43rd Indiana, the acting brigade commander, or Colonel Kittredge of the 36th Iowa would have been put in charge of this brigade-size operation. But both of them were sick. The command fell to Lieutenant Colonel Drake of the 36th Iowa. He put Maj. A. H. Hamilton in charge of his regiment.

On the morning of April 23, Drake reported in person to Steele, who provided him with a guide and traced on a map the route the column would follow. Steele seemed worried almost as much about the terrain they would have to cover as about the possibility of enemy attack. He pointed out a large swampy area known as the Moro Bottom that they would have to struggle through and warned Drake that he should not under any circumstances try to cross the swamp in the dark. Then he ordered him to get moving immediately.

Chapter Fifteen

Death at Marks' Mills

When Drake returned to his camp, he found that his troops had already been alerted and were preparing to move. Before dark they tramped across the pontoon bridge over the Ouachita and made camp in a cane patch a mile east of the river.

Early the next morning, as the teamsters were busy getting their mules harnessed and preparing to move out and the soldiers were finishing their meager breakfast, Maj. Mark McCauley trotted across the bridge at the head of a column of 240 cavalry troopers from his own First Indiana Cavalry and the Seventh Missouri Cavalry.

With the arrival of the cavalrymen, which a worried Steele had added to the train, Drake had under his command a total of nearly 1,200 men: 500 from his 36th Iowa; 300 from the 43rd Indiana; 400 from the 77th Ohio; and 50 men manning two sections of guns from the Second Missouri Light Artillery.

The 520 men of the First Iowa Cavalry who had earned a furlough at home by reenlisting were not ready when Drake left, but they expected to catch up with him before the column reached the Saline River.

At 5 A.M. Drake gave the order, and the long column, headed by McCauley's cavalry, moved out on the road leading northeast toward Pine Bluff, the snap of the teamsters' whips and their profane encouragement to their mules ringing out in the morning air.

Riding up and down the line, Drake soon found that his little army was not alone. Traipsing along behind, desperate to get out of the trap at Camden, was a strange collection of camp followers, later described by Drake as "a large number of citizens, cotton speculators, Arkansas refugees, sutlers, and other army followers, and also some 300 Negroes." The Negroes were former slaves who had heard of the Emancipation Proclamation from black soldiers accompanying Steele's column and who had opted to accompany Drake as the quickest route to freedom.

Drake could not have been happy to have these camp followers along, as they added one more complication to his already difficult job of escorting his long wagon train through difficult and perhaps dangerous country the 70 miles to Pine Bluff. But now that they were on the move, there was little he could do about them.

The first sign of trouble came late in the morning, about 12 miles from Camden. Drake's scouts reported they had found a spot where enemy cavalry had camped the night before. Looking ahead, Drake saw that the road ran through a dense grove of blackjack trees: an ideal place for an ambush.

Drake galloped up to McCauley at the head of his cavalry detachment. Pointing out the possibility of an ambush, Drake ordered him to have his men draw their sabers and make a cavalry charge through the grove. If they ran into trouble, Drake promised, he would send the infantrymen of the 36th Iowa to their aid.

Drawing their sabers, McCauley's troopers galloped into the grove of trees and almost immediately ran into a small detachment of dismounted enemy horsemen. The Rebel soldiers fought briefly, then mounted their horses and rode away, taking with them two of McCauley's officers. Drake was right in suspecting enemy soldiers in the grove of trees, but instead of planning an ambush on the large Federal train, they had simply been scouting out its progress. Drake later learned that the two captured officers told their captors the Union column was the vanguard of Steele's entire army, fleeing from Camden. This bit of disinformation, he concluded, had encouraged the Rebels to prepare for an attack on his force. Actually, the Confederate commanders were not deceived. They already knew that the column Drake headed was a supply convoy, and in fact they had stepped up their probing attacks on Camden to keep Steele pinned down there.

The soldiers the Union troops had encountered were part of General Shelby's brigade, which had crossed the Ouachita some 15 miles north of Camden on April 19, four days before Drake began his march.

While leaving small detachments to watch the supply convoy, Shelby and the rest of his brigade rode south along the east side of the Ouachita to El Dorado Landing, about 25 miles southeast of Camden. There the remainder of General Fagan's force crossed on April 24.

This put some 4,000 Rebel troopers and mounted artillery on the east side of the river but many miles south of Drake's slow-moving column.

Fagan organized his force into two divisions. One division was headed by General Cabell. Under him were his own brigade plus a brigade headed by Brig. Gen. Thomas P. Dockery. Shelby commanded a second division made up of his own Iron Brigade plus the brigade of Col. William A. Crawford.

Fagan's orders from General Kirby Smith were aimed at isolating Steele at Camden. Fagan's job was to make hit-and-run attacks on Steele's bases of supply at Pine Bluff and Little Rock and then concentrate on felling trees across the road from Camden to Little Rock. This would leave Steele in increasingly desperate straits at Camden while Kirby Smith moved the three infantry divisions he was bringing north from Louisiana into position around Camden.

But for Fagan, Shelby's news of a big, slow-moving column of Union supply wagons, guarded by a force strung out over as much as five miles and encumbered by a large body of camp followers, was too much to resist. He decided to forget about his orders to raid Steele's supply bases and to concentrate instead on the empty supply train. He concluded that he would have to stop Drake before he reached and crossed the Saline River roughly halfway to Pine Bluff. If the supply convoy crossed the river and came within reach of support from Union forces at Pine Bluff, Drake would probably be home free.

Looking at the map, Fagan found what was probably the last place where he could successfully catch and destroy the Federal column: the point where the Camden–Pine Bluff road was intersected by a road between Warren and Fordyce. The intersection was near a tiny settlement known as Marks' Mills.

The mills had been established in 1834 by John H. Marks, who moved to the area from his home in Alabama. He and his two sons had operated the mills for a number of years, sawing timber, grinding corn into meal, and ginning cotton.

In 1860, just before the war began, five members of the Marks family owned 142 slaves—71 of them male and 71 female.

Part of the area around the intersection was open cotton fields in a plantation owned by Mrs. Amelia Urquhart, who lived in a two-story house. Although larger than other homes in the area, it was still a modest house, much smaller than the great mansions that dominated other plantations farther south. Mrs. Urquhart owned 94 slaves—42 male and 52 female. Together the Marks and Urquhart families owned more than a third of the 619 slaves in the county. The remaining area near the crossroads and close to the mill site was covered with pine trees with underbrush, indicating that the area had not been burned over in recent years.

Gauging the distance his men would have to travel, Fagan saw that his opening was narrow. His forces would have to push their horses as hard as they dared to cover more than 40 miles in a day. For men on foot, it would be impossible. But Fagan's infantry and artillery were both mounted. They could do it, although it would be a severe strain on both men and horses—all of them near starvation.

But Fagan had two important factors in his favor. Except for Shelby's brigade, his entire force was made up of Arkansas men and boys, and even Shelby's Missourians had spent weeks crisscrossing Arkansas. Together they knew every back road and byway on the route they would have to cover. Fagan's other advantage was that the bulk of his force—his Arkansans—were literally fighting to protect their homes. The "invaders" from Iowa, Indiana, and Ohio were, on the other hand, fighting for more abstract causes, such as preservation of the Union.

The adventures of one of Fagan's youngest soldiers illustrate the kind of force Drake faced. William Franklin Avera, a Camden boy, joined the Fifth Arkansas Artillery company when he was 16 years old—even younger than Andrew Brayman had been when he enlisted. When Steele began his march south from Little Rock, Avera's company was stationed at Lewisville, near the southeast corner of the state. The artillery company had no guns; theirs had been given to another unit. And although they were supposed to be mounted, they had no horses either. Avera, whose home was on a farm outside Camden, and a friend who lived in the town decided to go home on a two-day pass to get a couple of horses so they could get into the war.

As they walked cross-country on April 18, they heard cannon fire in the distance and realized they probably couldn't make it through the Federal lines into Camden. They later learned that what they had heard was the fighting at Poison Springs. Instead of continuing on

toward Camden, the two teenagers sought out General Price's headquarters at Woodlawn, southwest of Camden. They boldly presented
themselves to the general, told him their story, and asked for permission to join a cavalry unit. He not only gave them the orders but
invited them to have supper with him and his staff—the first food they
had had since morning. After eating, the boys spread their blankets
and went to sleep in a hallway at Price's headquarters.

The next morning they found the unit to which they had been
assigned: the Arkansas artillery battery attached to General Cabell's
brigade.

On the following day their march took them within a mile of the
farm where Avera's mother, father, and sisters lived. Although Avera
could not break away for a brief visit, other members of the unit did
manage to spend a little time with the "home folks" during their
march.

Avera's unit met at the El Dorado crossing with the rest of Fagan's
army. Early the next morning they crossed the Ouachita on a pontoon
bridge and joined the race to cut off Drake before he could reach the
Saline River.

They traveled all day and on into the night, the men and horses
stumbling along like sleepwalkers. About midnight they were ordered
to halt. But instead of resting they were confronted with the frame-
work of a bridge across a narrow stream. The planks had been torn up,
making the bridge useless. The tired soldiers fashioned torches to light
the scene and were able to find some of the timbers that had been
removed from the bridge. They gathered up enough planks to replace
part of the bridge deck so the gun carriages, caissons, and wagons could
be manhandled across the creek. They then swam the horses across.

It was nearly 3 A.M. on the morning of April 25 before they were
permitted to halt, with orders to feed their horses and then rest themselves until daylight. They ate what little food they carried with them
but were not permitted to make any fires in the dark for fear of alert-
ing the Union troops. Avera, with only one blanket, slept from
exhaustion despite the cold. Finally, as dawn broke, the men were
awakened and told they could make fires and boil coffee.

As the sun rose, they were on their way again, urged by their officers to hurry—to walk their horses uphill but to trot on all the good
roads and downhill. Avera was the only nonveteran in the artillery
battery, but it was obvious even to him that they were about to go into
battle. His conclusion was confirmed about 10 o'clock, when they

were halted at a small stream and told to water their horses, fill their canteens, and light the wicks they would use to fire their cannons.

While Fagan's troops were racing to get ahead of the Bluecoats, Drake was pushing his ponderous train as fast as he could—but not nearly as fast as his mounted adversary. Following Steele's stern instructions, Drake camped on the afternoon of April 24 on the Camden side of the Moro Bottom. During the night, he put a force of some 70 men, most of them former slaves trying to escape from Camden, to work felling trees and placing them crosswise to form a bumpy corduroy road through the swamp. Working with only 12 axes, they had taken care of the worst parts of the road by dawn and had even rebuilt a small bridge.

The entire column was tense after the brief brush with Shelby's scouts. Shortly after Drake had lain down to rest, Maj. Wesley W. Norris, the commander of the 43rd Indiana, woke him to report that he had heard noises and suspected the enemy was near. Drake grumpily assured him no enemy were nearby and told him to go back to sleep. Still, Drake was concerned enough to send cavalry to patrol the roads in front of and behind the column and to ride down side roads for several miles to protect the column against a surprise.

Despite the work done during the night by the pioneers, as work parties were called, crossing the swamp was still a major challenge. At some places the soldiers had to put their shoulders to the wheels and push the wagons through the muck—which was so deep, Drake complained with understandable hyperbole, that only the mules' ears were visible.

As the wagons began to emerge from the mud on the north side of the Moro Bottom, Drake placed the 43rd Indiana at the head of the column with two of Lieutenant Peetz's guns. The 36th Iowa marched alongside the wagon train, while the 77th Ohio, with the other two guns, brought up the rear.

The train had just gotten under way when the soldiers in the lead had a sudden shock: A large column of cavalry was heading directly toward them. But as they saw the stars and stripes carried by the Seventh Missouri Cavalry, arriving from Pine Bluff with 150 men and a mountain howitzer, they heaved a general sigh of relief. The Seventh Missouri brought good news: The road they had just come down was clear all the way to Pine Bluff. They had been accompanied by the Eighteenth Illinois Infantry, which had remained on the north side of the Saline River to assist the wagon train at the crossing.

Norris was still nervous. His scouts told him there were enemy soldiers to his front. He halted his column and ordered his men to build barricades with fence rails.

As they set to work, Drake rode up and demanded, "Why have you halted?"

"There are Rebels to my front," Norris replied.

Drake, still angry at having had his sleep disturbed the night before, cursed Norris and shouted, "There is no enemy in front!"

"Yes, there is," Norris replied. ". . . I have seen them. . . ."

Drake ordered him to "advance your line and feel of the enemy—if there is any in front."

Norris turned his horse over to an aide and ordered his men to advance. They had gone no more than the distance of a city block when they ran into a heavy line of enemy skirmishers.

Drake became a true believer.

He ordered most of the cavalrymen to dismount and join the Indiana infantrymen and sent officers galloping back to alert the 36th Iowa and the 77th Ohio and to order them to hurry forward.

In the woods a short distance ahead, members of the Marks family heard the sounds of impending battle. One of the Marks women took her two small daughters, Fanny and Amelia, with her and hid in the creekbed. But Ella Marks, a teenager, and her cousin remained at home, peeking over the windowsills to see what was going on.

They saw gray-clad soldiers tearing down their fences and using the rails to erect a barricade across the road. Benjamin Floyd Knowles, a Confederate soldier whose home was only a short distance away, was

The Battle of Marks' Mills, April 25, 1864, about 10 A.M. The vanguard of the column headed by Colonel Drake emerged from the Moro bottom. The 43rd Indiana Regiment (1) moved forward and took a position where the Camden–Pine Bluff road crossed the Warren-Fordyce Road. The 36th Iowa Regiment (2) marched alongside the wagon train. The 77th Ohio Regiment (3) was still crossing the Moro bottom. The 43rd Indiana was attacked at the crossroads by Confederate General Cabell (4). Confederate General Dockery (5) stopped to feed his horses while Confederate General Shelby (6) hurried to get ahead of Drake's column. As the Indiana regiment came under attack, one battalion of the 36th Iowa was rushed forward as reinforcements. The other battalion, including Andrew Brayman, lay down on the field to the left of the road as a reserve.

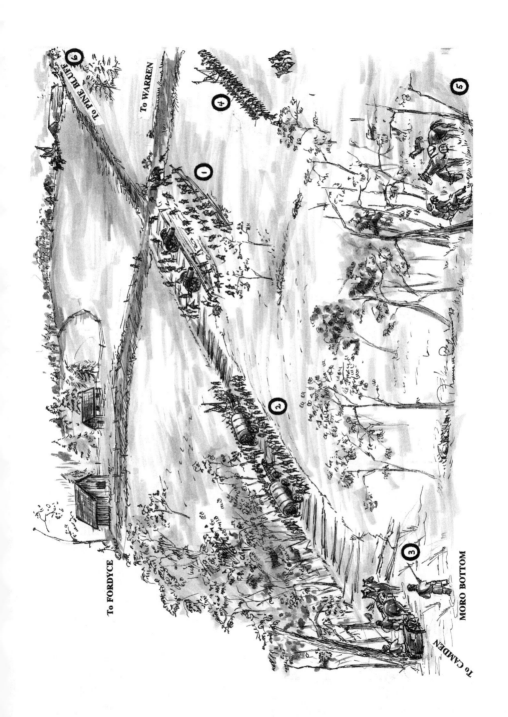

one of the soldiers on the line. As the first Union wagon trundled into view, he leaned his rifle across the wooden barrier, took careful aim, and killed the first mule and then the next, stopping the wagon and blocking the road. Soon the tiny Salty Branch that ran through the area was red with the blood of dead and dying animals.

General Fagan, the Confederate commander, had worked out the details of a set-piece battle that, if everything went well, would give him a quick and decisive victory over the slow-moving Federal wagon train.

General Cabell's troops—the unit of which young William Avera was a part—approached the crossroads near Marks' Mills on the road from Warren, putting him on the flank of Drake's column. Fagan sent Shelby on a long end run to get onto the Camden–Pine Bluff road in front of the Union train. Dockery was assigned to reinforce Cabell and hit the middle of the wagon column. In Fagan's plan, the three pieces of the trap would spring at the same time, dooming Drake.

But at the moment when Norris and his Indianans reached the crossroads, Shelby was still miles away. And Dockery, always independent, had spotted a barn full of feed and had stopped to let his hungry horses eat before joining the battle. Cabell feared that, if the column, now marching on a solid road, managed to pass him by, Drake would make it across the Saline River, only six miles away, before the Confederate forces could catch him. Cabell, cursing loudly, ordered the battle to begin a little after 10 A.M.

It was these first sounds of battle that Avera and his battery mates had heard. He quivered with nervousness, wondering about his chances of being killed or wounded. How sorry his mother and father and sisters would be if he were killed! And what would he do if he lost a leg or an arm?

The Rebel artillerymen were ordered to trot forward to a hill from which they looked down across a broad field. They saw the Yankees marching rapidly along a road about a mile away through what the natives called the Redlands because of the distinctive red color of the earth. The intensity of the musket fire to the front increased, and soon they saw wounded men being carried back to an aid station that had been set up near the artillery battery.

Still no order came to fire. Suddenly a messenger rode up and an officer shouted, in a loud voice, to move out. They trotted down a hill, across a small stream and to the edge of a large plantation in full view of the enemy. They were ordered to prepare the guns for firing and then opened up on the Union line. Avera became so busy listening to the gunner's commands and cutting fuses to the proper length that he forgot all about his fears of being killed or wounded.

A few miles away, on a nearby plantation, Mansfield Robinson, a young slave boy, was catching lambs for his father to shear. He heard the guns and knew there was a battle going on. But he figured there was nothing he could do about it. He went on catching sheep.

As the battle began, Andrew Brayman, along with the entire 36th Iowa, ran forward. Drake quickly divided the regiment into two battalions. One, under the acting regimental commander, Major Hamilton, was thrown into the battle. The other battalion, under Captain Gedney, who had been moved up from his normal spot as commander of Andrew's Company I, was held in reserve. Andrew was part of this reserve unit. The men were ordered to lie down in a field behind the wagon train. Lying down didn't give the nervous soldiers much rest, but it did make them virtually invisible to the enemy.

The veteran Indiana regiment, along with Hamilton's battalion from the 36th Iowa, fought fiercely, several times throwing Cabell's forces back. Losses were heavy on both sides. The artillery pieces were loaded with canister—a cylindrical tin case filled with cast-iron balls arranged in four tiers and packed in sawdust. Fired at a range of 100 to 200 yards, it took a terrible toll. But the Union troops began to believe that they might actually win this encounter. They still had Gedney's battalion in reserve, and the 77th Ohio should arrive anytime, breathless from their dash from the rear of the column.

It was then that the second prong of Fagan's trap snapped into place. Dockery, taking his own time and having fed his horses, galloped onto the scene to reinforce Cabell's embattled soldiers and attack the center of the wagon train. This put the new arrivals between the Ohio regiment and the main battle.

Drake sent orders to the Ohioans to push their way through, using their bayonets as they ran. Just then, a scout rushed up with news that a new column of Rebel cavalry was galloping toward them from the other direction, the road that led toward Pine Bluff. This was Shelby, arriving belatedly after his long end run, as the third prong of the trap.

The battle had now been going on for two and a half hours and it was well after noon. Drake, already in trouble, was about to be hit from both the flank and rear. He sent an aide to order McCauley to attack the oncoming Rebels with his cavalry, but the messenger did not get through. Drake, anxious to blunt Shelby's charge before he cut through the Union ranks, dashed off to deliver the message himself. As he passed across the enemy front, a minié ball caught him in the thigh. Drake kept on riding.

Reining up beside McCauley, he shouted orders to "charge with drawn sabres and a yell and make a letter S through that Rebel line and break it to pieces."

McCauley was startled: "We will obey orders, but there will be none of us left to report."

"You will go through them so rapidly that, in our opinion, you will suffer but slight loss," Drake replied.

McCauley then noticed the blood dripping from Drake's boot and asked, "Are you severely wounded?"

Drake glanced down. "Yes." But then he turned to the matter at hand. Promising to follow McCauley's attack with an infantry charge, he wheeled his horse and galloped away to find Gedney and order him to send his three companies charging against the enemy as soon as McCauley's troopers had disrupted the Confederate formation with his cavalry charge.

As ordered, McCauley's men drew their sabers and cut an S through the enemy line. Drake later reported that their losses were one man dead and a finger shot off McCauley's hand. But there was no follow-up from the infantry. The Rebels kept on coming.

Before Drake could reach Gedney with the vital order, he became so weak from loss of blood that he fell from his horse. Just as he was losing consciousness, he told an aide to have another officer take over command. But in the confusion of battle, that order was not passed on either. Thus, at a critical moment in the battle, the Union forces, each unit in its own part of the battlefield, were left without an overall commander.

This meant that as Shelby fell on the flank of the Union line, Gedney's men bore the full brunt of the attack. The soldiers rose up and fired into the oncoming Rebel units, but they were quickly forced back toward a large house, one of two buildings on the battlefield.

It was in this wild final stage of the battle that Andrew Brayman fell dead with a bullet in his heart.

The Battle of Marks' Mills, April 25, 1864: Scene at 1:30 P.M. *Early in the afternoon, after more than two hours of battle, the two other Rebel units joined the battle. Dockery (1) struck the road between the main battle and the Ohio regiment, preventing the Ohioans from reinforcing the two other Union regiments. Shelby (2) passed the mill buildings (5) and arrived on the scene in a cavalry charge on the flank of the Indiana and Iowa regiments, with the blow falling hardest on the portion of the Iowa regiment held in reserve (3). Remnants of the Union force were pushed back toward the two buildings on the edge of the battlefield (4). It was here that Andrew Brayman was killed. The Union forces, badly outnumbered, were overrun and forced to surrender.*

Soldiers will often fight to the death in support of their comrades. But soldiers also sense the tide of battle and can recognize victory or defeat. Slowly, in isolated units, white handkerchiefs, attached to Union rifles, were waving in surrender even while other units fought on.

Still there was hope for the Union troops. If the veteran Iowa cavalrymen, following along behind the main column, arrived on the scene in time, they might yet turn the tide. The march had been a tough one for the horsemen, who were used to riding rather than walking. About 2 P.M. they reached the bridge that had been built the night before over the creek flowing through the Moro Bottom. As they crossed through the swampy area, they were confronted by a panicky column of camp followers hurrying back toward Camden. They came streaming down the road, some two to a mule. A few stopped long enough to tell the troopers the train had been captured, everyone had been killed, and there were "more than a million Johnnies right behind them."

And then the horseless cavalrymen were in the fight, facing a Rebel line that flanked them on both sides. The Iowa cavalrymen gradually fell back, forming successive defensive lines, until they had passed a crossroads where they feared the enemy troops might get behind them. By then the fighting had tapered off and they camped for the night. The cavalry had indeed arrived—but not in time to change the outcome of the battle.

When Drake fell from his horse, he was carried to a small log cabin and laid on the floor. William Jasper Young, an 18-year-old private in the 36th Iowa, followed him in. He leaned his rifle in a corner and put a white cloth around his arm to signify he was acting as a medic and set to work fetching water and washing the wounds of Drake and the other injured men. As he worked, General Fagan, a tall man in Confederate gray with his hair curling down to his shoulders, strode into the room and asked where Drake was. Young pointed him out.

Fagan pulled off his glove and took Drake's hand.

"I am astonished at the stubborn resistance your men, so inferior in number, have made," he said. "Can you not arrange for their surrender?"

Drake told him he wasn't in command any longer and wasn't aware of the situation. Fagan gripped his hand again and then left. Fagan probably knew the Confederate surgeons had given Drake up as sure to die. Actually, he survived his wound and lived for many years as one of Iowa's most prominent citizens.

———

As the fighting tapered off outside, the victorious Rebels went through the wagons, hoping to find food and other supplies. Avera did find a little to eat—some hardtack, sugar, coffee, and bacon—and had the first full meal he had eaten in several days. A friend also found a box of cigars, and they each got a blanket and some clothing.

The wagon train was slim pickings. After all, the whole purpose of the trip was to obtain supplies from Pine Bluff, not to carry anything there. Perhaps in frustration, the victorious Rebels set fire to a number of the wagons. They also stripped the bodies of the slain Union soldiers. After all, they didn't need trousers or boots anymore. They also stripped some of the wounded, who did need clothing. Lieutenant Pearson of the 36th Iowa described the scene in his diary:

> The rebs robbed nearly every man of us even to our Chaplain & many of our dead they striped of every stitch of clothes even their shirts & socks & left them unburyed & the woods on fire & many of the wounded they jerked of their boots, blouses, pants & hats, & they would plead to have their garments left they would damn them for abolitionists or niger thieves, & they also took from many of the prisoners some of the garments they had on some they took their boots, some blouses, some pants & some hats & they had no respect for persons rank nor age, Old Capt Moss of the 43rd Indiana Infty they took his hat, & marched him bareheaded with his bald head & white beard in the burning sun, there was not an armed negro with us & they shot down our Colored servents & temsters & others what ware following to get from bondage, as they would shoot sheep dogs.

Some of the Southern troops—it was never clear exactly which ones—set upon the blacks accompanying the Union train and began beating and shooting them. One witness later claimed to have seen General Shelby himself beat a Negro with a rifle butt, then pull his pistol and shoot the man.

Shelby's adjutant, Maj. John N. Edwards, recalled after the war: "The battle-field was sickening to behold. No orders, threats, or commands could restrain the men from vengeance on the negroes, and they were piled in great heaps about the wagons, in the tangled brushwood, and upon the muddy and trampled road."

Although no one was ever able to make a precise count, probably a third of the 300 or so unarmed Negroes accompanying the wagon train were killed. Drake said his own black servant was shot and killed.

In this case—unlike Poison Springs, where the killing of blacks was done by the Texans, angry at their earlier defeat by the blacks of the First Kansas regiment, and the Indian soldiers—the killing was done by members of ordinary Southern units. Neither the Texans nor the Indians were present at the battle of Marks' Mills.

As the fighting gradually ceased, the battlefield was a melancholy scene. Lieutenant Pearson was permitted to walk across the area the following day. He recorded what he saw in his diary:

> The dead lay in every imaginable shape over the woods & many of them striped of every stitch of cloths & many of them burnt into a crisp next to the ground as the woods was burnt over, I think the woods took fire from the burning wagons as the Rebs burnt about half of them there are some 60 odd dead horses over the battle ground, & 30 odd dead mules, & the number of Negroes I could not get I saw perhaps near 30, & the Rebs pointed out to me a point of woods where they told me they had killed eighty odd Negroes men, women & children this is their report to me & it may be true & it may not, I did not see it nor was I in that part of the woods, but I fully believe they are hartless enough to do any act that wicked men or devils could conceive, they left our dead on the field until a flag of truce came out from Pine Bluff & burried them some 3 or 4 days after the battle & the negroes are not and never will be buried until the rains wash the sands over their bleached bones.

The battle was a victory of sorts for the Confederates. They had captured a large wagon train—albeit an empty one—and destroyed three Federal regiments. But the Confederates had left Steele's main force intact in Camden and his supply bases at Pine Bluff and Little Rock untouched. The ultimate outcome might have been much more favorable to the Southerners if Fagan had obeyed his orders to raid the warehouses at Pine Bluff and Little Rock and then put his force between Steele and Little Rock while Kirby Smith moved his infantry up to confront Steele at Camden.

An accurate count of the total casualties in the battle was never made. But the losses on both sides were very heavy, making it the bloodiest Civil War battle fought west of the Mississippi.

Of the total of 1,840 men Drake had in the battle, he provided an incomplete list showing 24 killed, 101 wounded, and 991 missing. A few of the soldiers managed to escape, but most of the missing were in fact prisoners, who were marched off to a camp near Tyler, Texas. Records of the 36th Iowa Infantry published after the war listed 32 soldiers killed in action at Marks' Mills with 26 men dying of wounds within a short time after the battle. Another 38 men died of disease while in the prison camp. The regiment, which had been mustered into the Federal service on October 4, 1862, simply ceased to exist as a fighting unit on April 25, 1864.

The force Fagan was able to commit to the battle was reduced by the number assigned as horse-holders—one of every four—and the unit sent to watch the river crossing near Mount Elba. Of the 2,500 soldiers actually involved in the battle, Fagan's incomplete tally of casualties was 108 dead, 272 wounded, and 143 missing, for a total of 523. With more than 20 percent of his force dead, wounded, or missing, it was a terribly costly victory.

No record remains of how or when Andrew Brayman's family was notified of his death. During the Civil War there was no formal system for reporting soldiers' deaths. In most cases that responsibility fell to the man's company commander, who wrote a letter in which he typically praised the soldier's courage and patriotism, assured the family that the dead man was now at peace with the Lord, and offered his condolences. After the defeat at Marks' Mills, however, it is unlikely that Captain Gedney, the commander of Andrew's company, who was taken prisoner, found the opportunity to write such a letter.

Accounts of the disaster that had befallen the 36th Iowa appeared in Iowa newspapers shortly after the battle, but they provided no lists of casualties. The Brayman family must have spent many anxious days worrying about the fate of their son and brother. Their concern was shared with many neighboring families, since Company I had been recruited in Appanoose County and the rest of the regiment had come from nearby counties. The Brayman family's worst fears would have been confirmed only if a soldier wounded in the battle returned home or a letter brought word of Andrew's death.

His family was probably told that Andrew died instantly of a bullet through the heart—at least that is what his service record indicates. But is that the truth, or was it simply an attempt to comfort the family with the thought that he had not died a lingering death on the battlefield?

An effort was made after the war to locate the bodies of the Union dead and move them to the national cemetery in Little Rock or to cemeteries near their homes. But the body of Andrew Brayman was never found. His family later erected an obelisk in the Miller cemetery, in a rural area near their home in Bellair (now Numa) Iowa. On the east side is this inscription:

> Andrew J., son of L. and M. Brayman, killed in the battle
> of Mark's Mills, Ark., Apr. 25, 1864, aged 18 years, 10 months,
> 17 days, of Co. I, 36th Regt. Iowa Volunteer Infantry.

Below the inscription is this verse, written by his mother, Mary Brayman:

HE GAVE HIS LIFE
HIS COUNTRY TO SAVE
BUT HIS BODY RESTS
IN AN UNKNOWN GRAVE

Chapter Sixteen

Escape from Camden

About midnight on the night of April 26, the day after the battle at Marks' Mills, the mockingbirds began to sing in the tall trees along Camden's Washington Street for the first time since the noisy Yankees had arrived ten days before. Several women along the street awakened and listened to the sweet song, thinking perhaps it was a good omen.

When Virginia Stinson looked out her window the next morning, she later recalled, "not a Bluecoat was in our town. They had silently folded their tents, wrapped the wheels of their wagons with cotton and left town without noise. It was daylight when the last wagon left. Camden looked like a deserted town—no noise or Yankees about. Oh! what a relief it was to be free of them."

Almost as soon as the first messenger arrived with the dreadful news of the disaster at Marks' Mills on the evening of April 25, Steele convened a council of war of his senior officers. Their men and animals were starving, the victorious enemy cavalry stood between them and fresh supplies from either Little Rock or Pine Bluff, and three divisions of infantry were marching toward them from Louisiana.

All but one officer voted for an immediate retreat to Little Rock. The holdout agreed they should abandon Camden but thought they should try to hold a position east of the Ouachita River and then guard the river carefully to prevent the enemy infantry from crossing. Steele ordered immediate preparations for the retreat to Little Rock.

Residents of Camden sensed that something was up and departure by the Yankees seemed likely, but it was not clear to them just what was happening. The city was sealed to prevent any of the civilians from slipping out to warn the Rebel commanders of what looked like preparations for a retreat.

Mrs. Stinson's servant, Aunt Sallie, was put to work cooking food for the soldiers to take with them. At about nightfall the Yankees began shooting every chicken they could find and adding them to Aunt Sallie's pot. Of Mrs. Stinson's own flock, they missed only one old sitting hen.

Any Confederate soldiers lurking in the darkness beyond the city's perimeter would have been confused by what they heard. Along the picket lines teams of Union men were noisily at work with picks and shovels strengthening the city's defenses. At 8 P.M. the drums loudly beat out tattoo—the familiar signal for troops to return to their quarters for the night. An hour later a deep bass drum sounded taps, the lights-out signal. All these activities were deliberately intended to mislead the enemy.

Far from turning in, the Union soldiers labored through the night, moving wagons across a 100-foot-long pontoon bridge over the Ouachita. Meager rations were distributed to the troops for their long march. Goods they couldn't carry were destroyed. Leftover harness was thrown into the river. Finally, the troops themselves marched across to the other side, one cavalry unit remaining behind to protect the residents against threats voiced by some of the soldiers that they would burn the city as they left.

By dawn on April 27, the last of Steele's army was across the river, and his engineers set to work tearing up the pontoon bridge and packing it on wagons to be used in crossing the Saline River, which lay across their route to the north.

At 9 A.M. the first Confederate soldiers ventured into the quiet, peaceful city and found not only that the enemy was gone but that he had taken his bridge with him, stranding them on the west side of the river. General Kirby Smith rode into town a short time later and set up his headquarters under the tall oak trees in Mrs. Stinson's large front yard. With the returning Rebels came her husband, who had lost an eye at Shiloh and had fled when Steele's army approached.

Kirby Smith had reason to be elated. Steele's long train of troops and wagons was barely out of earshot. Up ahead of the Union column somewhere were General Fagan's horsemen, the victors at Marks' Mills. Rapidly moving up from the south were the infantry divisions from Louisiana. The chances of catching Steele and defeating and capturing his army before he could cross the Saline to relative safety seemed remarkably good.

But first the Confederates would have to cross the Ouachita. Their own pontoon bridge was somewhere between Camden and Shreveport, so Kirby Smith set his troops to work constructing a bizarre makeshift bridge. While some of the soldiers cut trees and fashioned the logs into large rafts, another soldier swam the cold river with a line that was then used to pull a heavy hawser across the stream. The rafts were then floated out and tied to the rope end to end, making a barely usable floating bridge on which the men could cross the river at a trot. If they hesitated, the raft underfoot would sink beneath the surface.

It was at about this time that Kirby Smith made the first of a series of almost inexplicable errors. He called in General Maxey, whose Texan and Choctaw mounted regiments had done such terrible work at Poison Springs, and told them they could go on back to Indian Territory rather than accompany him in his race to catch Steele. He may have sensed that these notably independent-minded soldiers were about to head home anyway, regardless of his orders.

By the time the Confederate forces had made their way across their rickety bridge, assembled on the east bank of the river, and prepared to pick up the pursuit on the morning of April 28, they were not just a few hours but more than a day behind Steele. If they hurried, they could still catch up. Kirby Smith assumed, of course, that Fagan was where he should be, between Steele and his goal. But there was no communication between the two generals. Kirby Smith didn't really know where Fagan was, and Fagan didn't know that Steele had left Camden with the Rebel infantry in pursuit.

After the victory at Marks' Mills, Shelby, one of the war's most effective cavalrymen, urged Fagan to block the roads linking Camden with Little Rock, knowing intuitively that Steele would be heading in that direction. But Fagan, who was new to the cavalry, headed blithely off to the other side of central Arkansas, to the vicinity of Arkadelphia, looking for food for his men and animals and intending to follow, belatedly, his orders to attack the supply depots along the Arkansas River.

As Steele's men set out on their hurried march north, the weather was sunny and warm—so warm, in fact, that they quickly lightened their loads by throwing aside pieces of clothing, blankets, and other goods they thought they could do without. On the night of the twenty-seventh, they camped about 18 miles north of Camden and then rose early the next morning to resume their march. That night the vanguard of the Rebel force used the same campground, while the Federals camped near the small town of Princeton.

At 4 o'clock on the morning of April 29, Steele's army was again on the march. They expected to reach the Saline River and even get some units across before dark. Again, the skies were clear and the mood was good—except for the hunger that plagued both men and animals. The countryside had been scoured clean and the soldiers had only the meager rations they had drawn before leaving Camden— quarter rations or less.

And then, about noon, things began to go wrong. The skies had been clouding up as the morning wore on, and the first drops of rain fell at noon, gradually intensifying into a steady downpour. And at about the same time, the Confederate cavalry caught up with the army's rear guard and began harassing attacks that forced the Union soldiers to stop and go into battle formation. That night the cold, wet, miserable Bluecoats camped in the lowlands along the Saline River, their wet woolen uniforms giving off an inescapable sour odor.

When the Confederate forces, led by Generals Kirby Smith and Price, stopped for the night, their most advanced units were only nine miles back. But others were spread out for many miles behind them. The Confederate troops were just as uncomfortable as the Union men but even hungrier. Some of them tore down rail fences to make rough beds of wood—not very comfortable but enough to keep them up out of the water.

Steele had his men up well before dawn, pushing the wagon train across the pontoon bridge over the Saline as fast as possible. That was not very fast. The approaches to the bridge had become part of the river, and under the water, a foot or two deep, lay almost bottomless mud. Mules were double-teamed to pull the wagons toward the bridge. When that didn't work, long ropes were strung out and men added their brawn to the battle against the mud. To lighten the loads, army goods of all sorts—except ammunition, of course—were simply cast aside. When the wagons remained stuck, engineers broke out their spokes with sledgehammers and abandoned them.

As part of Steele's army labored to move the wagon train to safety, the rest took up defensive positions guarding the crossing point, known as Jenkins Ferry. Among the defenders were one officer and 60 enlisted men of the 36th Iowa, men who had been left behind when their outfit departed from Camden on its ill-fated mission. They were now all that remained of the regiment.

The Confederate onslaught was not long in coming. But here General Kirby Smith made his second mistake. Throughout the morning he fed his troops piecemeal into the center of the Federal line, where one after the other they were cut up and sent reeling back. Perhaps the soggy terrain made a successful attack on Steele's flanks impossible, but little effort was made to get around the sides of the Union army and avoid the Federal meat grinder.

The rain continued to pour down, cutting visibility. At one point Rebel soldiers spotted the shapes of what appeared to be Union soldiers on their flank and fired a heavy barrage with their muskets, only to learn a few minutes later that the "enemy" was a line of dead trees.

For the wounded, the watery battlefield posed a terrifying danger. If an injured man lost consciousness, he would slide down beneath the surface and drown. Badly injured men dragged themselves painfully to the nearest high spot, trying with their last bit of strength to keep their heads above water.

Aside from the water, which made life miserable for both sides, the battle was unusual in two other respects. Unlike most Civil War battles, cavalry played little role on either side. Fagan's Rebel cavalry force did not arrive until the fighting was over, while Steele had sent the bulk of his cavalry across the river to clear the road to Little Rock. Lacking the mobility provided by cavalry, the Confederate side had a particular problem, because it made any attempt to flank the enemy more difficult.

The battle was also unusual in that neither side was able to use its artillery effectively. Every time a section of artillery moved into position and got off a round or two, the recoil pushed the guns so deeply into the mud that they couldn't be aimed for another barrage.

Artillery did, however, play a role in one doleful episode.

The Second Kansas Colored Infantry, the unit whose officers had sworn after the massacre at Poison Springs "to take no prisoners," held a key part of the Union front, fighting bravely and effectively for hours. But in the early afternoon Colonel Crawford, the unit's commander, saw the Confederates bringing up two cannons only a short distance across a small creek from his troops. Fearful of the effect cannon fire might have on his men after all they had gone through in the morning's fighting, he asked for and got permission to charge the battery.

Lt. John O. Lockhart was just getting his two six-pounders into position to fire when he saw the black troops and white soldiers of the 29th Iowa swarming across the creek in a fierce bayonet charge. Without infantry support to meet such a determined attack, Lockhart surrendered.

The black troops, whose officers had told them of their oath to give no quarter, swarmed over the artillery position, shouting, "Poison Springs!" and bayoneted to death three of the soldiers whose hands were raised in surrender. The Iowans were able to save the lives of Lockhart and his remaining five men and take them prisoner.

By midafternoon the firing gradually tapered off. A rear guard of Union troops held a perimeter on the south side of the river, while the remainder of the wagon train and the rest of Steele's army crossed to the relative safety of the north side.

Many Union, as well as Confederate, wounded still lay on the soggy battlefield. Several units, including the Second Kansas, were detailed to round up as many of the Federal wounded as possible and help them cross the pontoon bridge before it was torn up. It was then that the men of the Second Kansas exacted a bloody revenge for the massacre of their sister regiment at Poison Springs.

As the Negroes went over the battlefield looking for Union wounded, they killed a number of helpless enemy soldiers. One of the soldiers in the 29th Iowa wrote home a few days after the battle: "The negroes want to kill every wounded reb they come to and will do it if we did not watch them. . . . One of our boys seen a little negro pounding a wounded reb in the head with the but of his gun and asked him what he was doing. the negro replied he is not dead yet! I tell you they won't give them up as long as they can kick if they can just have their way about it."

One Rebel soldier who managed to hobble away before they could reach him was Private John H. Lewis of the 18th Texas Infantry. "After awhile," he later recalled, "the firing ceased and our army was gone. Soon I looked around and saw some black negroes cutting our wounded boys' throats, and I thought my time would come next."

Other Confederates, arriving on the battlefield after the Federals had completed their withdrawal across the river, found evidence of the same thing. David S. Williams, senior surgeon in the 33rd Arkansas

Infantry, reported: "We found that many of our wounded had been mutilated in many ways. Some with ears cut off, throats cut, knife stabs, etc. My brother [acting Sergeant Major A. J. Williams] . . . was shot through the body, had his throat cut through the windpipe and lived several days. I saw several others who were treated in the same way."

Although the killing of prisoners by the Negro soldiers was widely known in Steele's army, no action was taken against them. In fact, several officers, in their after-action reports, went out of their way to praise the performance of the black soldiers. One officer said, "Particular praise is given to Kansas colored troops for their stubborn valor," and Steele himself wrote, "The conduct of the colored troops in my command proves that the African can be made as formidable in battle as a soldier of any other color."

With horses and mules dropping from hunger and exhaustion, Steele destroyed a good part of the wagon train he had worked so hard to preserve. He then marched safely to Little Rock, arriving back there on May 3 after five very long and unpleasant weeks. Food was so short on that last march that officers didn't even bother to halt the men at mealtimes. One soldier paid $2—a good part of his $13 monthly pay—for a single piece of hardtack. Another bought two pieces of the hard bread with a silver watch.

The Battle of Jenkins Ferry had clearly been a victory for Steele. He had beaten an enemy superior in numbers, and he had managed to extricate the bulk of his army—or what was left after the disasters at Poison Springs and Marks' Mills—from a very dangerous predicament.

At Jenkins Ferry the Confederate forces that were actually involved in the battle numbered about 6,000 men. Of these, 800 to 1,000 were killed or wounded. Steele, part of whose force was already across the river, had had about 4,000 in the battle. Of these, he lost about 700 killed, wounded, and missing, although a full official accounting was never made.

In the entire march to Camden and back, Steele suffered about 2,750 casualties and lost 635 wagons and 2,500 mules. He also lost General Rice, who, until he was severely wounded in the foot, was the actual battlefield commander at Jenkins Ferry. His injured foot was amputated, but he sickened and died of infection on August 8. The Rebel forces lost about 2,300 men, including a number of their most capable officers.

Steele's ill-conceived expedition—which, in fairness, he had resisted up to the moment he received explicit orders from General Grant—ended with him and his weakened army back where they had started, defending the line of the Arkansas River and trying to hold down the depredations of guerrilla bands north of the river.

Many of the men Steele had taken south with him lay dead—Andrew Brayman among them—and hundreds more, including the bulk of the 36th Iowa, had been marched off to suffer in a rough prison camp near Tyler, Texas.

Down in Louisiana, Porter had finally extricated most of his fleet from the Red River, and Banks had gotten what remained of his army back to New Orleans. A number of the cotton speculators had made their fortunes. But if Lincoln had hoped the Red River expedition would improve the political climate in Louisiana, the result was just the opposite. For miles on either side of the line of march, Banks's army had ravaged the country, taking food, stealing cotton, burning homes, barns, and entire cities.

The Rebels were still free to roam over much of Louisiana, Texas, and southern Arkansas—not that it made much difference. With the Union navy in control of the Mississippi, the Confederates west of the river were isolated, and nothing they could do would influence the outcome of the war—which was just as true before the foray up the Red River as it was afterward.

As far as the Union forces were concerned, the worst loss was Gen. A. J. Smith's 10,000-man force, which was stranded in Louisiana. This was an experienced force that Sherman needed and had counted on for his advance southward through Georgia. But Smith was ordered to remain in Louisiana long enough to protect Porter's priceless fleet. Thus, when the scene shifted back where attention should have been all along—on the great offensive—Sherman was short by thousands of troops he should have had.

Can anyone be held responsible for this harebrained expedition that cost the lives of Andrew Brayman and so many other simple farm boys—and the lives, too, of irreplaceable combat commanders—on both sides? Certainly Abraham Lincoln must share a part of the blame for permitting the greed of his cotton speculator friends and his own political interests to overrule sound military judgment.

General Halleck, as the top Union commander during the planning for the expedition, knew from his own military experience that the Red River expedition was the wrong thing to do, but he, too, let political considerations overshadow his military judgment.

General Sherman, who had already come to the sound conclusion that what happened west of the Mississippi was irrelevant to the outcome of the war, let his impatience and thirst for action overcome his otherwise sound military judgment.

General Banks, of course, must carry a major share of the blame for not recognizing his own military incompetence or insisting that someone more capable be selected to head the expedition.

General Grant is the one senior officer who comes off fairly well in this whole sorry affair. He recognized Banks's weakness as a commander and tried hard to have him replaced. He opposed the Red River expedition and instead insisted on using the forces available to seize Mobile. After he became the top Union commander, he gave his approval only when the expedition was already under way—and then he ordered that it be pursued vigorously.

The troops who marched forth from Little Rock, Fort Smith, and New Orleans and the Confederate forces who opposed them probably had little concept of how they fit into the broad panorama of the war. Many of them must have sensed, of course, the futility of some of the things they were asked to do—to march more than 200 miles from Little Rock to Shreveport without enough food for themselves or their animals, for example. One can only admire the bravery of Andrew Brayman and the other private soldiers who persevered through hardship and the blunders of leadership to carry out their duty and even to die, abandoned in unmarked graves, far from home.

When the remnants of Steele's army marched into Little Rock on May 3, the two great offensives designed to end the war were beginning in both the Eastern and Western Theaters. The Eighth Iowa Cavalry and Barney Brayman had been busy preparing for their part in the western offensive as General Sherman assembled his vast army in southern Tennessee in the spring of 1864.

Part Four

South Toward Atlanta— and Hell

PAGE 184: *Barney Brayman and unknown girl. This photo, apparently taken after the war, poses a mystery. The young woman is either too old or too young to be one of Barney's sisters. She wears a wedding ring, but there is no record that Barney ever married.* (Authors' collection.)

Chapter Seventeen

Offensive
in Georgia

When Barney Brayman and the Eighth Iowa Cavalry arrived in Nashville on March 13 after their winter chasing guerrillas in the western Tennessee wilderness, the troopers were hardly a credit to a great army. Their uniforms, issued five months before, were in tatters. Their shoddy blankets were threadbare rags. Many of their horses were worn out. The first order of business was to line up to draw new clothing, trade in their big bell tents for individual pup tents, and sign for 150 new horses.

The substandard uniforms they had been issued back in Davenport had used up a year's worth of their $3.50-a-month clothing allowance. By the time they were ready to leave Nashville with new uniforms, they were all solidly in debt to the government. Serving in the army was like trading at the company store—soldiers became another day older and deeper in debt.

Their march south from Nashville to Chattanooga, beginning on April 1, was one part military tourism and another part sobering reminder of what might lie ahead.

On their second night, they camped at the site of the Battle of Stones River, near the town of Murfreesboro, Tennessee. There, from December 31, 1862, to January 3, 1863, two large armies had fought. Together they had lost a total of nearly 25,000 men killed, wounded, and missing. Of the casualties, nearly 3,000 were dead.

The Iowans walked somberly among the long rows of headboards marking the graves of boys just like themselves. "I looked to our right," a member of the Eighth Cavalry wrote, "and could almost see that avalanche of Confederates that poured out of those swamps upon our surprised comrades, on that awful day about one year ago."

Their route took them on down over the Cumberland Mountains into northern Alabama. Crossing the mountains with their fourteen baggage wagons was one of the most difficult challenges they had faced. In some places as many as fifty men lined up to pull a wagon up a particularly steep, rocky part of the road.

At Bridgeport, Alabama, they crossed the Tennessee River on a long pontoon bridge—the first they had ever seen—and then marched east toward Chattanooga. At one point their route led through a mile-long section of the road that had been cut out of the mountainside, with Lookout Mountain on the right and the Tennessee River on the left. The narrow road was littered with the carcasses of horses and mules that had been left where they fell and then were ground into the mud by passing wagons and artillery. The soldiers called it "the valley of death" and were thankful the weather was not hotter and the stench worse.

That night they camped south of Chattanooga near Orchard Knob, a short distance from the foot of Missionary Ridge. It was on Orchard Knob that Grant had stood on November 25, 1863, only five months earlier, and watched as the 20,000 men of the Army of the Cumberland assaulted the foot of the sheer 500-foot-high ridge. The Army of the Cumberland had not done well in previous battles, so Grant had assigned them the relatively minor role of making a limited attack against the center of the enemy lines while two other armies were to do the major work of crushing the Confederate flanks. The Cumberland soldiers managed to drive the Rebels from their trench line at the foot of the ridge—and that was all they were supposed to do.

But as Grant watched in amazement—and some consternation—the soldiers rose up spontaneously, without orders, and charged up Missionary Ridge. Some of their confused officers took the lead, urging them on. Others shouted for them to stop and were ignored. The cliff was so steep that the Confederate artillery could not be lowered enough to fire on the cheering Bluecoats, and musket fire barely slowed them down. The veteran Confederate troops, looking down from their sturdy fortifications, saw the bayonets gleaming in the sun and battle flags flying as the Union horde came inexorably on. Suddenly the Confederate line broke and the defenders scrambled to the rear. Within minutes the Army of the Cumberland held the crest of the ridge, and the Confederate threat to Chattanooga was over.

As soon as they made camp, the men of the Eighth Iowa set out to explore the battlefield. They climbed the hill to the Confederate command post and looked down, finding it hard to understand how the Union forces had been able to storm such a seemingly invincible position. They found the slope of the ridge covered with the litter of war—broken guns, bits of clothing, and, of course, graves everywhere.

The Union practice was to bury the enemy dead where they fell. The Iowans saw hundreds of shallow graves along the Rebel lines at the foot of the ridge. In some cases a body had merely been rolled against a log, with some soil shoveled over it. In many places the deteriorating bodies were exposed to view.

The regiment remained only a few days near Chattanooga—not long enough to visit the nearby battlefield at Chickamauga. There, on September 19 and 20 of the previous year, two great armies had fought one of the bloodiest battles of the Civil War, with combined casualties—dead, wounded, and missing—totaling nearly 35,000 men. The battle had ended in victory for the South—but an overcautious Confederate general had failed to follow up his advantage and take Chattanooga.

From Chattanooga, the Eighth Iowa marched through pine forests over a range of mountains—much larger than any in their native Iowa—and traveled about 30 miles to the town of Cleveland, Tennessee, arriving there on April 13. It was a long march, but Colonel Dorr was a vigorous, energetic commander who believed in working his men and animals hard to get them ready for the combat that lay just ahead.

Even though they walked their horses both up and down the hills, however, some of the veteran noncommissioned officers in the regiment had begun to worry about the condition of their horses. One veteran sergeant forcefully predicted that half the regiment would be dismounted in less than a month if the regiment were "kept going helity scoot over the country when there is no occasion for it." He noted that the veteran cavalrymen in the First Tennessee, the Second Michigan Cavalry, and the Fourth Kentucky Mounted Infantry, with which the Eighth Iowa was joined to form a brigade, took it much easier on their animals, never riding their horses faster than a walk unless there was some good reason for a fast march.

It was twelve days after the Eighth Iowa arrived in Cleveland that Andrew Brayman was killed in the Battle of Marks' Mills. There is no record of how or when Barney learned of his big brother's death.

Barney probably was informed of Andrew's death very shortly after his family learned the bad news. During the Civil War news traveled remarkably fast. Urgent messages went by telegraph, which linked the larger cities and military headquarters. Mail flowed regularly up and down the rivers, and families at home often knew more about where their soldiers were and what they were doing than those at home did during World War II, when censorship prevented men from telling their families where they were.

Officers made frequent recruiting trips back home and brought news of the men in their units. Sutlers—merchants who attached themselves to a military unit—shuttled back and forth between the army camps and sources of supplies back home. They often carried money from the soldiers to their families and returned with packages of delicacies prepared by mothers and sisters.

According to his service record, Barney didn't even receive a brief furlough to return home to comfort his parents and his sisters after Andrew's death. One can only imagine his somber thoughts as he went about his duties in camp as his regiment prepared to march south into what promised to be some of the heaviest fighting of the war.

Despite their months chasing guerrillas west of Nashville—"playing war," as they later admitted—the Iowans were still considered "fresh fish" by the veterans in their neighboring regiments. They gave away their lack of experience in myriad little ways. When they passed another regiment, they always asked which regiment it was; veterans knew without asking. The veterans had a been-there-done-that look about them, reflected in the casual way they personalized their uniforms. Even General Sherman wore an old slouch hat and had only a couple of small stars on the shoulders of his common soldier's blouse.

But green as the Iowans may have been, they still had a pretty good idea of where they were and what they were expected to do. Their march into position at Cleveland had taken them across almost the entire front of the Union army, which stretched west from Cleveland some 150 miles to Decatur, Alabama, with the center at Chattanooga. This put the Eighth Cavalry on the far left or eastern flank of Sherman's vast army.

If the Iowans could have flown over that area of northern Georgia, just across the border to their south, they would have seen a distinctive

series of steep rocky ridges, running generally north and south, sepa-
rated by broad, fertile valleys. The ridges range in height from 655 to
820 feet.

As it was, looking south from Cleveland, they could see that they
were to the east of the last rocky outcrop of the ridge and valley system.
It was behind this ridge—known as Rocky Ridge—that the Confederate army had taken up its defensive position in the little town of Dalton, Georgia. The Eighth Cavalry was thus not only on the left flank of
Sherman's army but also in a position to threaten the right flank of the
enemy army.

Union officers who had known him at West Point and served with
him in the U.S. Army respected—perhaps even feared—the Confederate commander, Lt. Gen. Joseph E. Johnston. When Johnston took
over the Army of Tennessee (not to be confused with the Union Army
of the Tennessee; the Confederates named their armies for states, the
Union for rivers) a few months earlier, in December 1863, it had been
a badly demoralized force, plagued by desertions and short on every
kind of equipment. Johnston had spent the bitter winter of 1863–64
building up the army, restoring both its morale and its equipment.

His army's headquarters in Dalton stood in an almost impregnable
position behind Rocky Ridge. Some called it the "Confederate Gibraltar." Dalton could be approached from the west—where Sherman's
strength was centered—only through three narrow, easily defended
gaps in the ridge. It could also be approached from the north, from
Cleveland, where the Eighth Cavalry was stationed. But that approach,
too, offered the Confederates a series of strong defensive positions—
and to attack from that direction would require Sherman to shift the
center of balance of his whole vast army to the east.

As spring finally brought an end to winter, Johnston had under his
command a force of nearly 64,000 men, of whom 44,000 were considered "effectives"—men available to fight. He also had 144 cannons.
One of his greatest strengths was his cavalry, which had been assembled
in a corps under Brig. Gen. Joseph Wheeler. But many of Wheeler's
men had recently gone home to get new horses, following the Southern
practice in which cavalrymen provided their own mounts. This left
Wheeler with only 2,400 men as spring began, although his force would
gradually become stronger as his troopers returned to the ranks.

Perhaps Johnston's greatest handicap was his relationship with

President Jefferson Davis. The two men loathed each other, and Davis had put Johnston in charge of the Army of Tennessee only with great reluctance, because no one else was available. Johnston, a Virginia aristocrat, looked down on Davis, who was from Mississippi, as an uncouth westerner. Davis, overestimating the strength of Johnston's force, wanted him to take the offensive, to capture Chattanooga. Members of Johnston's staff speculated that Davis hated Johnston so much that he wanted him to go on the offensive and fail, even though such a failure would cost the South dearly.

Johnston proposed making an advance into western Tennessee that would at least disrupt Sherman's move to the south while avoiding the bloodletting that would be involved in an assault on Chattanooga. But the two men couldn't agree, so Johnston's army simply stayed in its fortress and waited.

On April 19 Johnston held a grand review of the Army of Tennessee on a parade ground in Dalton. Hundreds of ladies joined the general in the reviewing stand as some 40,000 men—all except those who couldn't be spared from their duties—marched in review. One of Johnston's officers, watching the men parade by to the cadence set by brass bands and the fife and drum corps, pronounced the army in the best condition he had ever seen.

Sherman, who was preparing for the spring offensive, had a much larger army than Johnston's, outnumbering him by more than two to one. He had 110,000 troops, of whom 99,000 were available to take part in the offensive. Even after trimming the size of his artillery force to make it more mobile, he still had 254 cannons, far more than Johnston.

To support and move his vast army, Sherman had 25,000 noncombatants and 5,150 wagons and 860 ambulances pulled by 32,600 mules and 12,000 horses—even after ruthlessly trimming his baggage train. Setting an example, he didn't even carry tents for himself and his staff.

Trailing along behind the army would be a vast herd of cattle. Each evening a number of them would be slaughtered and the meat passed out to the soldiers. The carcasses would be left by the side of the road to rot. With the abandoned carcasses, the offal of men and animals, and the sweat of a hundred thousand men in woolen uniforms, the stench given off by a Civil War army on the move was hard to imagine.

On paper, Sherman's cavalry arm was also much stronger than Johnston's. He had 6,000 horsemen, and another 6,000 were being outfitted and trained. But instead of concentrating his cavalry in a sin-

Lt. Gen. Joseph E. Johnston, CSA. (Library of Congress, Washington, D.C.)

gle corps under a single competent commander, as the Confederates did, Sherman had his cavalry in one corps of three divisions with a separate division under another commander. Barney's regiment was part of the corps. None of Sherman's cavalry commanders came close to matching the Confederates' Wheeler, and at least one of them was just plain incompetent. Sherman tried to make up for this defect by commanding the cavalry himself, but his own experience with horsemen was limited and his communications with the cavalry were poor.

Numbers alone do not accurately reflect the balance between the Union and Confederate forces. While Johnston remained in Dalton, he had the distinct advantage of fighting on the defense, which—at least in textbook terms—requires only a third as many troops as are needed for a successful offensive attack. And if Johnston did have to leave Dalton and retreat toward Atlanta, he would tend to grow stronger as he fell back and his supply lines became shorter, while Sherman would grow weaker as he moved farther and farther from his base of supplies.

Sherman and Grant had worked out their strategy for the spring offensive in their meeting at the Burnet House in Cincinnati back in March: They would both move south at the same time, in a bold effort to destroy, as quickly as possible, the South's ability, or willingness, to fight.

But Sherman seems to have been uncertain in his own mind just what his real goal was. Was it the minimal goal of keeping Johnston so busy that he couldn't send reinforcements to help Lee in his battles against Grant? Was it to destroy Johnston's army? Or was it to capture Atlanta, the South's vital communications and manufacturing center, even if Johnston's army remained in the field? In messages he wrote during the campaign and in reflections afterward, Sherman seems to have thought of each of these, at various times, as his goal.

Sherman's first problem, of course, was somehow to lure or force Johnston out of Dalton. To do so, in the first few days of May 1864, he set his vast army in motion in such a way that it would appear to Johnston to be threatening to attack him directly against Rocky Ridge and also down from Cleveland on Johnston's flank. As Sherman's troops assembled at the base of Rocky Ridge, soldiers on both sides were impressed.

The Union men looked almost straight up the rocky cliff. Hardly a tree remained standing—the Confederates had had plenty of time to cut them. Those they did not need in order to build redoubts for their artillery or to protect their trenches were felled and laid with their sharpened tops pointing downhill. To get at the defenders, the Bluecoats would have to not only climb over the boulders that dotted the hillside but also hack their way through the branches of the big pine trees. The broadest gap through the ridge—where Interstate 75 now runs—had been flooded, and the crests on both sides were heavily fortified.

Looking down from the fighting holes they had dug into the face of the cliff, the Rebel soldiers, who were always hungrier and less well clothed than the opposition, watched in admiration as the Union forces massed on the valley floor with their colors snapping in the breeze and the sun glinting off their weapons. The familiar patriotic tunes and the sight of Old Glory brought a lump to the throats of the Southern soldiers, many of whom were reluctant conscripts in the Confederate army.

As the bulk of Sherman's army massed at the foot of Rocky Ridge, Barney Brayman's unit, the Eighth Iowa, more than 40 miles away in Cleveland, mounted and began the march south in a column of fours. As they left Cleveland on May 3, they had a sweeping view over the pine-covered hills and valleys descending to the south. But the view was soon cut off as they moved downhill through the trees, paralleling the railroad from Cleveland to Dalton and generally following the route of today's Tennessee Route 60, which becomes Georgia Route 71 when it crosses the border at the tiny community of Red Clay.

Brig. Gen. Edward Moody McCook, pictured after his promotion to major general. (Library of Congress, Washington, D.C.)

The combined force of infantry, cavalry, and artillery moving south from Cleveland numbered some 10,000 men—only ten percent of Sherman's army but enough to leave the Confederate defenders unsure where the greatest danger lay. The Eighth Cavalry, which had remained in good health through the winter and had arrived at the front too late to take part in the bloody battles of the fall and winter, was one of the largest regiments in Sherman's army, with more than a thousand men. Many of the veteran regiments had been whittled down by sickness and battlefield casualties to a strength of only 300 to 500 men.

In Cleveland the Iowans met the man who was to be their commander for better—and eventually for worse—throughout the march through Georgia. They were assigned to a division headed by Edward Moody McCook, a 30-year-old lawyer and politician from the Pikes Peak region of what was then the Kansas Territory. McCook, who had joined the army as a lieutenant in May 1861, had been promoted rapidly, pinning on his one star as a brigadier general on April 17, 1864. He was the commander of one of the three divisions in the cavalry corps.

Lt. Col. Horatio G. Barner, acting commander of the Eighth Iowa Volunteer Cavalry during the march toward Atlanta. (State Historical Society of Iowa Library/Archives, Des Moines.)

With McCook's promotion, Colonel Dorr, the commander of the Eighth Cavalry, was moved up to command the First Brigade of McCook's division. The assistant regimental commander, Lt. Col. Horatio G. Barner, a 44-year-old Davenport man who had served earlier as a lieutenant and quartermaster of an Iowa infantry regiment, took over as the regimental commander.

As the column moved south, cavalry patrols rode out in front, looking for any sign of the enemy. During the first few days, they encountered little opposition. Then, on May 7—the day the bulk of Sherman's army began its offensive a few miles away on the other side of Rocky Ridge—they ran into their first serious opposition as they approached a tiny railroad stop known as Varnell's Station.

At this point the men marching south were entering Crow Valley, which stretched south toward Dalton. The "valley" is actually a series of vaguely connected valleys divided by low hills that are ideal for defensive positions. Johnston, the Confederate commander, fearing that Dalton would be attacked from this direction, had constructed a series of strongpoints across the valley. During the upcoming battle he would even spend a full day touring those positions, looking for signs that this would be Sherman's main line of attack. The Eighth Iowa, although it was on the fringes of the Union army, was thus marching into the area where the enemy commander had stationed much of his defensive force.

The Rebels gave up the village itself but held on to a strongly fortified position on a hill to the left of the railroad. Looking up, the Iowans could see the enemy soldiers pulling some kind of cart or wheeled vehicle up the hill. They didn't realize that it was a cannon being moved into position until they saw the smoke and heard a shell screaming toward them.

"I had heard cannons fired before," one cavalryman later recalled, "but I never realized how much louder a cannon shot sounded when the gun was aimed towards me."

In the skirmishing near Varnell's Station, several horses were killed and the Eighth Cavalry suffered its first battlefield casualties. George Allman was shot in the leg and died two months later of gangrene. Eli Rowley was shot in the arm and was discharged from the army.

As the Iowans moved south and saw more of the enemy, they lost much of their respect for the enemy artillery. Many of the Confederate guns were heavier than the Union guns and thus more difficult to move into position and aim. The Rebels also had trouble hitting their targets. Because of low-grade powder, their shells often wobbled in flight and then failed to explode. They even sounded different from the Union guns, making a tremulous ringing noise. The Federal guns, which had more reliable and more powerful powder, gave off a low bass roar.

As the enemy skirmishers advanced, the Iowans, fighting dismounted, slowly fell back, but in good order. Then they were relieved to see their division's Second Brigade, which had been formed around the veteran First Wisconsin Cavalry, sweep into position on their left. A six-gun artillery battery went by at the gallop, each gun drawn by eight horses, with the gunners, stripped to their undershirts, riding the caissons. This was the way the Iowa boys had imagined war would be.

All afternoon the guns hammered away, but the two sides maintained their positions.

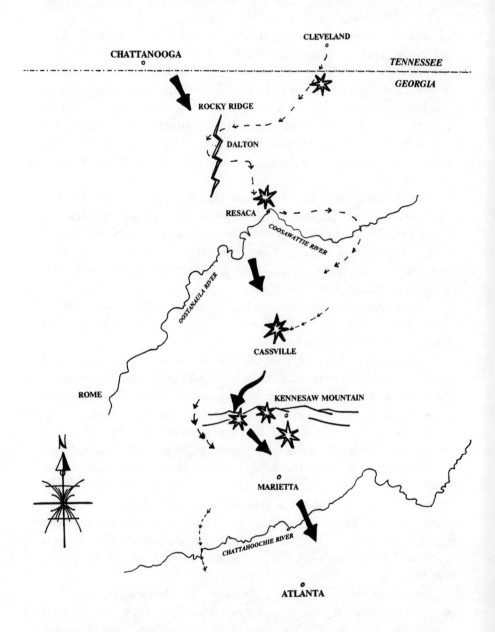

The route of the march of Gen. William T. Sherman's army from Chattanooga to Atlanta in May and June of 1864 is indicated by the large arrows. The Eighth Iowa Cavalry operated primarily on the periphery of the main army, as indicated by the smaller dashed lines. At Cassville, the Eighth Iowa played a key role when it happened upon the flank of the Confederate army, which was drawn up in preparation for a major battle, and forced its retreat.

The next day, the Union forces seized the initiative and pushed the enemy troops back about three miles. The Eighth Cavalry, moving along the railroad as part of the First Brigade, bore the heaviest fighting but suffered no serious casualties.

On their left, the Second Brigade had been fighting part of the time mounted and part of the time on foot. Then Colonel Oscar H. LaGrange, commander of the First Wisconsin Cavalry and acting commander of the Second Brigade, ordered his men to mount and led them in a headlong charge against the enemy position, sabers swinging wickedly. At first the Rebels scattered as the horses thundered down on them. Then troops hidden in earthworks on either side of the cavalry column opened up on the horsemen, halting their advance.

At this moment General Wheeler, who was personally leading a brigade of Texas cavalry, charged the flank of LaGrange's battered brigade. The attack required a tricky maneuver: The horsemen had to cross a swampy area before they could get to the Union column. They picked their way through the swamp in a column, four abreast. Then as they reached solid footing, they spread out "right into line" and charged the confused Federals, firing pistols and carbines. Unlike the Union cavalry, Wheeler's mounted infantry were not encumbered by sabers.

LaGrange's victorious charge had suddenly become a disaster. In moments the First Wisconsin lost 136 killed, wounded, and captured. LaGrange, who had two horses shot out from under him in the battle, was among the 120 men taken prisoner.

As the remnants of LaGrange's brigade fell back, Colonel Dorr ordered his brigade into position to protect their retreat. But Wheeler, who had only 900 men, broke off the engagement.

After the battle, Wheeler sought out LaGrange and complimented him on the gallant fight his men had made, but LaGrange could not be consoled. He was reported to have told Wheeler: "General Sherman gave me 2,500 men and told me he would make me a brigadier general if I captured you—and if I had had such men as yours I would have done it."

There is probably some truth in what LaGrange said. Over the previous few months, his Wisconsin cavalry had been in battle after battle, winning some, losing others. In one engagement back in October, they had even whipped one of Wheeler's units. But just before leaving Cleveland, the regiment had received 400 fresh recruits just in from Wisconsin. They were, of course, no match for the veterans they replaced.

———————

Around on the west side of Rocky Ridge, on the main battle front, the bulk of Sherman's army was moving in three columns toward three gaps in the ridge. Earlier in the year Union soldiers had probed the enemy defenses along the ridge. At the northernmost gap, men of the Tenth Missouri Infantry had charged a heavily fortified Rebel position on an outcropping known as Buzzards' Roost. In a few minutes the regiment, which had been looking forward to going on veteran furlough in a few days, lost 60 men.

But another probing effort five miles south at a pass through the ridge known as Dug Gap had found the defenses relatively weak. Now Sherman ordered an attack at this point.

Meanwhile the third column, commanded by Maj. Gen. James B. McPherson, was moving to the south. It approached the third gap, which was cut through the ridge by Snake Creek. Cautiously they felt their way along the narrow, twisting road through the gap. To their astonishment, they met not a single Confederate soldier. General Johnston had unaccountably left this vital hole in his defenses totally undefended. All the Union troops had to do was seize the little town of Resaca (named, incidentally, after the 1846 battle of Resaca de la Palma, during the war with Mexico). Doing so would not only allow them to penetrate the ridge, it would place them astride the railroad that linked Johnston's army to his sources of supplies in the south. It would also give them control of a bridge across the Oostanaula River. Making a bold move from there would trap Johnston, perhaps even end the war.

The little fort at Resaca was garrisoned with only 4,000 men under an ineffectual leader, and it could have been taken easily. But McPherson didn't know that. Afraid of a trap, he settled down at the exit from Snake Creek Gap and waited.

While he waited, Johnston, who by this time was aware of the threat to Resaca and was worried about the force moving toward him from the north, decided to give up his "Gibraltar" in Dalton and head south while he still could. Shortly after midnight on the morning of Friday, May 13, the exodus from Dalton began.

Up to this point, the Eighth Cavalry had played a subordinate role in the fighting, far from the center stage. But cavalry typically spends most of its time operating on the fringes of the main army, providing intelligence, creating diversions to confuse the enemy, and disrupting supply lines and communications. Now, as Johnston prepared to flee, the Iowans moved down closer to the center stage.

On the night of May 12, the regiment made an eerie all-night march, passing as quietly as they could through the camps of the sleeping infantry, their way lighted by the flickering of the soldiers' campfires. The only ones awake, aside from sentries, were the cooks, busy preparing food for the following day. Their march brought them from the far left of the army to a position near its center, where a road led up onto Rocky Ridge through the pass known as Dug Gap. There they set up camp and went to sleep.

On May 8 a Union infantry division had tried to fight its way through the gap. Some of the men had even made it to the top, dodging boulders rolled down the steep slope by the defenders. But the gap was already much more heavily defended than it had been when the probing effort was made back in February. The attackers had run into a trench line they had not seen and were sent reeling back down the slope with heavy losses.

On the morning of May 13, as the troopers of the Eighth Cavalry awoke after a brief rest, they were ordered to attack the enemy at the gap.

They moved out toward the gap expecting, as Colonel Dorr put it, "warm work." But the enemy soldiers had pulled out during the night, and the cavalrymen reached the top of the ridge without opposition. It looked to them as though a force of 500 men atop the ridge could have held off 5,000 attackers—which is about what had happened a few days before. As the Iowans reached the crest, they could see down on the other side of the ridge into Dalton, where Union infantry were already patrolling through the streets.

After moving cautiously down the eastern slope of the ridge, they entered the abandoned camp at Dalton. There they found an execution ground with 18 or 20 posts where Southern men had stood before Confederate firing squads. Alongside were graves. There were also sets of stocks, used for punishment of lesser offenses—all evidence of the stern measures Johnston had resorted to in dealing with desertion and other disciplinary problems in his own ranks.

The cavalrymen then trotted southward, falling in behind Johnston, pressing his rear guard as they fled toward Resaca, forcing the commander to put his army into defensive positions when he arrived there. Hundreds of enemy soldiers surrendered to the Bluecoats, although it seemed to the Iowans that the men had not been captured as much as they had seized on this opportunity to desert from the Confederate Army.

The Eighth Cavalry camped a short distance behind the infantry lines near the little town of Tilton. The two sides engaged in a furious battle, including a spectacular conflict in the dark with artillery and rockets lighting the sky. As the infantry fought, the Eighth Cavalry remained in line, ready to move forward as reinforcements. But they weren't needed. After two days the firing stopped, and the Rebel force pulled back into the open country across the Oostanaula River.

The battle at Resaca itself was a draw. But in the course of a week, Sherman had not only forced Johnston to abandon his "impregnable" position at Dalton but had cleared northern Georgia of the enemy and removed any immediate threat to Chattanooga, Nashville, and western Tennessee. Atlanta itself lay less than 90 miles to the south.

Chapter Eighteen

On to Atlanta

As soon as the Rebel army moved off to the south, the Eighth Cavalry joined in the pursuit.

Dorr put the Eighth in the advance of his brigade and swung to the east to cross the Conasauga River, about four miles above Resaca. Just east of Resaca, the Conasauga joins the Coosawattee River to form the Oostanaula. These three oddly named rivers thus posed a series of obstacles for an army on the move. After crossing the Conasauga, the brigade moved on down to the Coosawattee, about eight miles above the point where it joins the Conasauga at Resaca.

There they found a brigade of Union cavalry sitting idly along the riverbank. All along the opposite shore they could see the campfires of the enemy force. The colonel in charge of the waiting troops told Dorr there were two divisions of cavalry and one division of infantry just across the river. He had decided it would be too dangerous to attempt a crossing. But Dorr, always energetic, thought otherwise. He deployed two companies of the Eighth Cavalry at the crossing, then sent Company I charging across the ford.

As soon as they had crossed, the entire brigade streamed over to the other side as well. Patrolling up and down the river and along a road running to the south, they found that the enemy had left the campfires burning and moved out. They were camped about five miles away on the road to the neighboring town of Calhoun. The Union cavalry drove in their picket line but did not attempt an attack on their camp.

The next few days were a kind of minuet of giants. Neither general wanted a bloody head-on confrontation. Sherman, in fact, disliked battles because the outcome was always uncertain. Thus Johnston gradually moved back into a series of defensive positions, drawing Sherman farther from his source of supplies and sending Wheeler's horsemen to tear up tracks, raid depots, and burn trains in the Union rear. Sherman concentrated on outflanking Johnston and forcing him to pull back without a big fight.

It was during this ponderous dance that Johnston came up with a brilliant idea. His generals agreed that it had the potential to stop Sherman's advance to the south and might even force him to retreat all the way back to Chattanooga.

Johnston noted on the map that two generally parallel roads ran south from their present position. He split his force, sending a portion down each road, hoping to lure Sherman into splitting his force too. The ploy worked, and Sherman divided his force. Johnston then reunited his divisions near the beautiful little town of Cassville. With reinforcements that had just arrived, he had more than 70,000 men— the largest Confederate force ever assembled west of the Appalachian Mountains—ready to pounce on the badly outnumbered portion of Sherman's army that was headed toward Cassville.

On the morning of May 19, everything was in place. Then occurred one of those unpredictable events that make warfare such an uncertain endeavor. As a Confederate corps moved around to the north, positioning itself to make a devastating attack on the Union flank, a column of Federal cavalry suddenly appeared from the east, advancing on the flank and rear of the Confederate lines.

General McCook and Maj. Gen. George Stoneman, another Union cavalry commander, had just stumbled upon the Confederates while out on patrol. Conferring quickly, the two generals concluded they had chanced upon the flank of the entire enemy army. They decided to attack.

Colonel Dorr, commanding McCook's First Brigade, made a rapid assessment of the situation. One of his regiments was off on a reconnaissance mission. The Eighth Cavalry had only six companies on the scene; three were guarding roads elsewhere, and three were scouting for forage. The remaining six companies were ordered to attack. Looking west toward the enemy lines, Dorr could see that they would have to advance 300 yards over an open valley before reaching the line where the Confederates had hastily erected a line of breastworks of rails and earth. Dorr saw two artillery batteries in positions to the left and right of the valley.

As the horsemen of Companies G and M of the Eighth Iowa spread out in a long line and began their charge across the open field, the batteries on both sides opened up but didn't slow them down. But then the cavalrymen came upon a muddy creek that they had not been able to see when they began their charge. Reining back sharply, they stopped and reassembled into a column to ford the creek before resuming their charge. They then swept over the breastworks, driving the enemy back toward the town of Cassville. The remaining companies of the Eighth Cavalry then advanced on foot and drove the enemy out of an orchard and a building where their sharpshooters were stationed.

It is likely the veteran Confederate units had already been ordered to fall back before the Eighth Cavalry's assault began and were preparing to move away rather than offer stiff resistance. In any event, the losses to the Iowans were slight.

This sudden attack from an unexpected direction threw the Confederate forces into confusion, ending Johnston's effort to turn his brilliant strategy into battlefield victory. The Confederate forces retreated, and the cycle of retreat-and-pursue continued.

Ever since the Battle of Resaca, the two armies had been maneuvering in the relatively open area between the Oostanaula and Etowah Rivers. After the battle at Cassville, Johnston retreated again, this time moving south of the Etowah River into the mountainous, heavily forested area north of Marietta, which commanded the approach to Atlanta from the north.

On May 23, four days after they had precipitated Johnston's retreat from Cassville, the Eighth Cavalry crossed the Etowah and moved on south, skirmishing with enemy cavalry units and crossing the Allatoona range of mountains, then heading in the direction of the tiny community of Burnt Hickory.

The brigade advanced rapidly down the road, with the Second Michigan Cavalry driving a small force of enemy horsemen about eight miles. And then, as they approached Burnt Hickory, they found two brigades of cavalry blocking the way with two guns. Dorr brought up the Eighth Iowa to replace the weary Michigan unit on the front line. Despite the fire of the artillery, they pushed the enemy on down the road.

After moving back about four miles south of Burnt Hickory, the Rebel commanders found what they were looking for: a strong position where they could make a stand without being flanked.

Dorr called up Captain Walden, the commander of Company H—the unit in which Barney Brayman served. Instead of trying to get around the edges of the enemy position, Dorr ordered Walden to make a direct cavalry charge on the center of the strongpoint.

Forming up in a column four horsemen wide, the troopers galloped toward the Rebel breastworks, trying to ignore the shells from the enemy cannons. As Barney and the other Iowans reached the enemy entrenchments, they didn't slow. Urging their horses forward, they leaped over the barricades, firing their pistols and swinging their sabers. Enemy soldiers ran to escape the onslaught. After pursuing them a short distance, the Union men reined in their panting horses and turned to rejoin their regiment.

For the men of Company H, it was an exhilarating adventure—one shared by few Civil War cavalrymen. With the increase in range and accuracy provided by the rifled musket, a cavalry charge on an entrenched enemy was often suicidal. But in this case the unexpected attack on the center of the Rebel line not only succeeded but did so without the loss of a single man.

Having driven the enemy from their position, Dorr drew his men off a few miles and camped for the night.

For most of the time since the Iowans left Nashville on April 1, they had been on the go, and for three solid weeks since marching south from Cleveland on May 3, they had engaged in almost constant contact with the enemy. Except for a fertile area just south of the Etowah River, little forage was to be found. During one eight-day period, the regiment had received no food at all for the horses from army supplies. Yet, despite the warnings from veteran noncoms, Dorr had been pushing his men and horses hard. As the veterans had warned they would, the horses now began to fall by the wayside.

One trooper later recalled that his horse had become so crippled by saddle sores that it could not be ridden. And then the poor animal had simply lain down and refused to get up.

Horses were dying by the hundreds, Dorr now reported, not only in his brigade but throughout the cavalry. Hundreds of dismounted troopers had to be sent back to perform guard duty along the railroad line while waiting for more horses to be supplied.

The Eighth Cavalry thus remained on the sidelines as the bulk of the two great armies moved into the rugged, heavily forested area around Dallas.

While the Iowa cavalrymen had been pushing back the enemy horse-men, the larger part of Sherman's army had been engaged in a giant cartwheel movement, swinging around to confront Johnston, who was holed up in the mountains north and west of Marietta, from the west rather than from the north. With the Eighth Cavalry on the left, the main army marched eastward toward the community of Dallas, a cross-roads where New Hope Church stood, and a dot on the map known as Pickett's Mill.

When Johnston pulled back after his disappointment at Cassville, he had taken control of Allatoona pass, where the railroad from Chat-tanooga to Atlanta runs through the rugged mountains. The railroad was used by both armies but was especially crucial to Sherman, with his extended supply line. By swinging to the west, Sherman had moved his army away from the railroad. He had only a few days to fight his way back to the railroad before his troops began running short of everything from food to ammunition. His plan was to launch an offen-sive from Dallas, about 14 miles from the railroad. He had reason to hope that this move might fake Johnston out of position, forcing him to retreat to the south once more.

Johnston, however, saw what Sherman was doing. Instead of remaining in his strong defensive positions at Allatoona, he shifted his force west to meet the Union advance.

In the first clash, at New Hope Church on May 25, the Union infantry charged the dug-in Confederate line through a withering cross fire, losing 1,600 men in only a few minutes.

Both sides spent the next day catching their breath and preparing for renewed fighting on May 27. Late in the day, trying to get around the Confederate line, a Union unit launched an assault near Pickett's Mill, to the north of New Hope Church. The result was almost a rep-etition of what had happened two days earlier: another 1,600 were lost—dead, wounded, and missing.

The two sides then settled down into trench lines snaking through the woods for ten miles. Heat, rain, insects, the smell of rotting flesh, the shortage of food, the threat of constant death, all combined to cre-ate what the soldiers called the "hellhole." Snipers, hidden in trees, employed special rifles to pick off anyone on the other side who exposed his head for even a moment. Their favorite targets were offi-cers and cannoneers.

With his army running out of supplies, Sherman and his generals concentrated on trying to find a way to break the Confederate death grip, get around the Rebel force, and reach the railroad. Late on May 29, just as the Union soldiers were beginning a quiet withdrawal and a movement around to the north, the Confederates launched a series of furious attacks on the Federal trench line at Dallas.

The result was the reverse of the battles at New Hope Church and Pickett's Mill. "Braver men never shouldered a musket than those rebels that came up to drive us out of our works," one Union soldier wrote his wife. "We piled up their dead and wounded in perfect masses."

On May 31 Sherman's forces went ahead with their quiet withdrawal. They left only enough men in their fortifications to deceive the enemy while quietly pulling the rest of their troops out of their trenches and around the Confederate lines to the north.

By the afternoon of the next day, Union cavalrymen reached the railroad at the Allatoona Pass and found it undefended. Within a short time Sherman's army was back along the railroad, and Johnston had been forced to move once more toward Atlanta.

It would be only a matter of days, it seemed to the Union generals, before Johnston realized he would have to retreat once more—this time south across the Chattahoochee River, the last major water obstacle between Sherman and Atlanta. But instead of retreating across the river, Johnston dug in again on a series of distinctive mountains west of Marietta. Dominating the area was the eminence of Kennesaw Mountain, rising 691 feet above the surrounding territory, and its 400-foot neighbor, Little Kennesaw. Even though the engineers said it was impossible, Johnston's infantrymen manhandled the guns of an artillery battery to the top of Little Kennesaw. They also established defensive positions at nearby Pine Mountain, Lost Mountain, and Brush Mountain.

These enemy positions were not the only problem Sherman faced. Early in June it began to rain, and it continued to rain for nearly a solid month, turning the already inadequate roads through the area to mush. Instead of making a quick move across the Chattahoochee and down toward Atlanta, Sherman found himself almost completely bogged down.

On June 1 Iowa's Eighth Cavalry, which was gradually regaining its strength, took part in the capture of Acworth, one of the key points on the railroad line. On June 18 the troopers cooperated with Stoneman's men in an attempt to drive the Confederates off Lone Mountain. As they approached, the enemy forces withdrew. In the process Barney's Company H, under Captain Walden, captured a Confederate hospital and took a number of prisoners.

For the remainder of the month, the regiment remained camped quietly near Lost Mountain. At other points along the battle line, however, things were far from quiet. Word of one of the war's strangest episodes soon reached them.

On June 14, as the sun made a rare appearance through the clouds, Sherman set out for a look at the situation around Pine Mountain. Peering through binoculars, he saw a group of Confederates standing at the top of the mountain, and as a kind of "we see you up there!" message, he ordered an artillery battery to fire three volleys. From that distance Sherman couldn't make out the faces of the men on the mountain, but later he would learn that they were Johnston, the enemy commander, and two of his key subordinates.

The second shell that was fired as a result of Sherman's order scored a direct hit on Lt. Gen. Leonidas Polk, tearing away his heart and lungs and leaving a gaping hole in his chest. Polk, after graduating from West Point, had entered the Episcopal ministry and had risen to the rank of bishop. When war came, he traded his clerical collar for a general's uniform and entered the Confederate service. He had continued to fulfill both military and religious roles, and in recent weeks he had baptized two of his fellow generals, one of them Johnston, in moving candlelight ceremonies.

For the next few days, there was a lull in the fighting. Hundreds of women rode out from Atlanta to visit the top of Big Kennesaw to encourage their men and look down upon the hated Yankees encamped below. One young woman even stood on the ramparts and waved her hankie as a sign of defiance.

In addition to his personal tour of the battlefield—the one that resulted in Polk's death—Sherman had the advantage of new technology: For the first time, telegraph wires linked him to his subordinate commanders. Up until this point, he had had telegraph links to such distant points as Washington, but to communicate with his own generals he had to rely on signal flags and couriers.

After considering all the intelligence available to him, Sherman decided on what was for him an unusual move. This time, instead of repeating once again his pattern of outflanking Johnston and forcing him to pull back, Sherman decided to make a full-scale frontal assault on the enemy positions at the base of the Kennesaw mountains.

On the morning of June 17, the assault began. Wave after wave of Union troops surged forward—15,000 men in all. Time after time the Confederates, firing from behind heavy log and dirt barriers, beat them back. By day's end Sherman had lost 3,000 men. Johnston had lost about 700, most of them pickets overrun in the first moments of the offensive.

Sherman later justified the attack—and the slaughter—by explaining that it was necessary in order to convince Johnston that "I would assault, and that boldly." One of his more outspoken subordinates had a different explanation. Seeing Sherman after the battle, he told him to his face: "Well this is a damned appropriate culmination of one month's blundering."

In a letter to his wife after the bloody defeat of June 17, Sherman wrote:

> It is enough to make the whole world start at the awful amount of death and destruction that now stalks abroad. Daily for the past two months has the work progressed and I see no signs of remission till one or both and all the armies are destroyed. . . . I begin to regard the death and mangling of a couple thousand men as a small affair, a kind of morning dash—and it may be well that we become so hardened. The worst of the war has not yet begun.

For Johnston, beating back Sherman's assault had been a major victory, but it was not a very meaningful or decisive one. Sherman still threatened to outflank him—in fact, he was already preparing for such a move. Johnston decided to pull back once more, this time across the last remaining river protecting Atlanta. In the city the people observed a day of fasting and prayer and many of them packed up and left.

Sherman followed Johnston down across the Chattahoochee river, and the Eighth Cavalry was assigned the task of patrolling the fords up and down the river.

Johnston's series of retreats were causing consternation in Richmond, the Confederate capital. On July 17 Johnston was relieved as commander of the Army of Tennessee by one of his subordinates, John Bell Hood. The message that President Davis sent Johnston reflected the president's growing frustration with the general, whom he had never liked or trusted anyway:

> Lieut. Gen. J.B. Hood has been commissioned to the temporary rank of general. . . . I am directed by the Secretary of War to inform you that as you have failed to arrest the advance of the enemy to the vicinity of Atlanta, far in the interior of Georgia, and express no confidence that you can defeat or repel him, you are hereby relieved from the command of the Army and Department of Tennessee, which you will immediately turn over to General Hood.

The 32-year-old Hood had previously distinguished himself at the second battle of Manassas, Sharpsburg (Antietam), Gettysburg, and Chickamauga. He had an entirely different style of warfare from his predecessor. Where Johnston fought a battle of maneuver, giving up ground to save his army, Hood believed in carrying the battle to the enemy and hang the cost. His successes on the battlefield had been achieved at a terrible price, not only to the soldiers under him but to Hood himself. By the time he took over from Johnston in the defense of Atlanta, his left arm hung useless as a result of a wound at Gettysburg, and his right leg had been reduced to a four-and-a-half-inch stump as the result of a wound at Chickamauga.

In the Battle of Peachtree Creek on July 20 and the Battle of Bald Hill on July 22, Hood sent his forces charging out from Atlanta against the Union fortifications east of Atlanta while Sherman's artillery hammered the city in an artillery siege not unlike the Serbian shelling of Sarajevo 130 years later. But Hood's bold assaults simply piled up the casualties without changing the military situation. During these battles the Eighth Cavalry was on the other side of Atlanta from where the major fighting was taking place, protecting the western flanks of the army.

From their positions outside the city, Union officers could see trains pulling in from the south on two railroad lines. Despite the shelling, reinforcements and supplies continued to arrive. Frustrated, Sherman decided to try to cut the railroad lines and thus begin to starve out the Confederate army.

His plan called for making one of the largest cavalry raids of the war: He would send one large body of horsemen around Atlanta to the east and another around to the west. They would tear up the tracks as they went and meet together south of Atlanta, sealing off the city. When they came together, they would be a bigger and more formidable force than anything the Confederates had available to oppose them.

On July 22 Colonel Dorr was put back in command of the Eighth Cavalry and began to prepare his regiment for its part in the great raid.

Chapter Nineteen

"A Brilliant Success"

As July wore on with its appalling casualties, General Sherman may well have felt a growing disgust and impatience with the war. One recent battle before Atlanta had cost him 3,722 dead, wounded, and missing. The fighting in the Kennesaw Mountain area had taken another 9,000 casualties. At Resaca the loss had been 4,000. A wish to end the war quickly may have been at least part of his motive in sending thousands of horsemen looping south of Atlanta from two directions.

While the attack would be one of the largest cavalry raids of the war, it was still only a raid, involving fewer than 10,000 men and relatively puny in comparison with the vast campaign south from Chattanooga. Yet Sherman seems to have attached extravagant hopes to its outcome. If the raid were a complete success, he felt, it would achieve three objectives: cut off supplies to Atlanta and force the Confederates to abandon the city; destroy the enemy's cavalry; and free the thousands of Union prisoners held in abysmal conditions farther south, at Macon and Andersonville.

Striking south to the east of Atlanta would be General Stoneman, with his own division plus the division of Brig. Gen. Kenner Garrard, for a total of some 5,000 men.

Striking from the west would be General McCook with his division of some 4,000 men, including the Eighth Iowa Cavalry. McCook's force—in fact, all of Sherman's cavalry—had suffered heavily during the three months of the Georgia campaign, not so much from battlefield casualties as from sickness, injuries, and especially wear on the horses. The Eighth Cavalry, which had started out from Cleveland with more than a thousand men in the saddle, was down to just 24 officers and 292 troopers, among them Barney Brayman.

Under the circumstances, the choice of McCook to head the western force made sense. While he was not a brilliant cavalry commander—certainly not in comparison with Forrest and Wheeler, the Confederate cavalrymen who were causing Sherman so much grief—McCook had done well in the march south from Chattanooga, helping to push back the Rebel defenders north of Dalton. He could claim a large share of the credit for foiling what might have been a significant Rebel victory at Cassville.

But the choice of the 43-year-old Stoneman for the eastern force was a strange one. As anyone who looked at his record could tell, he was a defective leader and should long since have been sent home or to some place where he couldn't cause harm. An 1846 graduate of West Point, he had served mostly on the southwestern frontier until war broke out in 1861. As one of a small cadre of professional military officers, he was promoted rapidly, rising to the two-star rank of major general in 1862. For a time, he served as chief of cavalry for the Army of the Potomac. A 10,000-man raid on Richmond that he led did little harm but deprived the Army of the Potomac of its cavalry when it could have been put to better use.

After that raid, Stoneman had been tucked away at a desk job in Washington as chief of the cavalry bureau before being sent to Georgia to command a cavalry corps under Sherman. But the "corps" was part of Sherman's smallest army—the Army of the Ohio—and amounted to a single division. Stoneman still wore his two stars, but it was no secret in the army that his performance had been less than stellar and that he had, in effect, been demoted. Stoneman thus had a strong motive to do something spectacular to redeem his reputation.

On July 26 Sherman called his cavalry commanders to his headquarters and personally briefed them on what he expected them to achieve. The same day he outlined his plan in a report to General Halleck and spelled out his hopes of freeing the prisoners:

> I have also consented that General Stoneman, after he
> has executed this part of his mission [cutting the railroad], if

Maj. Gen. George Stoneman. (State Historical Society of Iowa Library/Archives, Des Moines.)

he find it possible, may, with his division proper, about 2,000 strong, go to Macon and attempt to release our officers and prisoners there, and then to Andersonville to release the 20,000 of our men there.

The proposal to attempt to rescue the prisoners had originally come from Stoneman himself in a note to Sherman. The commanding general agreed:

There was something most captivating in the idea, and the excursion was within the bounds of probability of success. I consented that after the defeat of Wheeler's cavalry, which was embraced in his orders, and breaking the road he might attempt it with his cavalry proper, sending that of General Garrard back to its proper flank in the army.

In the western leg of the raid, McCook got off to a shaky start. On the night of July 26, in the hours just before the raid was to begin, his men ran into an enemy force and engaged in an intense battle. Despite these rigors, McCook's men embarked on their raid the next day, July 27, as planned. They spent almost the entire day scouting along the Chattahoochee River for a safe place to cross, where they would not run into enemy soldiers as they tried to land on the opposite shore.

The First Brigade, to which the Eighth Cavalry was attached, finally halted and waited through much of the night for their pontoon train. On the morning of July 28, as soon as it was light enough to see, almost the entire brigade crossed the river, four men at a time, in a little boat. When the pontoon train showed up about noon, the Second Brigade crossed and went out ahead, and then the horses of the First Brigade were brought across.

By crossing the river with a boat and then a pontoon train rather than an existing bridge, their crossing point was not known and thus they avoided detection by the enemy division waiting on the other side of the river. As soon as the brigade was across the river, it headed down the road toward Palmetto, the nearest station on the railroad line that connected Atlanta with West Point, a major junction on the Alabama border, 45 miles to the southwest.

The troopers trotted into the town of Palmetto at about dusk on the evening of July 28.

A dozen miles to the south, the people of the little town of Newnan had, for days, been hearing frightening rumors that the dreaded Union army might be headed their way. The rumors were so realistic that on the night of July 13 residents went to bed convinced that, when they arose in the morning to cook breakfast, the Yankees would be there to eat it. Dawn came on the morning of July 14 and the rumors proved false. Still, the fears persisted.

Before the war Newnan, the quiet little seat of Coweta County, had had a population of fewer than 1,000 persons. The population of the entire county was about 15,000 in 1860, half whites and half slaves. Most of them lived in the countryside.

In September 1863 the Confederate authorities, to the distress of the townspeople, who hoped they could preserve their peaceful existence despite the war, decided to make Newnan a hospital center. All the major buildings in town were taken over and converted into hospitals, and when room ran out, 100-foot-long sheds were erected along the streets near the two-story brick courthouse, which stood in the

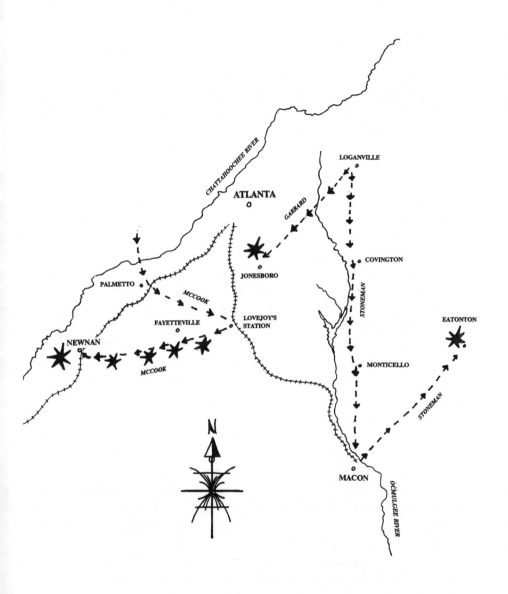

In late July 1864, as his army laid seige to Atlanta, General Sherman launched
a three-pronged cavalry raid south of Atlanta. Generals Stoneman and Garrard
moved down to the east of Atlanta while General McCook's forces, including the
Eighth Iowa Cavalry, struck from the west. Garrard was quickly turned back.
Stoneman, instead of linking up with McCook, as planned, headed south in an
effort to release Federal prisoners held at Macon and, farther south, at Andersonville. The divided Union forces were badly beaten. Barney Brayman was
captured during the battle at Newnan, Georgia, and taken off to Andersonville.

center of town surrounded by chinaberry and locust trees.

Day after day trains from the north brought pathetic loads of wounded men from the battlefields of Chickamauga and Missionary Ridge and the more recent bloody fighting at Resaca, Cassville, the hellhole near Kennesaw Mountain, and Atlanta. Many of the wounded were so badly crippled with spinal injuries that they could not even feed themselves. A few others received less sympathy: They had chopped off fingers or toes or otherwise mutilated themselves in order to avoid the fighting.

With the influx of wounded men and the streams of pitiful refugees from the fighting farther north, the population of the town grew rapidly until, in 1864, it may have held ten times as many people as it had four years before.

As the citizens of Newnan looked at the northern sky on the night of July 28, they were alarmed to see a bright glow. It could mean only one thing: The Yankees had crossed the Chattahoochee and were burning Palmetto.

That is exactly what was happening. In the early hours of the evening, McCook's men burned the depot and everything else that might be useful to the enemy. They managed to destroy 1,000 bushels of corn, 300 sacks of flour, slabs of bacon, and a large quantity of cotton, plus three freight cars. Work parties of troopers fanned out north and south of the town, tied up their horses, and destroyed two and a half miles of rails and telegraph wires.

Then, at about 9 o'clock, having done about as much damage as they could to block train traffic between Atlanta and West Point, McCook's men mounted and rode eastward through the night, heading toward their rendezvous with Stoneman and his men in the vicinity of Lovejoy, on the rail line between Atlanta and Macon.

It was an eventful night.

As the column moved toward the little town of Fayetteville, the troopers came upon mile after mile of wagons that were part of an enemy supply train parked beside the road. The soldiers quickly captured or drove off the teamsters and the few soldiers guarding the train. Looking quickly through the wagons, the troopers came upon trunks full of Confederate money. Laughing, they scattered it to the winds. They also found some 60 wagons stuffed with the personal baggage of high-ranking Rebel officers and took what they could carry. A number of Rebel officers were found sleeping nearby and taken prisoner.

There was no way, of course, that McCook's men could take the wagon train with them, which would mean escorting it safely the many miles through enemy territory back across Union lines. So they set about destroying it. First a few usable horses and mules were sorted out. Some of the soldiers traded their worn-out horses for new ones. Then the troopers, working in the darkness, killed the hundreds of remaining mules. But so as not to attract any enemy cavalry that might be within earshot, they kept their pistols in their holsters and killed the mules with their sabers.

For hours during that bloody night, the cavalrymen of the Second and Fourth Indiana Cavalry went about the sad duty of slaughtering hundreds of mules. When they were finished, the carcasses littered the road. No one bothered to count them, but the officers in command of the two regiments agreed that they had killed 1,600 to 2,000 mules. After working so quietly with their sabers, they set fire to the wagons, destroying about 600 of them and deliberately creating a beacon for any nearby enemy troops.

The enemy cavalry commander, having missed McCook's division at the river crossing, finally realized his mistake and hurried to catch up. As his men came upon the smoldering wagon train and the piles of dead animals, now stinking in the hot summer sun, they were appalled. They dashed ahead, angry and hungry for revenge.

Early in the morning of July 29, after their all-night ride and the slaughter of the "enemy" mules, McCook's force reached its goal of Lovejoy. Even though they had had only about three hours' rest, they repeated the destructive work they had done at Palmetto, tearing up the rail and telegraph connections between Atlanta and Macon. Working with another regiment, the Eighth Cavalry destroyed several boxcars, $300,000 worth of cotton and salt, and $100,000 worth of tobacco. The depot and water tank were both destroyed.

Their patrols scouted the surrounding area, looking for signs of enemy cavalry and, at least of equal importance, for signs of Stoneman's force. Anxiously checking their watches, McCook and his officers puzzled over Stoneman's absence. Had he run into enemy troops? Had he gotten lost? There was no obvious answer.

A patrol from the Eighth Cavalry rode off to check on the nearby town of McDonough, about ten miles to the east, searching for Stoneman. Finding no sign of the missing cavalry force, they hurried back with their negative report. As the hours wore on, it became obvious to McCook that, no matter what might have happened to Stoneman, he could not stay in Lovejoy much longer. His force's presence deep in enemy territory was certainly no secret anymore. The destruction they had wrought must have alerted everyone in the whole countryside south of Atlanta.

Captain Walden, the commander of Barney Brayman's Company H, listened anxiously as McCook and his brigade commanders debated what to do next. The vote went strongly in favor of continuing on to the east and north, swinging completely around Atlanta. Not only was it the shortest way back to friendly lines but it also offered the opportunity to join up with Stoneman. The army, however, was not a democracy. McCook pondered the question until late afternoon. To Walden, it seemed as though he was letting the golden moments when escape was possible slip away. Finally McCook made his decision: They would go back the way they had come. At least they knew the territory, and during their two days and nights of destruction, they had not run into any significant enemy opposition on that route.

It would be days before they learned what had happened to Stoneman.

Stoneman had headed south on schedule with his somewhat larger force. But instead of following orders to meet with McCook and then coordinate their operations, he divided his own force. General Garrard and his division rode toward the meeting with McCook. But Stoneman and his men headed directly for Macon—and glory. Stoneman thought that if he could release the Union officers held in Camp Oglethorpe at Macon and then swoop some 50 miles farther south to rescue the thousands of enlisted men at Andersonville, he would redeem his less-than-stellar reputation as a cavalry leader and become *the* hero of the war.

Releasing the officer prisoners at Macon was probably a plausible goal. There were only about 1,500 of them, and they were in relatively good physical condition. But Andersonville was another matter entirely. What would Stoneman do—overpower the weak guard force there and open the wooden gates of the compound? What would he do with thousands of starving men, many of them so sick they could hardly walk? After all, they were more than 100 miles behind enemy lines in an area without even enough food for the people who lived there. No one in Stoneman's party seems to have given any serious thought to this question, although Sherman, aware of the difficulty Stoneman would face getting back to Union lines, later said: "The difficulty will then commence for them to reach me."

From even a cursory look at the map, it seems obvious that Stoneman himself never intended to meet up with McCook. His route took him through the towns of Covington, Monticello, and Clinton to the outskirts of Macon. At no point did he even come as close as 25 miles to Lovejoy, where McCook was waiting.

The fact that Stoneman was on the move was no secret to the enemy. On July 27, the day he set out for the raid, Brig. Gen. Francis A. Shoup, chief of staff of the Confederate army in Atlanta, noted in his meticulous diary: "A large cavalry force moving around our right toward Flat Rock, evident intention to cut Macon and Western Railroad in vicinity of Jonesborough. Wheeler's cavalry in pursuit, Wheeler commanding."

Wheeler, whose horsemen had been dismounted and thrown into the defenses of Atlanta as infantrymen, pleaded with General Hood, the new Confederate commander, for permission to get his men back on their horses and set out after the raiders. Hood, after assuring himself that enough men would still be available to hold the defensive line, gave his approval.

Wheeler, personally heading his column, galloped south to head off what he thought were Stoneman's raiders north of Jonesborough, or Jonesboro, as it is now called, on the railroad near Lovejoy. His assumption that these were raiders was correct. But instead of Stoneman's full force, he met only Garrard, with about half their number. After a brief battle Garrard retreated back to friendly lines with more than 2,000 men and played no further role in the raid.

By heading straight for Macon, Stoneman probably left Wheeler as confused as McCook. By the time Wheeler realized what he was up to, Stoneman was well on his way to Macon.

As Stoneman and his troopers approached Macon, they encountered obvious signs that the citizens had heard of his coming and had panicked. Train after train of railroad cars were loaded with furniture, printing presses, private carriages, and horses. One of Stoneman's officers later recalled: "These were intercepted by our force, and, in the process of destroying the railroad and rolling stock, were necessarily swept out of existence."

Officials in Macon had even received sufficient advance warning of Stoneman's coming to move the officer prisoners from Camp Oglethorpe and send them off toward Charleston, South Carolina.

When Stoneman approached Macon, he was met by a quickly assembled force of militia backed by cannons well situated on a hill.

Blocked from entering Macon, he looked across the river in frustration and ordered a brisk shelling of the city—more from spite than for any useful military purpose. Then, about 3 P.M. on July 30, he signaled to his men to turn and head back north.

This order proved to be a fatal error, although it is not clear what alternatives Stoneman had. His line of march had taken him to the east of the broad Ocmulgee River, which now lay between him and McCook's force. Any hope he might have had that, by heading north, he could join up with McCook and that they would be able to fight their way through to friendly lines was a vain one.

Wheeler might have been perplexed by Stoneman's dash for Macon. But he did have part of his force waiting as Stoneman's men headed north. All during the night of July 30 until dawn of the next day, the Union troops encountered and pushed past one thin line of Rebels after another. At one point they found 35 Union men who had been captured while out foraging and locked up in a local jail. They freed their comrades and set fire to the jail, which lighted their way on up the road for a good distance. But through the long night they were never sure how large the enemy force was or even quite where it was.

At dawn on July 31, while they were still only about a dozen miles north of Macon, their way was blocked by a strong enemy force—how strong was not yet apparent. The two sides spent several hours feeling each other out. Then in late morning Stoneman ordered his men to advance on foot. They marched forward confidently. Suddenly, the enemy force launched a furious charge. It seemed to the frightened soldiers that they were badly outnumbered. One of Stoneman's brigades broke and ran for their horses. The Rebels surged through the opening in the line, cutting Stoneman's force into isolated units.

Stoneman prepared to surrender. He sent messengers to his subordinate commanders telling them of his intention but also giving them permission to try to fight their way out.

One of his brigade commanders was astonished: "Stoneman surrendered?" he exclaimed. "Never while I have a horse under me will I surrender."

Men in the units that had not surrendered stopped shooting and ran for their horses. What was left of Stoneman's army had turned into a huge mass struggling for possession of their horses. One can only imagine their desperation, caught a hundred miles behind enemy lines with their horses their only hope of escaping. Several hundred men did manage to mount their horses and dash through the enemy lines, swinging their sabers and firing their pistols and carbines. But many of those who escaped had thrown away their weapons in their frantic haste to claim their horses. They thus found themselves far from home and unarmed. Only a handful of the force that had set out a few days before was able to make it back to the Union lines safely.

To the astonishment of the Confederates, Stoneman himself surrendered, along with a large part of his force. With his dreams of glory gone, he sat down and cried. When his captors later read a letter he had written to his wife, they found it pathetic. Stoneman was exchanged as a prisoner a short time later. Yet he seemed to live a charmed life: Despite his disastrous performance in the raid, he received yet another command in the Union Army.

For a raid requiring the coordination of two large forces, one would assume that the commanders would synchronize their watches—or at least their calendars. But not only was there a large geographical gap between Stoneman and McCook, they were also operating on two different time lines. By the time Stoneman began his retreat from Macon, harboring hopes of linking up with the rest of the raiding force, Garrard had long since scurried for home, and McCook had given up waiting for him and had left Lovejoy on the previous day.

Up to the point where he left Lovejoy, McCook had had reason to pride himself on a successful—even spectacularly successful—operation. He had destroyed segments of both railroad lines linking Atlanta to areas farther south, and he had done so with minimal casualties. But just at the moment his forces headed back west again, his luck seemed to change. He sent the Second Brigade on ahead, with the First Brigade following a short distance behind. The troopers had been on their way only a short time when McCook received word that a force of Texas cavalry had suddenly appeared on the road between the two brigades. These were the same Confederate troopers who had missed McCook as he crossed the Chattahoochee and had been trying to catch up ever since.

The commander of the Union's First Brigade, Col. John T. Croxton of the Fourth Kentucky Mounted Infantry, called Dorr to his side and ordered him to charge the enemy force with the Eighth Cavalry. At that moment Dorr had with him something less than half the regiment; the remainder was following a short distance behind.

Dorr and the troopers trotted forward in column, four abreast, until they were a short distance from the enemy. Dorr could see some Rebels standing in column on the road and others spread out to the right of the road. He ordered the charge. As the Iowans thundered forward, the enemy on the road fell back rapidly. And then suddenly a group of Rebels hidden on the left side of the road—men Dorr hadn't been able to see when he ordered the charge—opened fire. As he later described the situation, the enemy "poured in a most deadly fire before which the head of the column went down like grass before the scythe."

Realizing that his men were caught in a trap, Dorr immediately ordered the remainder of the regiment, the men following a short distance behind, to hurry to the front. But these troops had been diverted off to the side of the road by Croxton as he assembled the brigade to face the enemy. Dorr was not happy.

"I had but two hundred and ninety men with me on the raid and by this order without notice I was left with about one hundred men to charge an entire Brigade and that the best Brigade in the Rebel service, composed of the 3rd, 6th and 9th Texas," Dorr wrote in his after-action report.

Actually, the initial clash—with the Ninth Texas regiment—was not as one-sided as it appeared to Dorr. The Texans were outnumbered and were armed only with rifles. They had neither pistols nor sabers, and they quickly began running out of ammunition. But then three more Texas regiments arrived on the scene and piled on. Dorr suspected he faced an entire division—and he was right.

Leaving their dead and wounded lying where they fell, the outnumbered Iowans fell back 150 yards to an angle in the road and hunkered down there until two other regiments came to their rescue. In the fighting, Dorr was wounded and Maj. Richard Root took over command of the regiment. Dorr resumed command on several occasions during the subsequent fighting.

The charge by the Iowans had given the rest of the brigade time to move into position and halt the enemy advance. Toward evening the firing died down, and the Union's First Brigade managed to slip around to its left and get onto the road behind the Confederate force.

McCook's little army moved forward—the Second Brigade in front, the First Brigade in the rear, and the train of pack mules in between. The road, as Croxton, commanding the First Brigade, described it, was "a narrow devious path, crossing innumerable ditches and bogs." McCook, some eight miles ahead at the front of the column, sent several aides back to urge Croxton and the First Brigade to hurry up. Croxton simply pointed at the pack train blocking his way. At one point forward movement stopped entirely. Finally, one of the officers worked his way forward and found both mules and teamsters sound asleep—so deep in sleep that it took the point of his saber to rouse them. At about daylight on July 30, the mule train took off at a gallop, and the First Brigade followed.

They had not gone far when a messenger hurried up to inform Croxton that his own regiment, the Fourth Kentucky, which he had left behind as a rear guard, had been surrounded. Croxton and his aides had not heard the sounds of battle because of the din made by the hooves of their galloping horses. He decided it was futile to go back to help his regiment. His real challenge now was to save the remainder of the force from the Texans, who had pushed past Croxton's rear guard and who were rapidly approaching from the rear. He left one regiment and a detachment of the Eighth Iowa to destroy the bridge over a small stream and then to serve as rear guard as the brigade raced toward Newnan.

By this time, the troopers in McCook's force had been on the move for almost four days and had engaged in the hard labor of tearing up rail lines when they were not in combat with the enemy. Newnan offered them a chance for at least a brief rest, something to eat and drink, and perhaps a defensive position from which they could hold off the pursuing enemy while preparing to slip away across the Chattahoochee to safety.

At about noon the advance elements of McCook's force galloped into town from the east, following a dirt road that crossed the railroad tracks, went by the depot, and continued up Depot Street—now East Broad Street—to pass the courthouse in the center of town. To their dismay, they found the depot area teeming with Confederate soldiers. A train carrying 550 mounted infantry—without their horses—had just pulled into the station from West Point. They had halted in Newnan, ironically, because the rails through the Palmetto station, which had been torn up by McCook's men, had not yet been repaired. The troops waiting at the Newnan station were commanded by General Roddey, the same officer whose crossing into Tennessee had put the Eighth Cavalry on the alert months before.

The Confederates scurried into defensive positions, but they were really not ready for battle and McCook's troopers were in no mood for one. As the Union column streamed on through the town, only a few harmless shots were fired by citizens from cellars, second-story windows, and rooftops. The bulk of McCook's force detoured south of the town. Wheeler, having left part of his force to lie in wait for Stoneman, had personally taken up the chase for McCook. As the Union regiments had moved off toward the south, he had arrived in Newnan from the north and set up his headquarters in a home its owners called Buena Vista, at what is now 87 LaGrange Street.

McCook's men were now only a few miles from the Chattahoochee and the chance of safety, but with enemy units behind them and on their flank, they could not avoid a battle. They hurriedly set up defensive positions about five miles south of town along Ricketyback Road. Today's Millard Farmer Road runs generally along the line of battle. Although Union records refer to the conflict as the Battle of Newnan, the people of Newnan call it the Battle of Brown's Mill, for a mill that stood near the site at the time.

It was a hot, steamy Georgia summer day, and the fighting began shortly after noon, at the hottest part of the day.

The Eighth Iowa Cavalry was ordered to dismount and set up barricades along the road, at about the center of the Union formation. The troopers rested there for what seemed a long time without seeing any sign of the enemy. Then they were ordered to mount, trot forward about half a mile, and charge the enemy, which had hastily erected barricades across a road running through a dense woods. The purpose of the charge was to break through the enemy line so that McCook's men could dash for the river.

Although it was not clear to the Iowans what was happening, their attack fell on the flank of a Confederate cavalry brigade commanded by Brig. Gen. L. S. Ross.

Ross's men, who had left their horses at the rear, had just finished driving a Union force from a woods when the Iowans struck. Not only had Ross been hit on the flank, but the Union troops had gotten between his men and their horses.

Ross gave the command, "'Bout face!" and turned to confront the threat from the Iowa cavalry. For an hour the battle seesawed back and forth. The fighting—often hand to hand—was done in brush so thick it was difficult to see more than a few feet. The Iowans captured many of Ross's horses and officers and men. At one point Ross himself fell into their hands. But then Ross's men got the upper hand, rescued their commander and the other captives, and reclaimed their horses.

The Iowans looked around. There were no friendly forces in sight.

As the Iowans fought to hold open the road, Colonel Croxton, the brigade commander, had moved part of his force along the road toward the river and halted on a rise, expecting the Eighth Cavalry to join him there. When they didn't arrive, Croxton, with two orderlies, rode back to find them and hurry them up. He soon found the road blocked by enemy soldiers. He and the orderlies turned and headed for the river to save themselves.

By this time the Eighth Iowa was reduced to fighting desperately to keep their cannons, which were firing canister at short range, from falling into enemy hands. About 5 P.M. McCook sent word to Colonel Dorr to disable his artillery by loading the guns with percussion shell and driving blocks of wood into the muzzles, knock the spokes out of the artillery carriages, abandon the wounded, and try to get away.

No one knew where Croxton was. Dorr was ordered to take over the First Brigade. But all he could find was the remnants of the Eighth Cavalry, by then down to about 100 men. A few of them were wounded, and many of them had lost their weapons in the fighting.

As Dorr and his men left the battlefield, McCook himself rode up and asked Dorr if he could form the Eighth on the brow of a hill and "check the enemy" to protect the division's retreat.

"I can," Dorr replied, and ordered his men to dismount and set up defensive positions. The road was filled with "fragments of regiments, stragglers and skulkers," as Dorr later put it. Remnants of one division seemed to be in a "stampede," blocking the road. The enemy could be seen clearly advancing on their flank.

"The enemy," Dorr later reported, "had thrown a Brigade on this our only outlet from the scene of battle and disaster, and after a few more fruitless efforts the fragment of the Regiment exhausted—worn out with fighting and lack of sleep—gave up to the overwhelming force around them."

Bitterly, the Iowans tied white kerchiefs to their carbines and waved them to signify their surrender. Barney Brayman was one of the exhausted, hungry men taken captive. Only much later would they understand how their fierce rearguard action had made it possible for a portion of McCook's raiding force to make it back across the river to safety.

The Confederate General Ross, who accepted the surrender, described the scene in his after-action report:

> I now proceeded to take possession of the prisoners and captured property, and, this done, bivouacked on the field during the night. Next morning, summing up the fruits of the victory, I found my command had captured 587 prison-

ers, including 2 brigade commanders, with their staffs, several field and a number of company officers, 2 stand of colors (the Eighth Iowa and Second Indiana Regiments), 2 pieces of artillery, 11 ambulances, and a large number of horses and horse equipments and small-arms. We also recaptured the colors of the Second Regiment Dismounted Arkansas Cavalry, and those of another regiment, number not known.

Of the 316 officers and men of the Eighth Iowa who had set out with McCook on July 27, only 20 escaped the disaster and made it back to Union lines.

As soon as the remnants of McCook's force got back across the Chattahoochee, rumors of what had happened reached Sherman's headquarters. But it was not until two days later that he received this message from Marietta confirming the disaster: "Col. James P. Brownlow has just come in here with a very few straggling cavalry, entirely demoralized. Brownlow is barefooted."

The report caused something close to panic in Sherman's headquarters.

Sherman passed the news along to Halleck: "I can hardly believe it, as he had 3,000 picked cavalry." The loss of cavalry, he added, is "a serious one for me." He sent off a series of frantic messages appealing for more cavalry to replace the men and horses that had been lost in the raid.

By August 3 the news seemed to be somewhat better. Sherman learned that McCook and about 1,200 of his men had made it back across the river. And he was still optimistic about Stoneman's chances. In a message to Halleck, he said:

> I think General Stoneman has a chance of rescuing those prisoners. It was a bold and rash adventure, but I sanctioned it, and hoped for its success from its very rashness. I think that all Georgia is now in my front, and he may meet but little opposition and succeed in releasing those prisoners. The difficulty will then commence for them to reach me.

Sherman was one of the last to know the full extent of the disaster. By that time, of course, Stoneman and many of his men had joined the sad company of the other Union prisoners and the news had reached as far as Richmond. On August 3 the Richmond *Dispatch* reported:

Maj. Gen. William T. Sherman at Atlanta. (National Archives, College Park, MD.)

Our cavalry under General Iverson attacked the enemy
yesterday near Clinton [Georgia]. The Yankees, commanded
by General Stoneman, were routed, and Stoneman, 25 officers and about 500 prisoners, with 2 pieces of artillery, surrendered, and have just reached the city [Macon]. The rest
of the Yankee force is scattered and flying toward Eatonton.

On the Confederate side there was jubilation. General Shoup
noted in his diary on August 1: "Today deserves to be marked with a
white stone. Good news flowed in from all distant points." He quoted
a message from Wheeler: "We have just completed the killing, capturing, and breaking up of the entire raiding party under General
McCook."

A message from another Confederate general summarized what had happened to Stoneman: "General Stoneman, after having his force routed, yesterday surrendered with 500 men. The rest of his command are scattered and flying toward Eatonton. Many have been already killed and captured."

Shoup reported that damage done to the rail lines during the raid was more severe than first reported but that repairs would be completed quickly. In fact, during and after the raid, Sherman's men, looking into the city from a crow's nest built in a tree, could see trains coming and going in Atlanta.

Sherman himself, in a report of the campaign written in mid-September, admitted that the attempt to cut the enemy's supply and communication lines into Atlanta with a cavalry raid was futile and that a much larger effort was required:

> On the whole the cavalry raid is not deemed a success, for the real purpose was to break the enemy's communications, which though done was on so limited a scale that I knew the damage would soon be repaired. . . . I had become satisfied that to reach the Macon road and thereby control the supplies for Atlanta, I would have to move the whole army.

In an extreme case of seeing the glass half full instead of half empty, McCook gave this assessment of the raid:

> I regard the raid as a brilliant success, and had the forces of General Stoneman been able to unite with mine near McDonough, as I understood was contemplated by the general commanding the military division, I think we might have successfully carried our arms wherever desired, and accomplished more magnificent results than any raid in the history of this war.

Chapter Twenty

A Summer
in Hell

The shooting in the battle south of Newnan tapered off at about five o'clock in the afternoon. A heavy, acrid haze of gunpowder smoke hung over the battlefield, especially at one swampy end of the area. Weary soldiers of both sides slumped in small groups, talking over the day's fighting.

Fannie Beers, a Confederate nurse, went to the battlefield to do what she could for the wounded and later described the scene:

> The dead lay around us on every side, singly and in groups and piles; men and horses in some cases, apparently inextricably mingled. Some lay as if peacefully sleeping; others, with open eyes seemed to glare at anyone who bent above them. . . . Duty now recalled me to my patients at the hospital. My hands and dress and feet were bloody, and I felt sick with horror.

All afternoon ambulances had been shuttling the five miles from the Brown's Mill area to the hospitals in town. If a soldier had to be wounded in a Civil War battle, Newnan was probably one of the better places. Hospital beds were available—Confederates were taken to whichever hospital had room, while wounded Union soldiers were concentrated in the Buckner hospital—and there were doctors and nurses, trained on the job over the last two years treating the flow of casualties that came in waves after each battle.

The battle could have gone even worse for the Yankee raiders. General Roddey's men, surprised at the depot and unaccustomed to marching rather than riding, took a long time to get in formation and march to the battlefield. By the time they arrived, the fighting was almost over and General Wheeler decided not to throw them into the battle. Critics would later say that he thereby missed the opportunity to give the Confederacy an even greater victory, but it is hard to see how Roddey's men, arriving late and on foot, could have had much success in chasing the frightened remnants of the Union cavalry. In any event the people of Newnan were thankful to Wheeler and erected a sign, which stands to this day, hailing him as the "savior of Newnan."

Barney Brayman and the other Iowans had suddenly been reduced from dashing cavalrymen to abject prisoners of war. Over the next few days, they were marched back into town and quartered in empty cotton warehouses. At least they had shelter from the sun and the thundershowers that were common in the humid afternoons. The citizens of Newnan, happy that the fighting had occurred out in the countryside and had left their town and its people unharmed, set about providing food from their own limited supplies for the soldiers of both sides.

The events of the next few days were filled with irony. The blue-coated prisoners were herded into railroad cars and trundled slowly back over the route they had followed on their destructive raid a few days before. They passed over some of the very railroad lines they had torn up, which had quickly been repaired and were already back in service. The whole raid suddenly seemed an exercise in futility. Their journey took them east to Macon and then south toward Andersonville—the same notorious prisoner-of-war camp whose population Sherman and Stoneman had hoped to liberate. The would-be liberators were soon to be inmates.

When Barney and the remnants of his regiment arrived in Andersonville in the early days of August, they could hardly have picked a worse time. Camp Sumter, as the prison at Andersonville was known, had received its first prisoners on February 27, 1864, as the Confederacy scrambled to move men from camps near the front lines to safer areas where it was less likely that Union raiders could liberate them. Most of the early prisoners came from the camp at Belle Isle, on an island at

Richmond. They brought with them smallpox and a group of urban toughs, known as the "raiders," who preyed on the other prisoners.

The site selected for the new prison, just north of the small town of Americus, seemed an ideal location. It was hundreds of miles from the front lines. It was set in a dense pine forest that gave it an endless supply of lumber that could be used for construction of a palisade and barracks and as firewood for cooking and heating. Sweetwater Creek, a refreshing stream, would provide ample fresh water for drinking and washing. As the stream passed under the palisade, it would carry away the camp's wastes.

What seemed ideal at first, however, soon became anything but. The timber was there, but the Confederates had too few axes and saws to cut it quickly and efficiently. Once trees were finally cut, they had to be taken to a sawmill, which would turn them into lumber. But prison authorities were authorized to pay sawmills only $50 for a thousand feet. The price that local sawmills could get on the open market was $100 a thousand. Therefore the mill owners gave the camp's lumber the lowest priority, if they milled any of it at all. When and if the mills finally did deliver lumber, the camp did not have enough nails to fasten the boards together.

To help in the construction, camp officials appealed to area plantation owners to provide slaves, horses, and wagons. But the local population didn't want the camp in their county in the first place. Not-in-my-neighborhood is not a recent phenomenon. Despite repeated assurances, the plantation owners didn't believe that if they sent their slaves and their horses and wagons to help at the camp, they would get them back—so many of them didn't help out.

When camp officials located materials that they needed in Macon or other nearby cities, they found it next to impossible to arrange for transportation. They were reminded that there was a war on and that the soldiers at the front had priority. Prison officials were authorized to buy beef on the hoof in Florida, but they couldn't find anyone to drive the animals to the prison.

The result was that when the prisoners from Belle Isle began to arrive at the rate of some 400 a day, the Andersonville prison had no barracks, no tents, no kitchens, and no sanitary facilities to accommodate so many men. Slaves were still busy building the stockade. To avoid milling, they hewed the long pine trunks into logs from eight to twelve inches thick with broadaxes and then set them upright in a trench, making a solid wall 15 feet high. Since the trees that had covered the prison site had been cut down to provide timber for the stockade, there wasn't even any shade.

The first prisoners made rough huts for themselves out of scrap wood from the branches and tops of trees that had been left lying about. They plunked down their shelters wherever they felt like it, setting aside no streets or passageways and making no attempt at order. As more and more men arrived, this haphazard arrangement added to the misery of the inmates in the heat of the Southern summer.

The growth of the stockade population was explosive as prisoners were moved from other locations and more men were captured in the heavy fighting in the spring and early summer of 1864. In March there were 7,500 men at Andersonville; in April, 10,000; in June, 22,291; at the end of July, 31,678. This rough patch of rural land contained one of the largest concentrations of population in the entire South, and certainly the most densely concentrated.

The pressure on Andersonville was compounded by the breakdown of a system of prisoner exchanges between the two sides in the early part of 1864. When Grant took over as commander of the Union forces, he was in no hurry to resume exchanges. He explained his position in a letter:

> It is hard on our men held in Southern prisons not to exchange them, but it is humanity to those left in the ranks to fight our battles. Every man we hold, when released on parole or otherwise, becomes an active soldier against us at once either directly or indirectly. If we commence a system of exchanges which liberates all prisoners taken, we will have to fight on until the whole South is exterminated. If we hold those caught they amount to no more than dead men. At this particular time to release all rebel prisoners North would insure Sherman's defeat and would compromise our safety here.

Crowding was particularly acute at Andersonville. Even after one wall of the stockade had been moved to enlarge the prison area, it contained only 26 acres. On average, it allowed only 36 square feet for each man—a little plot of land six feet square. Even this figure understates the degree of crowding. An area 17 feet from the stockade was marked off by a "deadline" of two-by-fours fastened to upright posts. Any prisoner who went into this area was liable to be shot by guards stationed on top of the stockade—and many of them were. Several more acres were taken up by the fetid swamp that had developed along Sweetwater Creek.

As the boxcars slowly ground to a halt at the small railroad station near the stockade, Barney Brayman and the other surviving members of the once-proud Eighth Iowa Cavalry peered out at their new home. The first sensation that struck their senses was not visual but olfactory.

Andersonville stank.

The men emerged from the cars and lined up for the short march to the prison stockade. They were a sorry sight: The uniforms they had been wearing for more than a week of hard riding, fighting, and imprisonment were torn and filthy. Having had no chance to wash during their trip to the prison, their bodies were crusted with dirt and soot from the steam engine.

Led by their own sergeants, they were ordered to halt before a high wooden gate. There a Confederate noncom who didn't appear old enough to be in the army at all instructed them on the few rules that governed life in the stockade. The most important concerned the deadline: Anyone approaching the stockade wall would be shot. Looking up at the top of the stockade, the prisoners saw soldiers armed with what looked like Revolutionary War–era muzzle-loaders. Some of the guards looked so young, they should have been home with their mothers.

In small groups the new prisoners were herded through the big gateway into a kind of holding pen. After a group had passed through the first gate, it was shut. Only then was another large gate opened, on the opposite side, to admit them into the stockade.

The interior was a depressing sight. Thousands of men clad in rags wandered among the little huts, or "shebangs," as they called them. Others huddled on the ground, too sick or depressed to move. Still others gathered in clusters at the prison version of a flea market, where odds and ends of goods were sold to those who had some money or traded to those who had something of value. A sutler offered for sale an odd assortment of fruits, vegetables, cakes, pies, and condiments— all at exorbitant prices.

Little prison businesses flourished. Here was a barber, there a man who took in laundry. Several men used the Georgia clay to make ovens and turned out bread that they sold to the others.

Andersonville prison. (State Historical Society of Iowa Library/Archives, Des Moines.)

Looking about, Barney and the other newcomers were struck by how dirty everyone was. Their only source of heat for cooking was pine wood. With thousands of fires going almost constantly, everyone and everything was coated with a dark veneer of pine resin. There was no soap for washing, so the filth simply accumulated, layer on layer.

In a way, Barney and his friends were fortunate. If they had arrived a few weeks earlier, they would almost certainly have been set upon by one of the gangs known as "raiders." Operating in small rat-packs, the ruffians used knives and clubs to intimidate the other inmates, stealing everything from food and blankets to the clothing off their backs. At first confining their attacks to the nighttime, they had become increasingly bold, attacking where and when they wanted, even in broad daylight. When anyone offered resistance, a gang signal quickly called up more raiders, who were better fed and therefore stronger than the other prisoners. Their victims were often left badly beaten or dead.

When the Iowans arrived, everyone in the camp was still talking about the events of the previous few weeks, which had brought a sudden end to the raiders' depredations. On June 29 a man badly beaten by raiders had dragged himself to the prison gate. The sergeant at the gate called over Capt. Heinrich Hartmann Wirz—Americanized to Henry Wirz—who was in charge of the interior of the prison. The 40-year-old Swiss-born Wirz, whose normal way of speaking was full of profanity, promised that, if the prisoners pointed out the thieves, he would "clear the stockade of every son of a bitch." To underscore his determination, he told the prisoners they would get no rations for a week if they did not bring in the assailants.

This was all the encouragement the other prisoners needed. Eagerly they led the guards to the shebangs of the men they accused of being gang members, who were then herded outside the prison. Gen. John Henry Winder, who was in charge of the Confederate prison system, authorized the prisoners to form their own court to try the accused men. At these trials, the sentences imposed on those found guilty varied. Some were forced to wear a ball and chain. Others were placed in stocks or strung up by the thumbs. At one point the prisoners were provided with clubs, and the convicted men were forced to run the gauntlet. Several were beaten so badly, they died.

Six ringleaders were convicted of murder and sentenced to death. On July 11 the six men were marched into the compound and turned over to the leaders of the prison community. Looking up, they saw a scaffolding with six nooses awaiting them. One man exclaimed, "This cannot be," and broke away. He got clear through the cesspool along the banks of the stream before he was caught and brought back to join the others.

After prayers by the Catholic priest who was a frequent visitor to the prisoners, the supports were knocked from beneath the platform on which they stood. Five of them died almost instantly. But the sixth rope broke and the man fell to the ground, still alive. He pleaded for mercy, but the rope was quickly fixed, the platform was set up again, and he was hanged.

In the process of catching and punishing the raiders, the prison authorities had encouraged the creation of a kind of inmate police force known as the "regulators." After the executions the regulators were able to impose order and prevent a recurrence of the kind of lawlessness that had become such a threat to the peaceful inmates.

The stench that had assailed the nostrils of the newcomers when their train pulled into the station became overwhelming as they entered the compound. Sweetwater Creek was now anything but. Before the sluggish little stream flowed into the stockade area, it first passed the camp of the 3,000-man guard force, carrying with it the effluent from their sinks. It then passed the cooking area, picking up a load of grease and refuse.

With the pressure of the growing prison population, any attempts at maintaining sanitary discipline had collapsed. Most of the men relieved themselves in the fetid swamp along the stream's edge. But many simply did their business wherever they were, often just outside their shebangs. On a number of occasions, as thirsty prisoners leaned across the deadline, trying to get a cup of the already polluted water before it mingled with the camp's refuse, they were shot.

Looking about, the Iowans were struck by the way the whole landscape seemed to be pockmarked with holes and piles of dirt, almost as though the area had been subjected to an intense artillery barrage. They soon discovered the reason for all the holes. Many of the prisoners, unable to find enough cloth or scrap wood to make huts, had dug themselves little pits, where during the day they could huddle for shelter from the oppressive 110-degree heat of the summer sun and at night curl up to sleep. Other mounds of earth marked the sites of wells that prisoners had dug in their search for clean water. A visitor to the prison site 20 years later easily located 20 wells, some as deep as 30 feet. If the prisoners dug deep enough, their efforts were rewarded. But the water they found was a strange bluish color, smelled of sulfur, and seemed to cause dysentery.

For the prison authorities, the wells were a constant source of concern. Many of them, especially those close to the stockade wall, were also the entrance points to tunnels leading, the prisoners hoped, to freedom outside the walls. On a number of occasions prisoners succeeded in burrowing out beyond the walls. Typically, those who had constructed the tunnel went first. Then everyone who dared was welcome to follow them to freedom. The theory was that the first ones out had a better chance of getting away if the guards—and their bloodhounds—had to pursue a number of fugitives rather than just a few.

Most of those who managed to escape this way didn't get very far. Of all the thousands of men held at Andersonville, only 329 made good their escape. When men were caught and returned to the stockade, they were shackled to a ball and chain that made it a chore to carry out the simplest tasks and certainly made it much harder to run away again. One of the few who did get away was one member of the Eighth Cavalry—22-year-old James A. Benson. He later rejoined his regiment, was promoted twice, and served until August 1865.

On the afternoon of August 9, just about the time of the arrival of the survivors of the battle at Newnan, a violent thunder, lightning, and rain storm swept over the area. In the midst of the storm, a gushing spring of fresh water suddenly erupted from a sandy area near the banks of Sweetwater Creek—a gusher of water still flows there to this day. The prisoners, many of whom had been gathering to pray and sing hymns, took the opening of the spring as an answer to their prayers and named it Providence Spring. Old-time residents of the area, however, cast doubt on the miraculous source of the water. They recalled that the spring had always been there, but had been covered up with dirt during the construction of the stockade. The rush of storm water had simply reopened it.

The storm water did more than reopen the spring. It also tore a gaping hole in the stockade. Winder and Wirz were almost in a panic: While the prisoners feared them, with good reason, they also feared the prisoners, with perhaps even better reason.

When the first prisoners had arrived at the stockade, the guard force had been made up of reservists who had a semblance of military training and discipline. But as the war drained the South's limited supply of manpower, the reservists had been replaced by poorly trained, undisciplined militia. Many of them were boys no taller than the old muskets with which they were armed. Others were men too old or decrepit to join the fighting forces. There were not enough weapons to go around, and ammunition was in limited supply. The guards, outnumbered ten to one by the prisoners, constantly feared a mass escape.

For weeks, as Sherman's forces approached Atlanta, Wirz and Winder heard rumors that a Federal raid would be made to free the prisoners. In late July, when Stoneman began his sweep south toward Macon, Winder frantically appealed for more soldiers to defend the prison, both from raiders and from an outbreak by the prisoners. Outside the compound a long earthen berm was dug that would permit the Confederate defenders to face either way—toward a threat from the outside or one from the inside.

Sixteen cannons were arrayed around the compound, again arranged in such a way that they could be swiveled to fire outward or turned inward to mow down prisoners. At the time of the Stoneman raid, a rumor swept through the camp that Winder had issued orders that, if raiders got within seven miles of the camp, the cannons should fire on the prisoners. No evidence was ever produced that that rumor was true. But there was enough basis in fact to make it believable. In mid-July Wirz posted a notice warning against any attempt at a mass escape, concluding: "No choice would be left me but to open with grape and canister on the stockade, and what effect this would have in this densely crowded place need not be told."

A few days later Wirz made a similar threat in a meeting with a group of sergeants among the prisoners. Shortly after the meeting two cannons were fired as a signal for the guards to man their stations. Many of the prisoners fell to the ground, fearful that this was the beginning of a massacre.

It was in this atmosphere of fear that Winder and Wirz confronted the crisis occasioned by the hole in the stockade caused by the storm. While a large workforce of Negroes repaired the damaged wall, Winder kept his guard force under arms for sixty hours.

Barney and the other Iowans were probably a little worse off than many of the other prisoners had been when they arrived. As cavalry-men, losing their horses meant losing almost everything else they had. They arrived without blankets, a change of clothes, or cooking uten-sils. Many of the infantrymen had managed to retain a pup tent, a spare shirt and underclothes, and a blanket; with a good deal of inge-nuity, they managed to sew together scraps of clothing, blankets, and pieces of canvas to provide some shelter from the elements. But the cavalrymen had little more with them than the clothes they had been wearing when they were captured.

Once Barney and the Iowans had managed to find some shelter, their primary challenge was to stay healthy—or at least as healthy as they could in such an unhealthy environment.

By the time they arrived, the food ration—never adequate—was barely enough to sustain life. Some days no food was issued at all. On a good day each prisoner received a piece of cornbread about half the size of a brick. The bread was made from corn that had been ground, cob and all, and was so full of roughage that it tore at the men's bow-els. With the bread came a small piece of salt pork or bacon. Occa-sionally they received a few beans but no fresh vegetables. The diet was almost perfectly designed to produce scurvy and diarrhea, which it did.

The filth was another problem—and there was little to be done about it. Once Providence Spring started flowing, clean water was available for washing, but the prisoners had no soap to cut the grime. Mosquitoes were a constant presence. Some of the soldiers had so many bites, they looked as though they had measles. Even a tiny scratch or splinter could become infected, fester, and turn to gangrene. An act as simple as scratching a sunburned arm could prove fatal.

As in both armies, diarrhea or dysentery—no clear distinction between the two was made—were the great killers. Typhoid fever struck some of the prisoners, but most of them had already survived in the army long enough to gain immunity to the disease. This was not true of the recruits in the guard force, who suffered much more from typhoid than the prisoners did.

In the early days at Andersonville, a hospital area had been set aside within the walls. But as the population grew, the hospital was moved outside the stockade. Each morning surgeons or their aides would set up shop at the entrance to the compound. Those who were not too sick to walk hobbled to the aid station; others were carried by their friends. On many days the wait to see a doctor was as long as six hours. The sickest of all simply lay in their shebangs, wasted away, and died.

When a man died in the compound, he was often stripped of his clothing and his meager possessions were divided up. Sometimes the prisoners fought brutally over the spoils. The body was then carried to the gate, where it was placed in a line with the other corpses. Being chosen for a burial detail was one of the "perks" of prison life. Members of the burial detail carried the bodies outside the walls and deposited them in long trenches, with one body touching the next, and covered them with earth. They then had the opportunity to gather firewood or trade with members of the guard force before returning inside the walls.

On August 2, when an inspector from Richmond visited the prison, he found more than 20 percent of the prison population listed as sick: 5,010 men in the stockade and another 1,305 in the hospital.

Many of the ailing prisoners seemed to have little to choose between going to the hospital and dying in their own shebang. Some 75 percent of those sent to the hospital died there. For most of the patients, being hospitalized was the equivalent of receiving a death sentence.

Most of the hospital patients lay two to a bed on straw that crawled with vermin. But there were not enough bunks or even straw for all the sick. As a result, some of the men simply lay on the bare ground.

When Dr. Joseph Jones, a Confederate surgeon from Augusta, Georgia, visited the prison in August, he was appalled by what he saw:

> Large numbers were walking about who were not reported sick, who were suffering from severe and incurable diarrhea and scurvy. I visited 2,000 sick, lying under some long sheds—only one medical officer in attendance—whereas at least twenty should have been employed. From the crowded condition, bad diet, unbearable filth, dejected appearance of the prisoners, their systems had become so disordered that the slightest abrasion of the skin, from heat of the sun or even a mosquito bite, they took on rapid and frightful ulceration and gangrene.
>
> The continuous use of salt meats, imperfectly cured, and their total deprivation of vegetables and fruit, caused scurvy. The sick were lying upon the bare floors of open sheds, without even straw to rest upon. These haggard, dejected, living skeletons, crying for medical aid and food, and the ghastly corpses with glazed eyeballs, staring up into vacant space, with flies swarming down their open mouths and over their rags infested with swarms of lice and maggots, as they lay among the sick and dying—formed a picture of helpless, hopeless misery impossible in words to portray.
>
> Millions of flies swarmed over everything and covered the faces of the sick patients and crowded down their open mouths, depositing their maggots in the gangrenous wounds of the living and in the mouths of the dead.

Of the 42,646 prisoners held at Andersonville—most of them between the end of February and mid-October 1864—12,853 died. Their graves are now marked by a forest of white monuments set on a broad green lawn. Statues and monuments commemorate the sacrifices of soldiers from the various states. One tall monument, carrying the names of dead soldiers, lists 182 members of Iowa regiments, including 11 troopers of the Eighth Cavalry. The whole gardenlike area is strikingly reminiscent of the cemeteries at Antietam, Gettysburg, Chickamauga, and Shiloh, sites where men died fighting rather than as prisoners.

The 11 deaths in the Eighth Cavalry occurred within the course of a single month. On September 2 Sherman finally took Atlanta. On

September 5 the prison authorities, who had been seeking to lessen the crowding at Andersonville, began shipping men to other locations farther from the Union lines. Within a few weeks, only the most seriously sick were left at Andersonville.

Members of the Eighth Cavalry were sent first to Charleston, South Carolina, despite the protest of the prison commander that he had no room for them. They were herded into the grounds of the city jail, and within a few days the overflowing sinks were as bad as the swamp at Andersonville had been before the eruption of Providence Spring. The food they received was far superior, however: They were issued wheat bread, rice, hominy, flour, beans, salt, and molasses. Perhaps best of all, they received soap to wash away the grime of months.

At Andersonville just about their only contact with the outside world had been the frequent visits of several Catholic priests. Residents of the area often came to the prison, but they merely stared down at the inmates, like animals in a zoo, from the walkways occupied by the guards. A notable exception was one charitable young woman who was permitted inside to visit the prisoners. Wirz later reported that, without doubt, she had had sexual intercourse with at least seven prisoners. She refused payment, Wirz reported, and said she had come to see how she could help them. At Charleston charitable women of a quite different kind—the Sisters of Charity—went among the prisoners, bringing them medicines and gifts. Later, the men of the Eighth Cavalry thought back on Charleston as a kind of oasis in their captivity.

Unfortunately for the Iowans, the stay in Charleston was brief. By the end of the first week in October, they had all been shipped off to a stockade still under construction at Florence, South Carolina. Arriving there was almost exactly like being thrown back into Andersonville, with the filth, the lack of shelter, the inadequate rations, and the sickness. By October 12 Florence had 12,362 prisoners jammed into its 23-acre compound. Three quarters of them lacked blankets, and many had little clothing. Eight hundred were sick in the hospital, and they were dying at a rate of 20 to 50 a day.

The ration was supposed to be a quarter pound of meat or its equivalent in peas or rice and three gills—about four ounces—of molasses. But there was seldom meat or molasses to be had. By the end of January, the men were receiving barely enough food to prevent starvation. But with the Confederacy rapidly collapsing both militarily and economically, Richmond said it had no money to provide more food—and the ration would have to be cut.

With the war drawing to a close, an exchange of prisoners was resumed in February 1865. On February 26 Barney Brayman was among the members of his regiment who were handed over to Union officers in Wilmington, North Carolina.

While the very word *Andersonville* has become synonymous with brutality toward prisoners, the Georgia prison was not the only place where prisoners of war suffered. Neither side had been prepared for war on such a long and brutal scale, and neither was able to provide for thousands of prisoners for months and even years. Yet during the four years of the war, nearly half a million men were taken captive—214,865 by the North and 193,743 by the South. As word of the suffering at Andersonville made its way to Northern newspapers, the authorities in Washington reacted by cutting rations and otherwise trying to duplicate Andersonville conditions in Northern prisons. Of the prisoners held by the North, nearly 26,000, or more than 12 percent, died in captivity. Of those held by the South, some 30,000, or more than 15 percent, died.

The members of the 36th Iowa Infantry who survived the Battle at Marks' Mills and were marched off to prison remained for nearly ten months at Camp Ford, near Tyler, Texas. Conditions in the camp, which had initially been fairly pleasant, deteriorated with the arrival of the men captured in Louisiana and Arkansas as a result of the Red River expedition. The conditions seem not, however, to have been nearly as bad as at Andersonville or some of the other prisons in the east. When the men were finally released on February 15, they were pointed eastward and sent on their way.

They marched for six days, reaching Shreveport, Louisiana, on February 21. There they boarded Confederate steamers for the trip down the Red River to the Mississippi, for transfer to a Union ship that would take them on to New Orleans.

After General Lee's surrender to General Grant on April 9, Northern anger at the treatment Union prisoners had received in Confederate custody remained high. Calls for trials of those responsible filled Northern newspapers.

John Henry Winder, who would certainly have been at the top of the list of those to be tried by the victorious North, died during a New Year's dinner on January 1, 1865. The report soon passed among the prisoners that his last words were: "My faith is in Christ; I expect to be saved; Wirz, cut down the Yankees' rations."

With Winder gone, Wirz survived as the symbol of Southern brutality toward prisoners. He was seized, brought to Washington, tried, and hanged on November 10, 1865.

When Barney Brayman arrived home on leave, his appearance was a shocking sight to his mother, Mary, his father, Lewis, and his two sisters, Tory and little Belle. The strapping youth who had gone off so confidently only two years before now had the shrunken look of an old man. A doctor who examined him shortly after his return found him "suffering from general debility and irritability of system" and concluded he was unfit for military duty. He was discharged from service on July 12, 1865.

If his parents and sisters were shocked at Barney's appearance, he was equally discomfited by the condition of his father. Lewis Brayman had not been well when Barney left and had been managing the family's small hotel rather than farming. But now he was obviously much sicker. Lewis, grieving for the loss of one son and worried about the health of the other, died on July 30.

For a few years Barney tried to operate the Brayman House hotel, but his health did not improve. In 1869 he moved to Rushford, Minnesota, in hopes of improving his health. There he worked with a cousin manufacturing wooden pumps. But his health continued to deteriorate. He died in Rushford on October 31, 1871, probably of tuberculosis contracted in prison. He was 24 years old.

Tory and Belle lived on and had children of their own. But the dream of a bright future in their new farm home that Mary and Lewis carried with them to the Iowa frontier began to dim with the coming of war and faded with the loss of Andrew and his father. With the death of Barney, the dream was at an end.

EPILOGUE

When the Civil War began, the United States was still predominantly an agricultural society, with more people living on farms than in the cities. Americans could still think of themselves in Jefferson's terms as "the chosen people of God."

By the time the war ended in 1865, the balance was shifting sharply. Immigration from Europe was swelling the eastern cities. And while slightly more Americans still worked on farms than in shops or factories, industry for the first time contributed more to the national economy than the nation's farms.

Washington, which to many Americans had been both remote and insignificant before the war, assumed a more visible and more important part in the nation's life. As the federal government expanded to fight the war, it assumed a greater role in stimulating and regulating the economy. The era of big government had arrived, although the government was still small by today's standards.

Jefferson's dream of a peaceful, self-governing agrarian society with a small and weak federal government was dead.

The frontier, which had been such an important part of Jefferson's dream, still existed, however—and Americans were still busy conquering it. Four years after the war ended, the transcontinental railroad was completed, linking the eastern and western sections of the country and helping to open up the territory in between.

The vast armies that had fought the war were quickly disbanded. The 36th Iowa Infantry continued in existence until the end of the war but never recovered from the disaster at Marks' Mills. The Eighth Iowa Cavalry was reconstituted after its defeat at Newnan and took part in operations in Tennessee and Alabama toward the end of the war.

In its final year—the year in which Andrew Brayman died and Barney Brayman suffered as a prisoner—the war became more than ever a bloody test of wills. Militarily, the Confederacy can be said to have lost the war when Vicksburg fell in the summer of 1863. The South fought on in the hope that the North would lose its will to fight and repudiate Abraham Lincoln in the election of November 1864. But military success, especially Sherman's march through Georgia, buoyed Northern morale and Lincoln's Republican administration was given another four years in office. Only then did the war finally grind to a halt.

The nation had suffered a terrible loss, not only in terms of physical destruction but in human terms. Six hundred thousand young men lost their lives during the four years of the war. It is impossible to measure what marvelous things they might have been able to do if they had survived.

Among those who did not survive was Colonel Dorr, the newspaper-editor-turned-soldier who commanded the Eighth Iowa Cavalry. After being captured at Newnan, he was exchanged and then resumed command of the reconstituted regiment. In May 1865, however, while in camp at Macon, he became ill with what was diagnosed as neuralgic rheumatism. Despite his illness, he went about his duties until May 28. He arose that morning as usual. Then, feeling suddenly ill, he lay down on his bed and died.

Many of those who survived the war remained broken in both health and spirit. Kittredge, the commander of Andrew Brayman's 36th Iowa Infantry, was court-martialed in March 1865 for drunkenness on duty, conduct prejudicial to good order and military discipline, and conduct unbecoming an officer and a gentleman—all apparently arising from a New Year's Eve party. The military court found him not guilty, but his commanding officer overruled the court, found him guilty, and dismissed him from the service. Kittredge fought the case all the way to Washington and won an order from President Andrew Johnson restoring him to command of the regiment. But by that time the war was over and the regiment was soon disbanded.

After the war Kittredge returned to Iowa and became a manufacturer of wagons. But he apparently never fully recovered from the wound in the groin he had received during his first tour of duty at the Battle of Belmont in January 1861.

For others, the war experience was the prelude to successful careers and even significant accomplishment. Grant, of course, went on to serve two terms as U.S. president. Stoneman, who seemed to make a hash of everything he attempted as a cavalry commander, went to California after the war and was elected governor.

Francis Marion Drake, who was in command at the disastrous Battle of Marks' Mills, where Andrew Brayman lost his life, flourished after the war. He founded Drake University and went on to serve as governor of Iowa.

General Wheeler, the Confederate cavalry commander who defeated McCook's force at Newnan, later returned to Federal service and at the end of the century, sporting a bushy snow-white beard, commanded American troops in the Spanish-American War.

With her husband and her two sons dead, Mary Brayman had increasing difficulty making ends meet. She gradually sold off the land the family had accumulated and used the money to live on and to educate her youngest daughter, Belle.

Shortly after the war, Mary and Belle moved to Centerville to live with Tory, her husband, Gilbert Goodenough, and their children, Mary Genette, 9, who was named for her grandmother, and Polina, 3.

Over the years Mary sent, through an agent, a series of ever more desperate appeals to the authorities in Washington in an attempt to obtain a pension based on Barney's service and imprisonment.

The answers from Washington—when the appeals were answered at all—were negative. Mary was forced to live with one or the other of her two daughters. In 1891 she was living with Tory in the small community of Farmington. She died there, destitute, on February 28, at the age of 76. She was buried beside her husband in the little rural Miller graveyard a mile and a half from Bellair. An obelisk marking the grave carries the names of Mary, Lewis, and their two sons, although the sons were not buried there.

Despite the family's increasingly perilous financial condition, Belle managed to obtain a good education, first at the Kirksville Normal School in Kirksville, Missouri, just across the border from Bellair, and at the Hamilton Female Seminary in Hamilton, Illinois.

At Kirksville, Belle met Alfred Randall Orr. (Everyone who knew him called him Orr, rather than Alfred.) They were married on August 5, 1879, then left for California, where Orr had founded the Visalia Normal School.

At the time of her wedding, Belle passed around a small autograph book in which friends wrote their good wishes and signed their names. Mary Brayman, her mother, who loved to write poetry, inscribed a brief verse that assumes added poignancy in light of the deaths of her two sons:

To Belle

Thou art going to leave me, my darling
My youngest, my loved one, my pet
Thou art going to the house of another
Whose love has not been tested as yet.

Will his love be like the love of a mother?
Will it shield thee through sickness, pain and
If not these; a love above all other
Which to trust will not be in vain.

May the clouds ever have a silver lining
That obscure thy horizon from view
And the sun be more brilliantly shining
And earthly beauties forever be new.

May the richest of heavenly blessings
Ever rest upon thee; and on thine
Is the prayer of your poor lonely mother,
Will be her prayer for all coming time.

Belle and Orr prospered in Visalia, where he was an educator and later mayor. The couple had four children: Alice, born in 1880; Austin, born in 1881; Zelma, born in 1882; and Edith, born in 1887.

Zelma died at the age of nine in 1891. Less than two years later, Belle herself became ill with tuberculosis and died on January 14, 1893, shortly after her thirty-sixth birthday.

Her widower later married a woman with three children. On October 3, 1897, while the boys were playing with a revolver, 16-year-old Austin was accidentally shot and killed by his stepbrother.

Alice and Edith grew into adulthood. Edith married Charles John Kelly in 1917 while he was serving as a sergeant in World War I, and they had two children, Alfred Orr Kelly and Charles John "Jack" Kelly, both born in San Luis Obispo, California. Alice died in 1942 and Edith in 1950.

Jack Kelly died in 1945 at the age of 20. Orr Kelly is the co-author of this look back through the shadows of time to catch a glimpse of two Iowa farm boys who marched off to war and gave their lives for their country.

Notes on Sources

Chapter 1: A Call to Arms

Much of the basic biographical information about the members of the Brayman family is the result of research done by the late Pearl Gordon Vestal of Keokuk, Iowa. Mrs. Vestal, a great-granddaughter of Mary Genette Gore Brayman, obtained the large autograph album in which Mary Brayman kept family records.

We have not seen the album itself, but Mrs. Vestal copied the material Mary Brayman had recorded therein and made it available to the Illinois Genealogical Records Committee of the Daughters of the American Revolution, which compiled a list of church histories, baptisms, and cemetery, Bible, and marriage records in the 1940s.

In 1934 Mrs. Vestal wrote a detailed family genealogical history for Harold Crown, a resident of Farmington, Iowa. Both Mrs. Vestal and Mr. Crown were great-grandchildren of Lewis and Mary Brayman.

In the fall of 1991, we happened to visit the small town of Farmington and learned that Mr. Crown's home and possessions were to be auctioned in a few days. Through the courtesy of Mary Jo Smith, the conservator of the estate, we obtained the genealogical history written by Mrs. Vestal, as well as pictures of Andrew and Barney Brayman and a number of letters comprising the correspondence between their sister, Victoria Ichebenda Brayman Goodenough, and her granddaughter, Mrs. Vestal.

We have been able to verify much of the information provided by Mrs. Vestal through census reports and records in the Appanoose County Courthouse in Centerville, Iowa.

The quotation from the Ottumwa *Courier* was obtained from the microfilmed copies of the newspaper in the Iowa State Historical Society Library in Des Moines.

General background information on the Civil War was obtained from a number of sources, primarily Bruce Catton, *The Civil War* (Boston: Houghton Mifflin, 1988), and Col. R. Ernest DuPuy and Col. Trevor N. DuPuy, U.S. Army (Ret.), *The Compact History of the Civil War* (New York: Time Life, 1960).

Background information on the regiments in which the Brayman boys served—the 36th Iowa Volunteer Infantry and the Eighth Iowa Cavalry—was obtained from the *Roster and Record of the Iowa Soldiers in the War of the Rebellion*, published by authority of the General Assembly, under the direction of Brig. Gen. Guy E. Logan, Adjutant General, Des Moines, in 1910 and 1911, and Lurton Dunham Ingersoll, *Iowa and the Rebellion, History of the Troops Furnished by the State of Iowa to the Volunteer Armies of the Union, Which Conquered the Great Southern Rebellion of 1861–5*, (Philadelphia: J. B. Lippincott, 1867).

The account of the recruitment effort in Appanoose County is drawn from Edgar R. Harlan, ed., "Benjamin F. Pearson's War Diary," *Annals of Iowa* 15, nos. 2, 3, 5, 6 and 7 (July 1925–April 1927). Pearson, a lieutenant in Company G of the 36th Iowa Volunteers—the unit in which Andrew Brayman served—kept a detailed and perceptive diary from the time when the regiment was being formed until it was discharged.

The description of Andrew Brayman was obtained from his enlistment papers, which are available on microfilm at the National Archives in Washington, D.C.

A history of Appanoose County and biographical information on the officers of Andrew's Company I are contained in Anon., *Early Pioneer Days* (Centerville, IA: Appanoose Genealogical Society, n.d.) and *Biographical and Historical Record of Wayne and Appanoose Counties, Iowa* (Chicago: Inter-State Publishing Co., 1886). Both are available at the public library in Centerville.

Chapter 2: The Dream Is Born

The material on Thomas Jefferson was drawn from Adrienne Koch and William Peden, eds., *The Life and Selected Writings of Thomas Jefferson* (New York: Modern Library, 1944).

An account of the history of Appanoose County is contained in the *Biographical and Historical Record of Wayne and Appanoose Counties,* cited on page 252.

Lewis Brayman's land purchases are detailed in records available at the Appanoose County Courthouse in Centerville, Iowa.

The depression beginning in 1857 is described in *Early Pioneer Days,* cited on page 252.

Chapter 3: You're in the Army Now

The frosty reception received by the first troops arriving in Keokuk is contained in E. F. Ware, *The Lyon Campaign in Missouri: Being a History of the First Iowa Infantry* (Topeka: Crane & Co., 1907).

Benjamin Pearson's diary, cited on page 252, is the source for the description of the regiment's arrival in Keokuk and Camp Lincoln.

The delays in issuing uniforms and blankets and the sickness of many men in the 36th Iowa are detailed in a series of letters from the regimental commander, Col. Charles W. Kittredge, to the state adjutant general, dated October 24, 27, and 30 and November 3 and 21, 1862. The originals of the letters are contained in the Iowa State Archives.

Biographical information about Lt. Col. F. M. Drake is contained in *Early Pioneer Stories,* cited above. Material concerning Colonel Kittredge's career was obtained from his service record and pension papers at the National Archives.

The telegram from N. B. Baker attempting to prevent Kittredge's commission from reaching him and Kittredge's letter to the governor are in the files of the adjutant general at the Iowa State Archives.

A description of the tactical training of Civil War infantry is contained in Grady McWhiney and Perry D. Jamieson, *Attack and Die: Civil War Military Tactics and the Southern Heritage* (Tuscaloosa: University of Alabama Press, 1982).

A description of the Austrian rifle issued to the regiment is contained in Earl J. Coates and Dean S. Thomas, *An Introduction to Civil War Small Arms* (Gettysburg, PA: Thomas Publications, 1990).

An account of the problems of supplying the Union Army as it grew from a few thousand is contained in Erna Risch, *Quartermaster Support of the Army: A History of the Corps 1775–1939* (Washington, D.C.: Quartermaster Historian's Office, Office of the Quartermaster General, 1962).

A soldier using the pseudonym of "Typo" described conditions when the regiment arrived at Benton Barracks in St. Louis in a letter to the editor of the *Weekly Ottumwa Courier*, December 13, 1862, on file at the Iowa State Historical Society Library.

Chapter 4: Down the Big River

The account of General Grant's campaign against Vicksburg is drawn from *The Civil War* and *The Compact History of the Civil War*, cited above, William S. McFeely, *Grant: A Biography* (New York: W. W. Norton, 1981); William T. Sherman, *Memoirs of General William T. Sherman*, with introduction by William S. McFeely (New York: Da Capo Press, 1984; originally published in 1875); and FM 100-5 *Operations*, Headquarters Department of the Army, May 1986.

Conditions in Helena when the 36th Iowa served there are described in *Historic Helena—West Helena*, 2nd ed. (Helena, AR: Phillips County Historical Society, 1978). Other details of Helena in that period are contained in two articles appearing in the spring 1993 issue of the *Phillips County Historical Review*: "Ella King Newsome, Confederate Nurse" and "Adventures on a Hospital Boat on the Mississippi," by Margaret Elizabeth Breckinridge.

Iowa soldiers wrote a series of letters from Helena published in the *Weekly Ottumwa Courier* on March 19, May 7, and May 21, 1863.

Pearson, cited above, described the Yazoo River expedition in his diary. Other details are provided in the diary of Capt. Allen W. Miller, Company C, 36th Iowa Infantry, on file at the Iowa State Historical Society, and in *Letters Home From an Iowa Soldier in the Civil War*. The letters from Newton Scott, a member of the 36th Iowa, to Hannah M. Cone, were posted on the Internet at http://www.ucsc.edu/civil-war-letters/home.html by Bill Proudfoot, pfoot@sj.znet.com.

Andrew's visits to the regimental surgeon and his eventual hospitalization were recorded in the regimental records available at the National Archives.

Chapter 5: "The Tennessee Quick-Step"

The dates of Andrew Brayman's hospitalization at Jefferson Barracks and Keokuk are contained in his service record, available at the National Archives.

Almost everything known about Civil War medicine is contained in the monumental six-volume *The Medical and Surgical History of the War of the Rebellion*, with surgeons Joseph J. Woodward and George A. Otis as the major editors. It was issued over an eighteen-year period (1870–88) by the U.S. Medical Department. The report was reprinted in 1992 as *The Medical and Surgical History of the Civil War* by Broadfoot Publishing Co., Wilmington, North Carolina. It was this version that we consulted at the National Medical Library at the National Institutes of Health in Bethesda, Maryland. The report lists the names of thousands of Union soldiers and describes their wounds, or illnesses. Unfortunately, Andrew Brayman was not one of those included, perhaps because his ailment—diarrhea—was both the most common and the most deadly.

The statistics concerning the number of patients treated at the two hospitals where Andrew was treated were obtained from this source.

A valuable summary of information on Civil War–era medicine is contained in George W. Adams, *Doctors in Blue: The Medical History of the Union Army in the Civil War* (New York: Henry Schuman, 1952).

Other sources of information on Civil War medicine consulted were Dr. Charles F. Ballou III, "Civil War Medicine, the Confederate Side," *Washington Post*, January 23, 1996; and Otto Eisenschiml, "Medicine in the War," *Civil War Times* 1, no. 2 (May 1962).

We also attended a series of lectures on "Civil War Medicine: Doctors in Blue and Gray," sponsored by the Smithsonian Institution and the National Museum of Civil War Medicine at the Smithsonian Institution in Washington on March 15 and 16, 1996. The moderator was Burton K. Kummerow, then head of the National Museum of Civil War Medicine in Frederick, Maryland. The keynote lecture was delivered by Dr. Alfred J. Bollet, clinical professor of medicine, Yale University.

Other lecturers were Jonathan O'Neal, M.D., an Air Force flight surgeon; Dr. Gordon E. Dammann, D.D.S.; Paul Sledzik, curator with a specialization in forensic anthropology from The National Museum of Health and Medicine; and Dr. Thomas P. Lowry, M.D., a psychiatrist from the University of California at San Francisco.

Chapter 6: Reunion in Little Rock

Four books provided background information on Arkansas and Little Rock during the Civil War: Harry S. Ashmore, *Arkansas: A History*

(New York: W. W. Norton, 1984); William W. O'Donnell, *The Civil War Quadrennium* (North Little Rock, AR: Horton Brothers, 1985); Leander Stillwell, *The Story of a Common Soldier of Army Life in the Civil War: 1861–1865*, 2nd ed. (Franklin Hudson Publishing Co., 1920); and Barry Popchuck, ed., *Soldier Boy: The War Letters of Charles O. Musser, 29th Iowa* (Iowa City: University of Iowa Press). Available at the Robert W. Woodruff Library, Emory University, Atlanta, Georgia.

The march of the 36th Iowa from Helena to Little Rock and life in Little Rock are described in Pearson's diary, cited on page 252, and in other letters, diaries, and newspaper articles, among them:

Letter from W.H.C., *Weekly Union Guard*, Bloomington, Iowa, October 24, 1863, Iowa State Historical Society Library.

Letter from J. H. McVay, *Weekly Ottumwa Courier*, October 22, 1863, Iowa State Historical Society Library.

Daily Pocket Diary for 1863, handwritten by Capt. Martin Varner, 36th Iowa Infantry, on file at the Iowa State Archives, Des Moines. This is one of the most poignant documents, taking Varner from command of a regiment through his final illness. The last few lines were written by friends, recording Varner's death and their decision to use the money found in his pockets to buy a metal casket so his body could be sent home.

Carl H. Moneyhon, ed., "Life in Confederate Arkansas: The Diary of Virginia Davis Gray, 1863–1865, Part I," *Arkansas Historical Quarterly* 42, no. 1 (Spring 1983), available at Arkansas History Commission.

Edward G. Longacre, "Letter From Little Rock of Captain James M. Bowler, 112th United States Colored Troops," *Arkansas Historical Quarterly* 11, no. 3 (Autumn 1981).

Larry Wesley Pearce, "The American Missionary Association and the Freedmen in Arkansas, 1863–1878," *Arkansas Historical Quarterly* 30, no. 2 (September 1971).

Frances Mitchell Ross, "Civil War Letters from James Mitchell to His Wife, Sarah Elizabeth Latta Mitchell," *Arkansas Historical Quarterly* 37, no. 4 (Winter 1978).

Mary P. Fletcher, ed., "An Arkansas Lady in the Civil War: Reminiscences of Susan Fletcher," *Arkansas Historical Quarterly* 2, no. 4 (December 1943).

Leo E. Huff, "The Union Expedition Against Little Rock, August–September, 1863," *Arkansas Historical Quarterly* 22, no. 3 (Fall 1963).

Michael B. Dougan, "Life in Confederate Arkansas," *Arkansas Historical Quarterly* 31, no. 1 (Spring 1972).

Clara B. Kennan, "Arkansas's Old State House," *Arkansas Historical Quarterly* 19, no. 1 (Spring 1950).

Chapter 7: The Hanging of David Dodd

The case of David Dodd is referred to in the books cited in Chapter 6 and is described in detail in LeRoy H. Fischer, "David Owen Dodd: Folk Hero of Confederate Arkansas," *Arkansas Historical Quarterly* 37, no. 2 (Summer 1978).

We also discussed the case with Gregory J. W. Urwin, professor of history at the University of Central Arkansas in Conway, Arkansas.

The problem of paramilitary or criminal gangs is described in Leo E. Huff, "Guerrillas, Jayhawkers and Bushwhackers in Northern Arkansas During the Civil War," *Arkansas Historical Quarterly* 24, no. 2 (Summer 1965).

The hanging of Jeremiah Earnest and Thomas Jefferson Miller was reported in the March 26, 1864, issue of *The National Democrat* of Little Rock. It was examined at the Library of Congress in Washington, D.C.

Chapter 8: Another Son Goes to War

Background information about the Brayman family is drawn from the sources cited for Chapter 1. General background information about the progress of the war and the political situation is drawn from Catton and DuPuy, cited above, and from Albert Castel, *Decision in the West: The Atlanta Campaign of 1864* (Lawrence: University Press of Kansas, 1992). Specific information about the situation in Iowa was drawn from Dan Elbert Clark, *Samuel Jordan Kirkwood* (Iowa City: State Historical Society of Iowa, 1917).

The history of the Eighth Cavalry is covered in *Roster and Record of the Iowa Soldiers in the War of the Rebellion* and *Iowa and the Rebellion, History of the Troops Furnished by the State of Iowa to the Volunteer Armies of the Union, Which Conquered the Great Southern rebellion of 1861–5*, cited on page 252. Other details of the service of the regiment are covered in Capt. M. M. Walden, *A Brief History of the Eighth Iowa Volunteer Cavalry* (Des Moines, IA: Register and Leader Co., 1889), and a handwritten "History of the 8th Iowa Cavalry for 1863 and

1864," prepared by Col. J. B. Dorr, the regiment's founder and commander. Dorr's report is available at the Iowa State Archives.

Newspapers consulted at the Iowa State Archives contained many references to the war and the efforts to recruit new regiments. Among them were:

The Weekly Union Guard, Bloomfield, Iowa, October 24, 1863. Proclamation by President Lincoln setting draft of 300,000, detailing how states will respond.

The Weekly Union Guard, November 7, 1863. Proclamation by Governor Samuel J. Kirkwood, October 26, urging support of Lincoln's call.

The Weekly Union Guard, February 20, 1864. Statement from Governor W. M. Stone, dated February 5, noting draft of 500,000 scheduled for March 10. Says he promised Iowa would meet its quota: "There must be no draft in Iowa." Number of Iowans needed should not exceed 6,000.

The Weekly Union Guard, February 27, 1864. Proclamation dated Des Moines, February 14, from office of Governor Stone. He complains that men are going beyond the Missouri to escape military service; refers to men going to the goldfields of Colorado, Nevada, Utah, the Rocky Mountains; forbids anyone to move out of Iowa before March 10; and orders guards on river crossings between Leavenworth, Kansas, and Sioux City, South Dakota.

The draft riots in New York and other cities are described in Eugene C. Murdock, *One Million Men: The Civil War Draft in the North* (Madison: State Historical Society of Wisconsin, 1971), and James McCague, *The Second Rebellion: The Story of the New York City Draft Riots in 1863* (New York: Dial Press, 1868). Both books are available in the library of the National Archives.

Chapter 9: Cavalrymen at Last

General information about the Eighth Cavalry in this chapter is drawn from the same sources cited for Chapter 8.

An especially useful source was the biography of George Monlux, a member of the regiment. It is available in an undated, typewritten version at the Iowa State Historical Society Library. Most of the detail about the regiment's service to the west of Nashville during the winter of 1863–64 is drawn from Monlux's diary.

Background information on the military situation in the winter of 1863–64 is drawn from the Sherman and Grant biographies; *Decision in the West,* cited on page 257; and Richard M. McMurry, "Atlanta Campaign: Sherman Plunges into a North Georgia 'Hell Hole,'" *Blue & Gray* 6, issue 4 (April 1989).

The description of life in Nashville was drawn from Walter T. Durham, *Nashville: The Occupied City. The First Seventeen Months— February 16, 1862 to June 30, 1863* (Nashville: Tennessee Historical Society, 1985); James A. Hoobler, *Cities Under the Gun: Images of Occupied Nashville and Chattanooga* (Nashville: Rutledge Hill Press, 1986); John Egerton, *The Faces of Two Centuries: 1780–1980* (Nashville: Plusmedia, 1979); and Robert S. Henry, "Chattanooga and the War," *Tennessee Historical Quarterly* 19, no. 3 (September 1960).

Chapter 10: Thinking the Unthinkable

Like all serious students of the Civil War, we relied heavily on Robert N. Scott, chief compiler, *The War of the Rebellion: A Compilation of the Official Records of the Union and Confederate Armies* (Washington, D.C.: Government Printing Office, 1880–1901). This great collection, in 128 volumes, contains reports, messages, and correspondence of officers on both sides of the conflict. We examined the volumes at the Dorothy C. Starr Civil War Library at the Fort Ward Museum in Alexandria, Virginia, and relied most heavily on series I, vol. 34, part I, "Reports," and part III, "Correspondence," and on vol. 38, parts I, II, and III, "Reports," and part V, "Correspondence," for descriptions of the military situation in this and subsequent chapters.

In this chapter and the subsequent ones dealing with the war in Louisiana and Arkansas, we relied heavily on Ludwell H. Johnson, *Red River Campaign: Politics and Cotton in the Civil War* (Kent, OH: Kent State University Press, 1993).

Chapter 11: Fight for Elkins' Ferry

Brig. Gen. Frederick Steele's doubts about the wisdom of his participation in the Red River expedition were spelled out in a series of messages back and forth with other commanders throughout the winter of 1863–64 and were recorded in *Official Records* cited above.

The participation of the 36th Iowa in the campaign was described in a letter from Lt. Col. Francis M. Drake, the deputy commander of the regiment, to A. B. Baker, the Iowa State adjutant general, from Little Rock on February 28, 1865. His report is available at the Iowa State Archives.

Drake elaborated on his wartime experiences in "Personal Reminiscences of F. M. Drake, on the Campaign of General Steele Through Arkansas to Join General Banks on the Red River Expedition," contained in *War Sketches and Incidents, as Related by Companions of the Iowa Commandery, Military Order of the Loyal Legion of the United States*, vol. I (Des Moines: P.C. Kenyon, 1893). These reminiscences are the source of the quoted dialogue involving Drake in this chapter and in Chapters 14 and 15.

This chapter, like all those involving the 36th Iowa, relies on Pearson's detailed and perceptive diary, cited on page 252.

Chapter 12: Disaster at Sabine Crossroads

This chapter is drawn largely from *Official Records* and from Durham's account of the Red River expedition, cited on page 259.

Chapter 13: Flight to Camden

We visited the Prairie De Anne battlefield site and discussed the battle with John Teeter, who operates an historical museum in the small neighboring town of Prescott.

Pearson, in his diary, gives a vivid account of the stirring spectacle of the Union army drawn up in battle formation.

In Camden, we visited the Chidester house, which served as headquarters for generals on both sides at slightly different times.

Other details of the battle at Prairie De Anne are contained in J. H. Atkinson, "The Action at Prairie de Ann," *Arkansas Historical Quarterly* 19, no. 1 (Spring 1960); Alwyn Barr, "Confederate Artillery in Arkansas," *Arkansas Historical Quarterly* 22, no. 3 (Fall 1963); and General Clement A. Evans, ed., *Confederate Military History*, vol. 10, (Atlanta: Confederate Publishing Co., 1899).

Note: We encountered a number of spellings for Prairie de Anne, which apparently resulted from an attempt by French explorers to sound out an Indian name in French. For consistency, we have used Prairie de Anne, except where it is contained in a direct quote or the title of an article.

Chapter 14: Massacre at Poison Springs

The food-gathering foray by the 36th Iowa is described in Drake's 1865 report and in Pearson's diary.

Accounts of the Battle of Poison Springs by officers on both sides are contained in *Official Records*.

The most detailed account of what happened at Poison Springs is contained in an unpublished manuscript, "'We Cannot Treat Negroes . . . as Prisoners of War': Racial Atrocities and Reprisals in Civil War Arkansas," by Professor Urwin of the University of Central Arkansas.

Other accounts of the battle are contained in C. T. Anderson, ed. Roman J. Zorn, "Campaigning in Southern Arkansas: A Memoir," *Arkansas Historical Quarterly* 8, no. 3 (Autumn 1949); Edwin Bearss, "The Battle of Poison Springs," *Ouachita County Historical Quarterly* 25, no. 3 (Spring 1994); Virginia McCollum Stinson, "Yankees in Camden," *Ouachita County Historical Quarterly* 25, no. 3 (Spring 1994); Mrs. Hellice Gillespie Burton, "Battle at Poison Springs," *Ouachita County Historical Quarterly* 22, no. 2 (December 1990); and Ira Don Richards, "The Battle of Poison Spring," *Arkansas Historical Quarterly* 18, no. 4 (Winter 1959).

More general information relating to African-Americans is contained in John L. Jordan, "Was There a Massacre at Fort Pillow?" *Tennessee Historical Quarterly* 6, no. 2 (June 1947); Joseph T. Glatthaar, *Forged in Battle: The Civil War Alliance of Black Soldiers and White Officers* (New York: Free Press, 1990); Dudley Taylor Cornish, *The Sable Arm: Black Troops in the Union Army 1861–1865* (Topeka: University Press of Kansas); and Edward G. Longacre, "Letter From Little Rock of Captain James M. Bowler, 112th United States Colored Troops," *Arkansas Historical Quarterly* 11, no. 3 (Autumn 1981).

Chapter 15: Death at Marks' Mills

Information about the battle at Marks' Mills is drawn from *Official Records*; the history of the 36th Iowa, Colonel Drake's 1865 report and his later reminiscences; and *Confederate Military History*, all cited on pages 259–60.

A particularly valuable source of information was Anita Knowles, "110 Years Ago Thursday Salty Branch Ran Blood," reprinted in *Family Ties: Official Newsletter of the Marks-Barnett Family Association* 11, no. 1 (May 1995). We also interviewed Mrs. Knowles at her rural home a few miles from the Marks' Mills battle site on April 21, 1996.

Another valuable interview was with Townsend Mosely, a Camden native who has on a number of occasions walked the route of Steele's army, using his metal detector to determine not only the roads the soldiers took but the precise location of troop units in the various battles. It was through his guidance that we were able to determine, probably within a few yards, the spot where Andrew Brayman was killed.

The battle at Marks' Mills is also covered in Edwin C. Bearss, *Steele's Retreat From Camden and the Battle of Jenkins' Ferry* (Little Rock, AR: Democrat Printing and Litho Co., 1967), and E. R. Hutchens, *The War of the 'Sixties* (New York: Neale Publishing Co., 1912), which contains "The Battle of Mark's Mills" by William Jasper Young, Private, 36th Iowa Infantry Volunteers.

The intriguing view of the Battle of Marks' Mills through the eyes of a young Confederate soldier was drawn from Henry Cathey, ed., "Extracts From the Memoirs of William Franklin Avera," *Arkansas Historical Quarterly* 22, no. 2 (Summer 1963).

At the Iowa State Archives we found the following record of the inventory of the effects of Andrew Brayman:

Head Quarters Co. I, 36th Regiment Iowa Volunteer Infantry, Little Rock, Arkansas, August 16, 1864.
To the Adjutant General of Iowa: Inventory of effects of Pvt. Andrew J. Brayman, late of Co. I, 36th Volunteer Infantry who was killed at Marks Mills, Arkansas, the 25th day of April, 1864. No effects. Last paid to 31 December, 1863. Drew clothing to the amount of $10.09 since last settlement, October 31, 1863.
(Signed) G. R. Huston, 1st Lt.
Commanding Co. I, 36th Regiment
Iowa Volunteer Infantry.

The diary of Hiram A. Pratt, Company B, 36th Iowa Infantry, is on file in the Iowa State Archives. The diary, which relates primarily to the period of the captivity of members of the regiment, is in such delicate condition that we could not use a copying machine to reproduce it. Instead, we transcribed it during a visit to the Archives on November 1, 1995.

Chapter 16: Escape from Camden

Information for this chapter was drawn from *Official Records*; Bearss's *Steele's Retreat From Camden and the Battle of Jenkins' Ferry*; and Urwin's unpublished manuscript about the Battle of Poison Springs, cited on page 261.

The quiet departure of Steele's forces from Camden is described in Virginia McCollum Stinson, "The Yankees in Camden," cited on page 261.

Chapter 17: Offensive in Georgia

This account of Sherman's march from Chattanooga and the involvement of the Eighth Cavalry in that campaign is drawn from the same basic documents listed for Chapters 8 and 9: the Official Records; Sherman's *Memoirs*; Castel's *Decision in the West*; McMurry's "Atlanta Campaign"; Colonel Dorr's history of the regiment; the Monlux diary; and Captain Walden's account of his experiences as commander of Company H.

Also useful sources were Steve Meyer, *Iowa Valor: A Compilation of Civil War Combat Experiences From Soldiers of the State Distinguished As Most Patriotic of the Patriotic* (Garrison, IA: Meyer Publishing Co., 1994); Homer Mead, *The Eighth Iowa Cavalry In The Civil War: Autobiography and Personal Recollections of Homer Mead, M.D.* (Carthage, IL: S. C. Davidson, n.d.); William Deloss Love, *Wisconsin in the War of the Rebellion: A History of all Regiments and Battles* (Chicago: Church and Goodman, 1866); Edward Hagerman, *The American Civil War and the Origins of Modern Warfare: Ideas, Organization and Field Command* (Bloomington: Indiana University Press, 1992); and Grady McWhiney and Perry D. Jamieson, *Attack and Die: Civil War Military Tactics and the Southern Heritage* (Tuscaloosa: University of Alabama Press, 1982).

During a visit to Georgia in February 1996, we traced the route of the Eighth Cavalry from Cleveland, Tennessee, to the disastrous battle at Newnan, Georgia. While in Dalton, Georgia, we toured the Rocky Ridge fortifications with Kevin McAuliff, a preservation planner in Dalton for the State Regional Development Center.

Chapter 18: On to Atlanta

The account of this phase of Sherman's march toward Atlanta is drawn largely from the same sources cited for Chapter 17.

Additional sources included Stewart Sifakis, *Who Was Who In the Civil War* (New York: Facts on File Publications, 1988), for biographies of Generals George Stoneman and Edward Moody McCook; *The Atlanta Papers*, compiled and arranged with notes by Sydney C. Kerksis, U. S. Army, Ret. (Press of Morningside Bookshop, 1980), available at the Atlanta Historical Society, Atlanta; Ezra J. Warner, *Generals in Blue: Lives of the Union Commanders* (Baton Rouge: Louisiana State University Press, 1964); and Ezra J. Warner, *Generals in Gray: Lives of the Confederate Commanders* (Baton Rouge: Louisiana State University Press, 1959).

Chapter 19: "A Brilliant Success"

This chapter again relies heavily on *Official Records*, which contain extensive reports on the McCook-Stoneman raid from officers on both sides.

Of particular interest is the account written by General McCook near the Chattahoochee River railroad bridge August 7, 1864, a week after the battle at Newnan. This report, in which McCook described the raid as a "brilliant success," is to be found at page 762 of *Official Records*, series I, vol. 38, part II—"Reports." Operations in North Georgia, etc., May 1–Sept. 8, 1864. A more detailed report of his operations, written at Cartersville, Georgia, on September 30, 1864, appears beginning at page 765.

The raid is also described in Atlanta Paper No. 27, "Stoneman's Raid to the South of Atlanta," read by Horace Capron, 14th Illinois Volunteer Cavalry, December 7, 1889; reprinted from War Papers #32, D. C. Commandery (Atlanta: Press of Morningside Books, 1980).

The situation in Newnan is described in Kate Cumming, edited by Richard Barksdale Harwell, *Kate: The Journal of a Confederate Nurse* (Baton Rouge: Louisiana State University Press, 1959).

The battle at Newnan is described in the *Newnan (Coweta Co.) Georgia Sesquicentennial Booklet* (Newnan, GA: Harden-Patrick); W. Winston Skinner, "Battle of Brown's Mill Was 130 Years Ago Today," and, "The Day Coweta Hosted 3,500 Troopers," *Newnan Times-Herald*, July 30, 1994.

Chapter 20: A Summer in Hell

Fannie Beers's account of her visit to the battlefield near Newnan is contained in Fannie A. Beers, *Memories* (New York: J. B. Lippincott, 1889).

We visited Andersonville at the time of a reenactment of the opening of the camp in February 1996.

Descriptions of the prison are contained in Ovid L. Futch, *History of Andersonville Prison* (Florida: University of Florida Press, 1968; ninth printing, 1988); William B. Hesseltine, ed., *Civil War Prisons* (Kent, OH: Kent State University Press, 1962); B. F. Gue, "Iowa at Andersonville," *Palimpsest*, June 1961 (reprinted from the *State Register*, dateline Andersonville, April 16, 1884); and Holland Thomas, *The Photographic History of the Civil War in Ten Volumes*, volume 7, *Prisons and Hospitals* (New York: Review of Reviews, 1912).

Barney Brayman's service record does not include his incarceration at Florence, but that fact is mentioned in his obituary, which appeared in the *Rushford (Minn.) Journal* on November 3, 1871.

INDEX

About the Authors

Mary Davies Kelly has written extensively in her field of genealogy. This is her first book. Orr Kelly, a veteran Washington reporter and Pentagon correspondent for *The Washington Star* and *U.S. News & World Report*, is the author of five books on military subjects, including *Never Fight Fair!: Navy Seals' Stories of Combat and Adventure*. The Kellys live in Washington, D.C.